BRICKWORK

BUILDING CRAFT SERIES

BRICKWORK   *By* J. K. MᶜKAY

CARPENTRY   *By* J. K. MᶜKAY

JOINERY   *By* J. K. MᶜKAY

BUILDING CONSTRUCTION
By W. B. *and* J. K. MᶜKAY
Volumes One, Two, Three and Four
(*These are also available as two separate books
in hard covers*)
Volumes One and Two together
Volumes Three and Four together

BUILDING CRAFT SERIES

BRICKWORK

BY

W. B. McKAY

M.Sc.Tech., M.I.Struct.E.

Formerly Registered Architect and Chartered Structural Engineer and
Head of the Department of Building and Structural Engineering in the
Manchester University Institute of Science and Technology

THIRD EDITION [Metric]
BY

J.K. McKAY
B.A., B.Sc.Tech., A.R.I.B.A., C.Eng., M.I.Struct.E., F.F.B.

WITH 173 DRAWINGS

LONGMAN
LONDON and NEW YORK

LONGMAN GROUP LIMITED
Longman House
Burnt Mill, Harlow, Essex, U.K.

Published in the United States
of America by Longman Inc., New York

First published 1945
Second edition 1968
Second impression 1969
Third edition 1974
Fourth impression 1979
Fifth impression 1981

ISBN O 582 42519 0

Library of Congress Catalog
Card Number: 73-86517

Printed in Hong Kong by
Wah Cheong Printing Press Ltd.

PREFACE TO THE THIRD EDITION

FOR a long time the craft of bricklaying has been a basic process in the building industry. This has continued during the time since the first edition was published in 1945 and there is no reason to doubt that it will remain so during the next twenty-five years.

It is a craft which, unlike some others, has seen very little change; the same skills and principles of bonding will always apply.

In this new fully revised edition the units have been converted to metric terms. Most of the dimensions given in the Figures are in millimetres when the abbreviation mm has not been added; some are given in metres and these are distinguished by the suffix m.

1973   J. K. McK.

PREFACE TO THE FIRST EDITION

IT is generally agreed that demands on the building industry immediately after the war, and for many years to come, will be greater than they have ever been in this country, and that to meet these demands will call for a substantial increase in numbers of skilled craftsmen. Accordingly, it is anticipated that there will be an increase in the number of students attending building courses at Junior Technical Schools for Building, Technical Colleges and the various Government Training Centres.

This book has been prepared with the object of assisting those who will be receiving technical training in the bricklayer's craft. It is intended for beginners, but it is hoped that certain chapters, such as that concerned with setting out, will be useful to more advanced students.

At the request of several teachers, a chapter on drawing has been included so that the student may attain that degree of skill in draughtsmanship which is so desirable, not only in the preparation of sheets of brickwork details in class and for homework, but also as an additional qualification when he has become skilled in his craft.

The author is greatly indebted for help in the preparation of several sections of the book to Mr Benjamin Smith, who has provided much practical information gained during a long experience as a craftsman in brickwork and as a master builder.

W. B. McK

CONTENTS

7

8   CONTENTS

Unless noted otherwise all dimensions in the Figures are given in
millimetres.

INTRODUCTION

BEFORE making a preliminary study of brickwork and the materials and tools employed in its construction, the apprentice should be aware of the nature of the work which the bricklayer is called upon to do and some of the qualifications which the efficient craftsman should hold. Hence the following brief survey.

One of the principal tasks of the bricklayer is, of course, that of constructing walls of bricks and mortar. Such must be soundly built on foundations of adequate strength. Outer walls especially are often required to be of a specified appearance. Detached walls must have their ends suitably finished. Outer walls of a building require special treatment at their external and internal angles to ensure stability and a desirable appearance, and inner walls must be properly tied to external walls. Brickwork over door and window openings must be supported by arches or lintels, and the bottom of such external openings must be provided with steps or sills.

Moisture from the ground must be prevented from rising up the walls by the provision of a damp-resisting material placed at a suitable level above the ground. External walls of a building not covered with a roof must be protected either by bricks, suitably arranged, or by stonework. Horizontal bands of bricks, arranged according to several patterns, are sometimes required at the top of a wall, and similar decorative features are also called for near the ground level, at intervals up the wall and at corners.

Special provision has to be made for fireplaces, including the formation of openings to receive kitchen ranges, etc., the construction of smoke flues and the building of chimney stacks which penetrate the roofs.

Concrete is required to be laid under basement or ground floors of wood. Concrete floors are sometimes required for kitchens, sculleries, larders, coal-houses, etc. Flat roofs are often constructed of concrete, and paths are formed of this and other materials.

Occasionally brickwork is required to be reinforced with metal rods or fabric. Certain walls are circular on plan.

Miscellaneous jobs of the bricklayer include (a) the bedding with mortar of door and window frames, and wood plates to which floor joists, roof members, etc., are fixed by the joiner, (b) pointing walls with mortar, (c) fixing metal windows to brickwork, etc., and (d) attending upon other trades, i.e., forming holes in walls for pipes and making good the brickwork round the pipes after they have been fixed.

The work of the bricklayer also includes that associated with alterations and additions to existing buildings. This may entail the construction of new walls, forming openings in existing walls and building up door and window openings. Not the least important type of addition is that concerned with the provision of basements necessitating the construction (called *underpinning*) of new walls up to the old. A common type of alteration job, known as a *conversion*, is that requiring the removal of the lower portion of an external wall to accommodate a shop front. For this class of work, wood or steel members (called *shoring*) are needed to support temporarily the upper portion of the wall, upper floors, roof, etc.

The foregoing does not by any means exhaust the list of work performed by the bricklayer. For instance, he is required to construct inspection, etc., chambers in connection with drainage work, and he may be called upon to lay drains. And in rural districts especially, the bricklayer may be required to construct walls of stone.

In addition to all this, the efficient craftsman must be qualified to set out buildings, *i.e.*, determine the position of the walls by measurement and insert wood pegs, etc., at salient angles. He may be expected to instruct and supervise the labourers when excavating trenches, excavating for basements, etc., and fixing timbers necessary as temporary supports to the sides of such excavations. He will also be required to supervise and assist in the erection of scaffolding, and take all precautions to ensure that such can be used with safety.

Besides having the ability to produce sound workmanship economically, he should have a wide knowledge of the materials which he uses to ensure their effective employment and in order that he may be able to distinguish between those of sound and inferior quality. The preparation of mortars and concrete to conform to required mixes is sometimes performed or supervised by the bricklayer.

The qualified craftsman must be able to read plans and have a knowledge of the Building Regulations or regulations of local authorities. The ability to prepare progress, etc., reports and sketches of constructional details is an additional qualification.

From the above brief summary the apprentice will gain some idea of the work carried out by the bricklayer. The first aim of the keen apprentice will be to become dexterous in the use of the tools, especially the brick trowel, as soon as possible. To this end he is usually first employed on the construction of internal walls, and as his skill increases he is gradually put on to more important work, such as external walls which require to be of good appearance in addition to being soundly constructed.

CHAPTER ONE

MATERIALS

Brief description of the manufacture and characteristics of bricks, cements and limes; lime and cement mortars; concrete.

As the apprentice should be conversant with the materials used by the bricklayer, it is proposed to give a brief description of these in the following pages. These materials include bricks, lime, cement, mortars and concrete.

BRICKS

MANUFACTURE.—Bricks are made from several materials, chief of which are clay and shale. Concrete, sand-lime and glass bricks are also manufactured, but in relatively small quantities, and these are briefly described on p. 17.

There are many classes of clays and those most suitable for brick-making are found in many parts of the country, including the counties of Berkshire, Durham, Hampshire, Lancashire, Leicester, Northamptonshire, Staffordshire, Sussex and Yorkshire.

The chief constituents of clay are alumina and silica or sand. Lime, iron, magnesia and salts (such as magnesium and sodium sulphate) may be also present, in addition to organic matter and water. One of the chief characteristics of clay, due to the presence of the alumina, is its plasticity. Sand influences the hard and lasting qualities of bricks, but brittleness will result if it is in excess. The lime serves as a binding material and also renders the bricks light coloured. Iron and magnesia also influence the colour, thus red and brown bricks may contain at least 3 per cent. of iron and blue bricks may have up to 10 per cent. of iron present. Salts may cause defects (see p. 16).

Shale, quarried in Durham, Lancashire, Yorkshire and elsewhere, is a hard laminated (capable of being split into thin layers) clay rock which is reduced to a powder by machinery and ultimately to a plastic condition after water has been added.

There are various methods of production, depending largely upon the nature of the clay or shale. The processes are (1) preparation of the brick-earth, (2) moulding, (3) drying and (4) burning.

1. *Preparation.*—After the top soil has been removed, the clay is excavated usually by a mechanical excavator, filled into bogies or

wagons, and conveyed to the grinding mill. Shale is generally loosened by blasting (gelignite or other explosive being used for this purpose), loaded and transported. Any vegetable matter, large stones, etc., are removed by hand (or the clay may be washed in a cylindrical tank) before being reduced.

One type of grinding mill, suitable for hard and dry clays, consists of a revolving pan in which two metal rollers are caused to rotate. Water is added to the clay or shale, the crushed material ultimately passes through holes in the bottom of the pan and hence through a fine screen from which it is conveyed by a moving belt to the moulding machine or bench. An auger machine may serve the same purpose; here a powerful metal screw working within a cylinder churns up the clay and forces it through the outlet. Clays of high plasticity are crushed between rollers and then screened.

2. *Moulding.*—Most bricks are moulded by (*a*) machinery, fewer are shaped by (*b*) hand.

(*a*) *Machine-moulded Bricks.*—Two kinds of bricks are moulded by machinery, *i.e.*, (i) wire-cut bricks and (ii) pressed bricks. The standard sizes of bricks are given on p. 47. The size of these rectangular slabs is considered to be 215 mm long by 102·5 mm wide by 65 mm thick.

(i) *Wire-cut Bricks* or *Wire-cuts.*—A diagram of one type of wire-cut machine is shown in Fig. 1. The prepared clay or shale is forced through

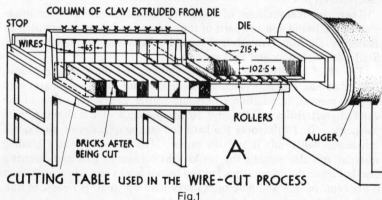

CUTTING TABLE USED IN THE WIRE-CUT PROCESS

Fig.1

the mouthpiece or die of the auger (or pug mill), and as a continuous band it passes over rollers to the cutting table. As clay shrinks when it dries, the dimensions of the mouthpiece (and consequently those of the cross-section of the band) are slightly in excess of the length and width of the finished brick. As shown, the frame of the cutting table contains vertical wires at a distance apart equal to the thickness of the bricks, plus shrinkage allowance. The frame is caused to rotate and the wires divide the band into slabs by a downward cut. Alternatively, the band may be cut to the length of the frame and pushed forward past the wires. The slabs are then placed on a barrow and wheeled to the drying floor.

(ii) *Pressed Bricks.*—There are many types of machines for moulding bricks by the pressure process. One type, which is power-operated, is shown diagrammatically in Fig. 2. The dimensions of the die-box or mould are that of the brick plus shrinkage allowance. The mould is charged with clay and the latter is consolidated as the plunger descends. The slab is removed after the hinged sides have been dropped; alternatively, the slab is automatically pushed up as the plunger ascends. Some bricks are further consolidated and rendered a better shape by being passed through a second press. Another type of the larger power-operated machines is capable of pressing four bricks at a time. A pressed brick usually has a *frog* on each of the larger faces (see Fig. 21 and p. 48).

Most so-called common or stock bricks and large quantities of facing bricks (those used chiefly on the outer faces of external walls) are machine-made.

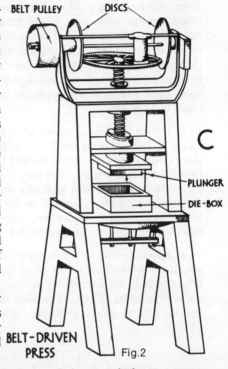

Fig.2

(b) *Hand-moulded Bricks.*—These are made by a much slower process than those described above and they are consequently more costly. There is, however, a demand for hand-made facing bricks because of their excellent appearance and durable qualities.

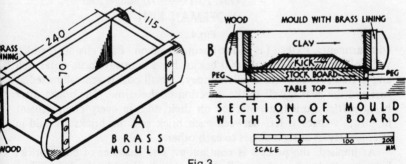

Fig.3

A metal lined wood mould used for the purpose is shown at A, Fig. 3. The moulding operations are done on a wood bench and the mould is usually placed on four pegs inserted at the corners of a rectangular-shaped

piece of wood, called a stockboard, fixed to the bench (see B, Fig. 3); as
shown, the stockboard has a raised centre, known as the kick, and this
forms the frog (see p. 48). The moulder sprinkles sand on the stockboard and the inside faces of the mould to prevent adhesion of the clay.
An assistant takes a piece of prepared clay, kneads it into a clot of sufficient size and hands it to the moulder. The latter dashes the clot into
the mould, presses it down with his fingers and removes any excess clay
by drawing a piece of wire across the top. The mould is lifted and the
slab turned out on to a pallet-board or flat piece of wood. The slabs are
taken to be dried.

3. *Drying.*—Artificial means of drying are now commonly adopted,
steam or hot air being used for the purpose. In one system of drying,
the moulded slabs are placed on end (with a space between each) on the
floor of the building in which they are moulded and under which steam
pipes are laid. The heat gradually dries the slabs which are then taken
to the adjoining kiln. Sometimes the slabs are placed on shelves to dry.
Bricks made from comparatively dry clay may be taken direct to the
kiln immediately after being moulded.

4. *Burning.*—The final process is carried out in a kiln. This is a brick
structure, the walls and top being lined with special bricks, called firebricks, which are capable of resisting very high temperatures. There
are several forms of kiln. The plan, in outline of one type, called a continuous kiln, is shown in Fig. 4. It is divided into several chambers or

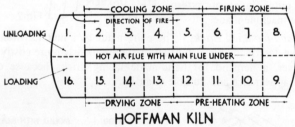

HOFFMAN KILN

Fig.4

compartments, sixteen (as shown) being common. Each chamber, which
will hold some 8,000 to 40,000 bricks, has a doorway in its outer wall
and a flue connected to a tall chimney. Small coal is generally used as
fuel and the heat travels in the direction of the arrow. The bricks, after
being partially dried, are stacked on their sides in every compartment
in turn; a space is left between each brick and the bricks are laid in
alternate layers at right angles to each other.

As implied, the process is continuous, one chamber of burnt bricks
being emptied and one being filled with partially dried bricks daily. Thus,
if to-day chamber 1 is being unloaded with bricks that have been burnt,
those in chambers 2, 3, 4 and 5 (called the cooling zone) will be cooling
as they have already been burnt, those in chambers 6, 7 and 8 (the firing

zone) will be burning at a high temperature whilst coal is added at intervals through holes at the top, those in the pre-heating zone consisting of chambers 9, 10, 11 and 12 will be subjected to the hot air from the firing zone, and the bricks in the next three chambers (the drying zone) will become gradually dried and heated as the hot air continues to circulate and finally escapes through the flue in chamber 15. As the burnt bricks in chamber 16 would have been removed yesterday, men will be busy charging it to-day with slabs from the drying floor. Only two doorways will be open (those in chambers 1 and 16), the rest being temporarily bricked up.

The above operations are maintained in the order stated but advanced by one chamber daily. During to-morrow, therefore, chamber 1 will be filled with partially dried bricks and chamber 2 emptied of the burnt bricks which will be sufficiently cool to permit of handling. The continuous kiln is economical as the hot air from the firing zone is utilized to gradually dry and bake the slabs preparatory to final burning.

Characteristics.—Good bricks should be well burnt and, to facilitate laying, those required for most internal work and certain external walling should be regular in shape and of uniform size. Some bricks, such as are needed for engineering work (p. 17), are often specified to have straight arrises (edges) and even surfaces, square (between adjacent faces) and of a uniform colour. On the other hand, some facing bricks, especially those which are hand-moulded, are highly prized for their slightly irregular arrises, variation in texture (surface finish) and mixed colouring. Good bricks should be free from cracks, chips and the defects referred to on p. 16.

Bricks which have been well burnt are generally hard, strong and durable (capable of lasting a long period without showing signs of defect). Underburnt bricks are weak and soon perish, especially if exposed to the weather. The experienced craftsman can generally tell the quality of bricks by their appearance. Underburnt bricks, because of their soft condition, are easily damaged and consequently a consignment of such bricks when delivered on the job will usually show a large proportion which are chipped and broken. In addition, underburnt bricks are generally abnormally light in colour. Any doubt as to their condition can usually be removed by striking two bricks together, a hard ringing sound indicating hard bricks and a dull sound underburnt bricks.

There is a big variation in the weight of bricks. Whereas wire-cuts may weigh from 2 to 2·7 kg, pressed bricks will weigh from 3 to 3·6 kg or even 4·5 kg each. In general, the heavier the brick the stronger it is.

Usually it is not difficult to classify the several types of bricks from their appearance. Thus, a wire-cut brick is of uniform shape and has straight arrises; it has no frogs and, as a rule, traces of the wire marks are visible on the 215 mm by 102·5 mm surfaces. A pressed brick is also of uniform shape and has true arrises, but it has generally two frogs, and is often heavier than a wire-cut. A hand-made brick has only one frog, and its slightly irregular arrises and rich texture are characteristic.

Bricks are obtainable in various colours, *i.e.*, white, grey, buff, brown, red, purple, blue and black with intermediate shades. Many of these, including the so-called *multi-coloured bricks* which are of varying shades, are often used for faced work. Several factors affect the colour, such as (*a*) the chemical constitution of the clay (careful mixing of clays and shales of varying iron content produce bricks of many attractive colours, white bricks have little or no iron present whilst blue bricks contain at least 7 per cent. of iron), (*b*) temperature during burning (a low temperature produces light coloured bricks, whilst blue bricks require a very high temperature—up to 1,200° C.), (*c*) atmospheric condition of the kiln (a smoky atmosphere is produced for dark brown and purple coloured bricks whilst white bricks must be protected from smoke) and (*d*) sand-moulding (different coloured sands used to sprinkle over the moulds used for hand-moulded bricks help to produce very pleasing colours). Bricks can also be stained on their surfaces by sprinkling over them, prior to burning, certain metallic oxides (such as manganese and cobalt), mixed with sand.

Defects.—In addition to those stated on p. 15, bricks are subjected to the following defects:—

Laminations.—Thin layers (laminæ) may scale off on exposure to the weather. The laminations are generally the result of air collecting between the particles of clay or shale during the grinding operation. Provision is made in modern machinery for the withdrawal of this air (the operation being known as *de-airing*) and the prevention of such defects.

Lime Nodules.—Any lime present in the clay should be very finely ground, otherwise it will expand if water is absorbed and cause the bricks to crack or flake.

Efflorescence.—This is a white deposit on the exposed faces of bricks when built due to the presence of salts in the clay. This condition gradually disappears in mild cases, but if there is a large proportion of salts the objectionable appearance may remain for a long time.

Scumming or Kiln White.—This is a brownish-white film which sometimes forms on the surface of bricks containing lime and iron and is produced in some types of kilns during the burning process. Such bricks are only suitable for internal brickwork or where the appearance is not of importance.

Crozzling.—Excessive heating in the kiln may produce badly shaped bricks, known as *crozzles*, which are only fit to be broken up for concrete (p. 22), foundations for paths, etc. If not too mis-shapen, they may be used for internal brickwork or that below ground level.

SPECIAL BRICKS.—These include: (*a*) Firebricks, (*b*) rubbers, (*c*) glazed bricks, (*d*) concrete bricks, (*e*) sand-lime bricks, (*f*) engineering bricks, (*g*) perforated bricks, (*h*) V bricks, and (*i*) glass bricks.

(a) *Firebricks.*—These are used for the lining of furnaces, fireplaces etc., as they are capable of resisting very high temperatures. The clay from which they are made contains a high percentage of silica, those known as *silica bricks* having as much as 97 per cent. of silica present. *Ganister bricks* are also of this class and are made from ganister, a dark coloured sandstone containing up to 10 per cent. of clay.

(b) *Rubbers or Cutters.*—These are chiefly of a uniform red colour. Because of their relative softness, they are easily cut and rubbed (on a hard stone) to any desired shape, and are therefore suitable for certain arches (see pp. 134, 135, 136, 138, 140, 142-144).

(c) *Glazed Bricks.*—As implied, these have one or more smooth glazed surfaces. They are usually pressed bricks, true to shape and with fine arrises. The glazing may be effected by salt which is thrown into the kiln at intervals during the burning of the bricks. Such are known as *salt-glazed bricks* and are of a brownish colour. If the glazing is produced after the bricks have been dipped in turn into several vessels containing various liquids and finally burnt, they are called *enamelled bricks* and are obtainable in many colours, white being common. Glazed bricks are used for walls of factories, dairies, class-rooms, areas, laboratories, etc.

(d) *Concrete Bricks.*—These are made of a mixture of cement and sand (see p. 22) and pressed into moulds. They are not much used, although large slabs of this material are often employed for partitions.

(e) *Sand-lime Bricks.*—Such are made of a mixture of lime (see below) and sand which is pressed into moulds (of the same size as for clay bricks) and then hardened in a steel cylinder to which steam is admitted. Their natural colour is grey, but pigments are sometimes added to give other colours. They are occasionally used instead of clay or shale bricks.

(f) *Engineering Bricks* are exceptionally strong and durable, and are used for piers, bridges and similar engineering work. Well-known examples are Accringtons (pressed bricks), Southwaters (pressed and wire-cuts) and blue Staffordshires (wire-cuts and hand-made).

(g) *Perforated Bricks.*—An increasing number of clay bricks are now available with perforations; the amount of perforation varies from 15 per cent. to 50 per cent. of the total volume of the brick. Perforated bricks produce a wall which is lighter in weight and has better thermal insulation than a wall made of standard bricks (see p. 168).

The perforations take the form of rectangular slots or cylindrical holes through the depth of the brick. An example of the latter type is shown in Fig. 21 where the brick has 16 holes each about 16 mm dia. (see also B, Fig. 161).

(h) *V Bricks.*—These are special perforated bricks used to produce the equivalent of an 280 mm thick cavity wall which is, however, 215 mm thick only and accomplished with one brick instead of two. A V brick is shown at A, Fig. 161 and the application of these bricks forms the subject of Chap. XV.

(i) *Glass Bricks.*—These are either solid or hollow blocks of glass of various sizes. They are built in mortar to form semi-transparent walls not required to take much weight.

LIME

Lime for mortar is produced by burning chalk or limestone in a kiln. One of the simplest forms of kiln, built at the side of the quarry, is shown in Fig. 5. A rough arch of blocks of limestone is formed at the bottom upon which is charged from the top both limestone and fuel to form alternate 450 mm thick layers of limestone and 230 mm thick layers of coke. A coal fire is started in the fireplace below the arch, and this gradually extends throughout the whole mass. It takes about four days to burn out, after which the lime (called *quicklime*) is removed through the eyes at the bottom of the kiln.

Another form of lime kiln is similar to the continuous brick kiln described on p. 14.

There are several varieties of lime, that used very largely for brickwork is known as *hydraulic lime*, as it has the property of hardening under water.

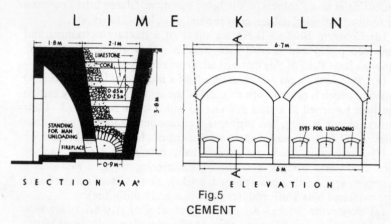

Fig.5

CEMENT

Of the various kinds of cement used by the bricklayer, that known as *Ordinary Portland Cement* is the chief. It is made of a mixture of chalk and clay in the approximate proportions of 4 parts chalk to 1 part clay. The following is a brief description of the manufacturing operations:—

MANUFACTURE.—The various processes include: (1) Preparation of the materials, (2) mixing and grinding, (3) burning and (4) grinding.

1. *Preparation.*—The chalk is quarried and conveyed to a powerful machine which crushes it to a size not exceeding 200 mm cubes. This is passed through a second crusher and reduced to particles of 20 mm maximum size from which it is conveyed by a moving belt to a large silo (cylindrical storage bin).

The clay is excavated, washed in a mill and delivered to a storage tank.

2. *Mixing and Grinding.*—The chalk and clay in correct proportions (about 4 to 1) are fed into a horizontal cylinder, known as a *wet grinding mill* (some 12 m long and 2·4 m diameter), in which there are many steel balls of varying size from 100 to 25 mm diameter. The mill rotates, and during this process the action of the balls upon the material reduces it to a creamy consistency, known as *slurry*, which is then passed through a fine sieve.

3. *Burning.*—The slurry is pumped to the kiln. This is a large cylindrical structure, approximately 90 m long and 3 m diameter; it is slightly inclined and revolves very slowly. The slurry automatically enters the kiln at its upper end and pulverized coal, or gas fuel, is blown in at its opposite end. The temperature within the kiln at its lower portion is very intense and it gradually decreases towards the top end. Hence the slurry is first dried, then heated and finally burnt as it gradually passes down the kiln. It leaves the kiln in the form of a very hard clinker (which, on cooling, is dark brown to black in colour) and is conveyed on a belt to a shed.

4. *Grinding.*—The clinker is fed into a *dry grinding mill*, which is similar to the wet grinding mill, and as it rotates the metal balls grind the clinker to an extremely fine powder which is passed through a sieve. This is the finished product, and is now grey in colour. It is forced by compressed air up a pipe to large silos.

PACKING.—The cement from the silos is caused to flow to the *packing machine* which automatically fills, weighs and seals it in paper or jute bags of 50 kg capacity.

This important building material must comply with various tests which are detailed in the British Standard Specification for Ordinary Portland and Rapid-hardening Portland Cements, No. 12.[1] Cement must be kept absolutely dry until required for use, otherwise it will set and become useless. As described on pp. 21 and 22, Portland cement is used for mortars and concrete, besides a number of other purposes.

SETTING AND HARDENING OF CEMENT.—When cement and water are mixed into a paste, the mixture remains in a plastic condition for a short while. The water combines chemically with the particles of cement to form *hydrates*, and this chemical process is called *hydration*. Gradually the plasticity disappears and the cement begins to stiffen or *set*. This is known as the *initial set* of the cement and the time taken to develop this condition is called the *initial setting time*, which, for ordinary Portland cement *must not be less than thirty minutes.* This allows time for mixing the cement when making mortar (see pp. 20-22) and concrete (see pp. 22-28) and applying it or placing it in position before the initial set commences. A piece of apparatus can be used for accurately determining the initial set, but, roughly, it may be considered as having commenced if a thumb nail drawn lightly across the surface of the cement fails to scratch it. After the initial set, the cement should *harden* quickly and increase in hardness and strength for some considerable time afterwards. *On no account must cement be disturbed after it has begun to set, as such disturbance will seriously affect the hardening process and decrease the strength of the mortar and concrete* (see pp. 21, 24 and 27).

SAND

Sand used for mortars and concrete should be clean and well graded (*i.e.*, particles of varying size—not exceeding 4·8 mm—with the smaller

[1] Published by the British Standards Institution.

filling the spaces between the larger). *Cleanliness is most important* as the presence of dirt (loam, clay, dust and organic matter) reduces the strength of the mortar or concrete with which it is mixed because it prevents the necessary adhesion between the sand and lime, etc. Clean sand, when rubbed between the thumb and forefinger, will not stain them. If sand is not sufficiently clean, much of the dirt can be removed by washing.

The sand is obtained from pits or quarries, banks or beds of rivers and sea beaches. Provided they are clean and well graded, *pit* or *quarry sand* and *river sand* are excellent for all purposes. *Sea sand* is used locally for concrete, but it is not suitable for mortar—because of the presence of salt which causes efflorescence (see p. 16)—unless the appearance of the brickwork is immaterial. *Crushed stone* is also used instead of sand; this is especially good for masonry as the colour of the mortar can be readily made to conform with that of the stonework. *Ashes* or *clinkers* from furnaces after being crushed are also adopted in lieu of sand to produce black mortar (see p. 21); such should be free from coal and dust.

MORTARS

Mortar is the binding material used in the construction of brickwork. There are several kinds, including: (1) Lime mortar, (2) cement mortar and (3) lime-cement mortar.

1. LIME MORTAR.—This is a mixture of quicklime (produced as described on p. 17), sand (or a suitable substitute such as crushed stone) and water. The latter must be clean, fresh and free from harmful chemical solutions and organic matter, otherwise it will have an adverse effect upon the mortar; this is a matter which should be considered when building operations are carried out in the country and a good water supply is not available.

The amount of sand mixed with the lime depends upon the type of the latter and the class of work to be constructed. A composition frequently used is 1 part lime to 3 parts sand. Sand is used because it helps to harden the mortar and prevent it cracking; it also reduces the cost of mortar.

The quicklime must be well *slaked* before use. This is done by sprinkling water over the lime which has been formed into a heap. This generates heat, causing the lime to expand and fall into powder. In order to retain the heat and moisture necessary to thoroughly disintegrate the lime, the heap is adequately covered over with the measured proportion of sand. Some limes slake more slowly than others, but in no case should lime be used within twenty-four hours after *slaking* (also called *slacking*). If unslaked nodules (small rounded lumps) were mixed with the mortar and built into the joints of a wall, delayed slaking might cause much damage to the brickwork. Hence, in order to remove any unslaked particles, it is necessary to pass the lime after slaking through a screen and only that which has passed through the screen is made into mortar.

The slaked lime and the sand must now be well mixed together. This is done either by hand or in a mortar mill. In hand mixing the slaked lime is turned over with a shovel on a proper boarded platform (it should not be mixed directly on the ground as earth would be shovelled into the mix), water is added and the mixing is continued until the mortar is brought to the required consistency. If mixed in a mortar or pug mill the lime and sand are placed in the pan and thoroughly incorporated by the action of the rotating and grinding rollers, sufficient water being added to ensure a mix which is neither too stiff nor too plastic. The mortar should be used fresh and it should therefore be produced in just sufficient quantity for each day's use.

Hydrated Lime Mortar.—Certain limes are now slaked by some lime manufacturers at the lime-works. Such lime is known as *hydrated lime.* This is produced in a special plant. Briefly, the burnt lime from the kiln is first crushed and then passed through a large tube in the form of a coil, a carefully regulated supply of water, just sufficient to slake the lime, falls on to the lime just as it enters the coil, and by the time it has traversed the tube the lime is slaked and is therefore in a powdered form. The powder is blown by a fan along a pipe and ultimately to a bunker from which it flows into paper bags and is automatically weighed and sealed. The common size of bags is of 25 kg capacity, although 50 kg bags can be obtained. Hydrated lime is therefore in the form of a dry, fine powder which is supplied in bags ready for use. When it arrives on the job, the necessary proportion of sand is added (and sometimes cement —see below) together with water, and these are intimately mixed to form lime mortar as described on the previous page.

Lime mortar is very rarely used now; cement mortar or cement-lime mortar being preferred. Some lime mortars are not suitable for work below ground level, although that made by hydraulic lime is excellent for this purpose.

Black Mortar.—This is a mixture of lime and ashes (see p. 20), a common proportion being 1 part lime to 1 part sand and 2 parts ashes or clinker. It is ground and mixed in a mortar mill. This mortar is hard-setting, and is suitable for internal walls and for brickwork where its black colour is not objected to.

2. CEMENT MORTAR is a mixture of Portland cement and sand. For general walling work the usual mix is 1 cement: 6 sand; but as this is harsh then an additive, to improve plasticity, can be included in the mixing water in the proportion of about 3 per cent. Cement mortar is stronger and more waterproof than lime mortar; it is therefore used in walls designed to bear heavy loads, piers (pp. 119-123), in chimney stacks, for walls in exposed situations and brickwork below damp proof course level when the mix would be 1:3.

Cement mortar sets and hardens relatively quickly, and it must therefore be used immediately after mixing (see p. 19). Any which has begun to set before being used must be discarded. Such waste of material is avoided if the cement mortar is made in small quantities from time to time as needed. Advantage is taken of its quick-setting property during winter as it is not so liable to damage by frost as weaker mortars.

3. CEMENT-LIME MORTAR.—This is also known as *compo* and is a mixture of lime, Portland cement and sand. The proportions vary from 1 part cement, 3 parts lime and 9 to 12 parts sand. As this mortar hardens relatively quickly, it is usual to first mix the lime and sand, as described above, and to defer incorporating the cement (an operation known as *gauging*) until just before the mortar is required for use. Only certain limes, such as the non-hydraulic variety, should be used for this class of mortar.

Compo is stronger than ordinary lime mortar, and because of its relatively quick-hardening property it is usefully employed in winter as it is less liable to damage by frost than the slower setting ungauged type.

Cement grout is cement mortar which has been reduced to a liquid paste by the addition of sufficient water. This is used occasionally for several purposes. Thus, brickwork and masonry may be grouted (*i.e.*, the grout is poured in to fill up spaces) and metal bars may be fixed by grouting their ends in the holes left or prepared for them (see also p. 130).

Waterproofed mortar (see p. 28) is sometimes used, *e.g.*, for brickwork constructed in exposed positions.

CONCRETE

Concrete consists of a matrix (or binding material), a fine aggregate (or body) and a coarse aggregate. As described on p. 23, sufficient water is added to these materials.

The binding material used for most concretes is ordinary Portland cement.

The fine aggregate is sand. The maximum size is limited and it is usual to specify that the sand must pass through a sieve having a 4·8 mm square mesh; fine dust should be excluded. Cleanliness and suitable grading (see below) are essential requirements.

Coarse aggregates include clean, hard broken brick or stone and gravel. The minimum size is 4·8 mm or equal to the largest grains of the sand. The maximum size varies according to the use to which the concrete is to be put. Thus, it is usually 38 mm (that passed through a sieve having a 38 mm square mesh) for plain or mass concrete as used for foundations, and 19 mm for reinforced concrete work (*i.e.*, concrete which is strengthened by the addition of steel).

Both the fine and coarse aggregates must be well graded to ensure a dense, strong and economical concrete. Therefore, there should be sufficient fine sand to fill the spaces or voids of the coarser sand, and the fine aggregate should fill all the voids in the coarse aggregate left after its smaller particles have packed the spaces between the larger; the Portland cement paste should fill the spaces between the fine aggregate, and, in covering every particle of fine and coarse aggregate, serve to bind the whole mass. Less cement is needed when the aggregates are well graded, and therefore the better the grading the cheaper the concrete.

PROPORTIONS.—The composition of concrete varies a good deal depending upon the desired strength, durability and class of work, characteristics of the materials, etc. The proportion of cement is specified by weight and that of both fine and coarse aggregates is usually expressed by volume (cubic metres). Thus the Building Regulations—see p. 82—state that site concrete (see p. 90) shall consist of not less than 50 kg of cement (being the weight of the contents of a bag) to every $0 \cdot 1$ m^3 of fine aggregate and $0 \cdot 2$ m^3 of coarse aggregate. Sometimes concrete is specified to be composed of so much cement (in kg) to the combined volume of the fine and coarse aggregates.

A mixture of the cement and aggregates is known as a *concrete mix*. A nominal mix is expressed in parts. Thus, a nominal mix often used for general reinforced concrete work consists of 1 part cement, 2 parts fine aggregate and 4 parts coarse aggregate. This is abbreviated and known as a "$1:2:4$ mix". As the weight of cement is approximately 1 442 kg per cub. metre, it follows that the volume of a 50 kg bag is about $0 \cdot 035$ m^3. Hence the qualities of materials required per cwt. of cement in the above $1:2:4$ mix are $0 \cdot 035$ m^3 cement:$0 \cdot 07$ m^3 fine aggregate:$0 \cdot 14$ m^3 coarse aggregate or, as it is usually stated, 50 kg cement:$0 \cdot 07$ m^3 fine aggregate:$0 \cdot 14$m^3 coarse aggregate.

The amount of water used in a concrete mix depends upon the nature of the work for which the concrete is required, the desired *workability* (*i.e.*, the amount of work necessary to mix the concrete and deposit it in position in a uniform condition and to the required finish), condition of dryness of the fine aggregate, etc. As a general rule, just sufficient water should be added to make the mix reasonably plastic and workable. It should be clearly understood that *too much water results in a considerable reduction in the strength and impermeability (watertightness) of concrete.* Sloppy mixtures must therefore be avoided. A practical test, called the *slump test*, for determining the required amount of water is described on p. 26.

MIXING.—It is absolutely essential that the materials shall be carefully measured in correct proportion and thoroughly well mixed. Measurement by shovelfuls of materials or by barrow loads should not be practised because of the inaccurate proportions which are bound to result. Hence batch boxes, described on p. 24, or their equivalent are used for measurement. The mixing should be continued until the concrete is of a uniform colour and consistency. Concrete is mixed either (*a*) by hand or (*b*) more usually, by machine.

(a) *Hand-mixing*.—This method is only used nowadays for small quantities of concrete or when the use of a machine is not practicable. It is slower, more costly and often less efficient than machine-mixing.

The mixing should never be performed on the bare ground as this results in earth being scraped up and incorporated in the mix. Hence it is usual to specify that the mixing shall be carried out on a wood platform or staging. Small quantities can be mixed on a conveniently situated and clean concrete, etc., floor or paving. A wood platform, some 2·5 to 3 m square, is formed of close fitting boards nailed to cross bearers. Sometimes the boards are covered with sheet iron to protect them from damage by the shovel. The platform should be level to prevent the water and liquid cement from draining off, and it should be situated near to the place where the concrete is to be deposited and adjacent to the water supply.

As stated on p. 23, careful measurement of the materials is essential. The type of measure usually adopted is a rectangular and bottomless wood frame or box having a handle at each corner. This is called a *measuring frame* or *batch box* (see

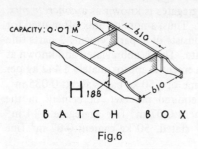

CAPACITY: 0·07 M³

H 188 610 610

B A T C H   B O X

Fig.6

Fig. 6). A batch of concrete is that formed after each mixing. The size of a batch depends upon the amount of labour employed and just sufficiently large to enable it to be mixed and deposited in position before the concrete begins to set, *i.e.*, within thirty minutes (see p. 19). The size of a batch box depends upon the proportions of materials used. Thus, that shown is suitable for a 1 : 2 : 4 mix (which requires 0·07 m³ of fine aggregate and 0·14 m³ of coarse aggregate (see p. 23) as its volume is 0·07 m³. See also p. 26.

The order in which the materials is measured varies with local custom or individual preference. Thus:—

1. Some prefer to measure half the required quantity of coarse aggregate first, followed by the whole of the fine aggregate, then the remaining half of the coarse aggregate and finally the cement. Hence, if the mix is required to be of the above proportions, the batch box of the size shown in Fig. 6 is placed on the platform at one end and at just sufficient distance from the edge to allow for the spreading of the materials. It is filled to the top with the coarse aggregate and then lifted. After this has been spread out and levelled off, the box is placed on the heap, filled with the fine aggregate and lifted. The fine aggregate is levelled over, the box is placed on it and again filled with coarse aggregate. Finally, after the latter has been spread, a bag of cement is emptied and uniformly distributed over the heap.

2. Others prefer to place all of the coarse aggregate on the platform, followed in turn with the sand and then the cement. Thus, after filling the box with the coarse aggregate and lifting it, a second measurement of the same material is made at the side of the first and the heap is levelled off. The sand is then measured on top of this, and after this has been spread a bag of cement is emptied over it.

3. The following order is often recommended: The whole of the coarse aggregate (two boxes) is measured on the platform and spread out.

A bag of cement is evenly distributed over it and a measured box of the fine aggregate completes the heap.

4. Another method consists of first spreading the measured sand on the platform. A bag of cement is emptied over it. Both are well mixed together. The measured coarse aggregate is then thrown over this mixture and the heap is finally mixed as described below.

The heap, made up according to any one of these orders, is then mixed at least "twice dry and twice wet". This expression is often used and its meaning will be evident from the following: The heap is shovelled by a man (or preferably two men) to one side, the materials being turned and sprinkled in the process. This is repeated and the heap thrown back to its original position on the platform. If the mixing has been thorough the colour of the heap should be uniform. Any brown and grey streaks indicate partial mixing only and the necessity for the heap to be turned over for a third time. The *proper amount* of water is then sprinkled on the dry mixture. As stated on p. 23, the quantity of water required varies (see also p. 183). As a rule, the water is measured from a 15 litre pail. It must not be thrown on direct from the pail, as this washes out the cement, especially if the whole pailful is dashed on. Preferably, it is sprinkled from a watering-can having a rose-head (perforated), which is filled from the measured pail. The mixing is now continued, the heap being turned over at least twice until the required uniform consistency has been obtained.

(b) *Machine-mixing.*—This has largely superseded hand-mixing. Mechanical mixing is essential when large outputs are required, and even when only small quantities of concrete are needed the portable type of machine, which can be readily transported from one job to another, is now often used. Machine-mixing is much faster and more economical than hand-mixing, and it generally produces a more thorough and stronger concrete.

There are several types of mechanical mixers, that shown in Fig. 7, called a *tilting drum concrete mixer*, is of the portable type. It consists of a hopper or charging skip, a revolving mixing drum, a water tank and a petrol or other type of engine. Correct quantities of the cement, sand (or fine

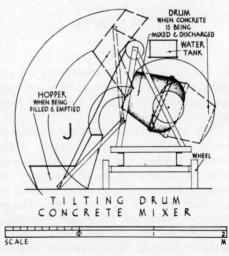

DRUM WHEN CONCRETE IS BEING MIXED & DISCHARGED
WATER TANK
HOPPER WHEN BEING FILLED & EMPTIED
J
WHEEL
TILTING DRUM CONCRETE MIXER
SCALE
Fig.7

aggregate) and coarse aggregate are loaded into the hopper. These materials are tipped into the drum when the hopper is tilted to the position shown by broken lines. As the drum revolves, the materials strike against projecting metal blades fixed to the inside and become thoroughly well mixed. *The period of mixing should be not less than one minute and not longer than two minutes after the materials have been added.* The drum, still revolving, is then tilted (see broken lines in sketch) and the contents discharged into barrows or other receptacles. The engine provides the power for revolving the drum, tilting the hopper, etc. The machine, being provided with wheels, is readily transported from one job to another or to various positions on a building site. The size of the drum varies, but one of 0·3 m³ capacity is useful for average work. A hopper is not always provided, and for this smaller type of machine the dry materials are fed directly into the drum; a batch box, having a wood base, is used for correct proportioning.

When large quantities of concrete are required *continuous mixers* are sometimes employed. Such consists of a large mixer into which the fine and coarse aggregates, cement and water are fed after being mechanically mixed and from which the concrete is continuously discharged.

SLUMP TEST.—Various tests are applied to concrete, but the only one that need be described here is the slump test, as this is a good and simple

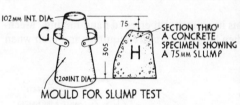

MOULD FOR SLUMP TEST

Fig.8

practical test for determining the desired workability (see p. 23) of concrete and the amount of water required. It is frequently adopted on the site during the progress of the work. The apparatus simply consists of a metal mould and a metal rod. As shown at G, Fig. 8, the mould is shaped like a frustum of a cone (and is often called the *cone*), both of its ends are open, it has two handles and its dimensions are as stated. The rod is 16 mm in diameter and 600 mm long.

When carrying out the test, the mould is placed on a flat non-absorbent board with the large end downwards. It is filled with the recently mixed concrete to a height of 75 mm. The concrete is rammed twenty-five times with the rod to expel the air. Another 75 mm layer is filled and consolidated, and this is repeated until the mould is filled. The surface is levelled off flush with the top by a trowel. This method of filling ensures uniformity. When full, the mould is carefully lifted *vertically* and placed alongside the concrete specimen left on the board which will have subsided or slumped. The decrease in height of the concrete, which varies according to the quantity of water added, is the amount of slump and is expressed in mm. It is found by placing a rule or straight edge across the top of the mould and measuring the vertical distance between its lower edge and the top of the concrete. Thus, for example, the slump indicated at H, Fig. 8, is 75 mm.

The values of the slump vary according to the class of work. For mass concrete it varies from 25 to 100 mm, a maximum slump of 50 mm being common for foundation concrete. The slump may be increased to 175 mm for certain reinforced concrete work which cannot be rammed or consolidated when placed in position.

In good class work the slump test is taken daily to check the condition of wetness (known as the *consistency*) of the concrete. Whilst several factors influence the slump, *it is important to note that, if after carrying out this test, the slump is greater than that required, it usually indicates that too much water has been added during the mixing of the concrete, and consequently the strength of the concrete will be reduced and its permeability increased.* Consequently, less water will have to be added in subsequent mixes. On the other hand, if the test shows a deficient slump, it will be less workable and the mixture may be honeycombed (spaces between the particles); additional water in the mix is therefore required.

A rough-and-ready test is to take a handful of the concrete immediately after mixing. A good concrete will retain its shape and become moist on the surface after being squeezed with both hands. A wet, sloppy and weak mixture will, of course, be easily "squeezed out".

PLACING AND COMPACTING CONCRETE.—Concrete must be taken from the mixer or mixing platform and placed in the desired position on the job as soon as possible and within half an hour of mixing. Small amounts may be conveyed by hand in buckets. Otherwise it is usually either shovelled from the platform or discharged from the mixing drum into specially constructed watertight steel barrows, wheeled to the place required and carefully tipped. It must never be thrown from a height as this would disturb the mix and separate the heavier from the lighter particles. If required for upper floors, the barrows are hoisted by special tackle.

The concrete after being placed in position is consolidated by *ramming* or *punning*. This must be done thoroughly in order to obtain a dense concrete, *i.e.*, one free from honeycombs or voids, although it must not be unduly prolonged and should be completed well before the concrete begins to set, otherwise the process of hardening (see p. 19) will be interfered with. *Rammers* used for this purpose are of various shapes and sizes. That shown at F, Fig. 9, is a common form for general work; it has a 225 mm by 225 mm by 75 mm wood base,

RAMMERS

Fig. 9

having metal protected edges, and a 1·2 to 1·5 m long handle. The metal *pummel* shown at G is another type. When the concrete is thick it should be laid in 150 to 300 mm layers and each layer should be rammed before the next is spread.

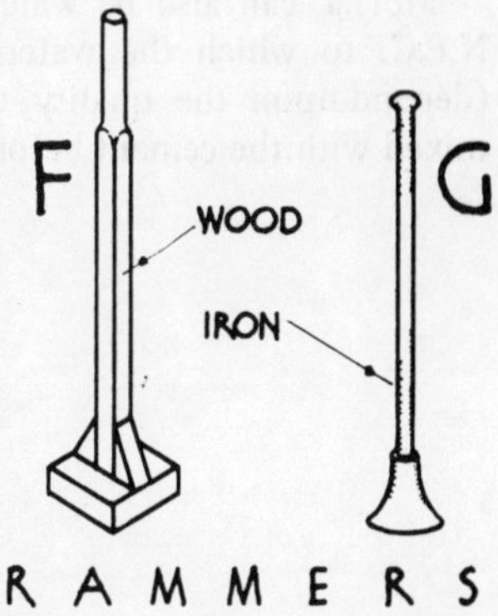

CURING CONCRETE.—It is improtant to keep the concrete in a moist condition for as long as possible in order that the hardening process (see p. 19) may be continued until the strength of the concrete has been fully developed. Once the concrete becomes dry, the hardness finishes, and rapid drying out of the water may cause a considerable reduction in strength. To prevent evaporation of the water from the concrete, it is usual to cover it with sacking about an hour after it has been compacted, and this is kept moist by regularly sprinkling it with water for a week or so. Sheets of waterproofed paper are sometimes used as a cover.

Concrete before it has hardened can be considerably damaged by frost, and concreting must therefore be suspended during frosty weather. To protect freshly placed concrete from frost, it is essential to cover it with sacks filled with straw, waterproof paper, etc. Such covering should always be provided at night if there is any suspicion of frost.

WATERPROOFED CONCRETE.—If concrete is composed of good quality cement and clean, sound, well graded aggregates it can be rendered sufficiently impervious for most practical purposes, provided the materials are suitably proportioned, thoroughly mixed, properly placed and con-solidated. Unless, however, all of these factors are rigidly controlled the concrete will be more or less porous. It is therefore now a common practice to use waterproofed cement; alternatively normal Portland cement to which certain substances, called waterproofers, can be added when the concrete is required to be impervious. There are several water-proofers on the market, including "Cementone", "Medusa", "Pudlo" and "Sika". Some are powders, others are pastes and liquids. The method of incorporating this material varies, but if in powder form it is usual to mix it with the cement before the latter is added to the fine and coarse aggregates. The quantity also varies, a common amount being 3 per cent.

Mortar can also be waterproofed by using waterproofed cement or N.P.C. to which the waterproofer is added. Thus, 2 to 5 per cent (depend-upon the quality of work) of the powder is added and well mixed with the cement before the latter is added to the sand.

CHAPTER TWO

DRAWING EQUIPMENT AND DRAWING

Instruments, paper; hints on draughtsmanship; methods of representation;
lettering, sketching; inking-in, tracing and colouring.

THE student should be conversant with the instruments and materials
used in the preparation of drawings related to brickwork. It should also
be the aim of the beginner to reach a satisfactory standard of draughtsmanship as early as possible. Hence the following brief notes which
should be considered before a close study is made of the details of
construction appearing in this book.

Students attending classes in Brickwork (theory as distinct from
practical) will be required to devote a certain amount of time to scale
drawing and freehand sketching. The general practice at each class
meeting is to commence with a clean drawing sheet upon which the
student draws to scale, or sketches, details of construction prepared by
the teacher on the blackboard; these details may be supplemented by
examples in the textbook, and if it is not possible to complete the sheet
in class the student is required to do so as part homework.

The student is therefore required to equip himself with certain
instruments and materials. The following are the minimum requirements:
Drawing board, tee-square, two set squares, scale, protractor, compass
with pencil point, pencil, rubber, drawing paper, four drawing pins and
a notebook or pad.

DRAWING BOARD.—A type of board quite suitable for the beginner is
made of three-ply (three thin layers of wood glued together). A convenient size is 605 mm by 430 mm as this will take an A2 size sheet of
paper (see p. 30).

TEE-SQUARE.—This consists of a hardwood blade screwed at right
angles to a short head. The standard length of blade for an A2 size
drawing board is 630 mm. The cheapest type, usually of beechwood, has
a thin parallel blade; it is satisfactory, although easily damaged if not
carefully looked after. A better, but more costly, tee-square has a
polished mahogany taper blade with a bevelled (sloping) edge in which is
inserted a narrow strip of celluloid which forms a transparent ruling edge.

SET SQUARES.—Two are required, i.e., a "45°" and "60°". The sides
adjacent to the right angle of the 45° set square should be about 150 mm
and the 60° set square should have its vertical side (that adjacent to the
90° and 30° angles) at least 200 mm long. Those of transparent celluloid,
having square edges, are best; the "open pattern" (having a central
triangular space) is preferred to the "solid pattern", as it is more easily
handled and is not so apt to soil the drawings.

An adjustable set square is a useful, but not essential, instrument; its sloping edge can be set to any desired angle.

SCALE.—A scale, of oval cross section, 300 mm long and made of boxwood is recommended. It has eight scales, *i.e.*, 1:10, 1:100, 1:20 and 1:200 on one side, and 1:5, 1:50, 1:1250 and 1:2 500 on the reverse. The edge of the scale containing the 1:1 and 1:100 scales is calibrated in millimetres and so can be used for full size (1:1) drawings. A 150 mm Armstrong pattern, having the same number of scales, is sometimes preferred, as it is handier to carry in the pocket. It is also made of ivory, boxwood with white celluloid edges, and ebonite (black with white divisions). Cardboard scales are not recommended.

PROTRACTOR.—This may be of the 150 mm rectangular type or, preferably, of the semi-circular transparent celluloid pattern of 100 or 125 mm diameter which is divided into degrees. This is not necessary if an adjustable set square (see above) is available.

COMPASS.—The student should take special care in selecting this. As a rule, very cheap compasses quickly develop defects and are responsible for inaccurate or untidy draughtsmanship. Whilst a pencil compass is all that he may require at first, he may later wish to acquire additional instruments as he advances in his studies. Several makers now produce sets of reliable instruments at a reasonable price specially to meet the requirements of students. Such instruments are standard and therefore any replacements of damaged or missing parts can be readily obtained at a minimum of cost. Instruments should be accommodated in a case for convenience and as a protection.

A case containing a 140 mm compass having a pencil socket, loose dividing point and a refill case for holding spare leads will meet the requirements of the beginner. When not being required for use as a pencil compass, the lead in the socket may be replaced by the dividing point for pricking off lengths or dimensions, etc.

Alternatively, a larger set which will serve the needs of the student for several years consists of a case containing the following: (*a*) 125 mm compass with pencil, pen and lengthening bar fittings, and a key for tightening joints; these fittings are interchangeable, thus the pencil is replaced by the pen fitting when curves are to be inked-in, and the bar is introduced when larger circles or arcs are to be described; (*b*) 125 mm divider; (*c*) 90 mm spring-bow pencil (for small circles); (*d*) 90 mm spring-bow pen (for inking-in small circles); (*e*) 125 mm drawing pen (for ruling lines in ink), and (*f*) refill case with spare leads.

PENCIL.—A good quality H. or H.B. pencil is recommended (see p. 32).

RUBBER.—This must be soft and free from grit, otherwise it will damage the surface when applied to drawing paper. An ink rubber is useful if, at a later stage of his training, the student inks-in his drawings or produces tracings.

DRAWING PAPER, ETC.—This is required for both class and homework. Good quality paper is essential. As stated on p. 29, the size of the sheets recommended for first year students is A2 size (594 mm by 420 mm).

Four drawing pins are needed for fixing the paper to the board, and some should be kept in reserve. A *sharp* penknife is also essential (see p. 32).

NOTEBOOKS AND PADS.—Either a notebook or pad is essential. The paper, which should be plain, should be of good quality and preferably of A4 size (210 by 297 mm). Ruled paper should not be used, as students from the outset should learn to sketch unaided by printed lines (see p. 43). If a pad is used, the sheets should be filed methodically in a suitable folio or folder.

Finally, instruments should be treated with care. Good work cannot be expected if the edges of tee-squares, set squares and scales are chipped or otherwise damaged, and if the joints of compasses become permanently loose or the legs bent.

HINTS ON DRAUGHTSMANSHIP, ETC.—A sheet of paper is pinned to the drawing board in the following manner: a drawing pin is inserted in the top left corner of the sheet and board. The sheet is "squared" (the tee-square being used to ensure that the top edge of the paper is parallel to that of the board), drawn taut by hand-pressing diagonally towards the bottom right-hand corner at which a second pin is inserted, stretched from the centre towards the top right corner which is then pinned, and tightened towards the remaining corner in which a pin is pressed home.

Most draughtsmen prefer to work on drawing boards which have sloping surfaces. Some boards are provided with shaped bearers which give the required inclination. Otherwise a board may be tilted by placing under its top edge a piece of wood (of the desired thickness and sufficient length), an old book, etc.

All horizontal lines should be drawn aided by the tee-square. The head should be pressed against the left edge of the board by the left hand, the tee-square is slid up or down until the blade is in the desired position, and this pressure should be maintained until the line has been drawn. The pencil should be held in contact with the *bottom* of the ruling edge of the blade as the stroke is made from left to right. Students are apt to acquire the bad habit of moving the tee-square with the left hand at the middle of the blade and keeping the hand in this position whilst drawing the line; this often results in the lines not being "square".

Vertical lines should be drawn with the assistance of a set square. The tee-square is placed in the desired position with its head pressed against the left edge of the board, as described above. The position is maintained as the left hand traverses and presses on the blade. The set square is placed with its base on the upper edge of the blade and its vertical side in the required position. Both tee-square and set square are held by the left hand whilst the vertical line is drawn with the pencil contacting the bottom of the vertical edge. Set squares are also used for drawing lines at 45°, 30°, 60°, etc. Long vertical lines, such as borders, may be drawn with the tee-square.

The scale should never be used as a ruler, as its edge will become damaged by the action of the pencil—or pen—against it.

Each line should be of uniform thickness. Students should practice drawing lines of varying thickness against the edges of the squares until they can with certainty produce lines of the desired strength.

It cannot be too strongly emphasized that *the quality of draughtsmanship is largely dependent upon the condition of the pencil, and blunt pencils are a common cause of drawings which are inaccurate and of unsatisfactory appearance.* Hence the pencil should be sharpened to a long (at least 20 mm with 6 mm lead exposure) and tapering point, and *it must be maintained in this condition by the frequent application of the knife.* Whilst drawing lines, revolving the pencil after each stroke will help to maintain the point. A blunt pencil is often due to a blunt knife. A stumpy pointed pencil must not be used as it blunts quickly and can only be applied against the bottom edge of the tee-square with difficulty (see p. 31). Short pieces of pencil, unless fitted in a suitable holder, should not be used as they are difficult to control.

Before commencing drawing, the student should see that the tee-square, set squares and scale are clean, otherwise the sheet will quickly become soiled. A clean duster or waste piece of plain paper should also be used for keeping this equipment clean as the drawing proceeds.

Until the student becomes reasonably efficient as a draughtsman, he should at first apply the pencil lightly to the paper. Apart from the difficulty in erasing firm lines drawn in error, he will find that heavy lines (especially when drawn with a soft H.B. pencil) will quickly become smudged by the constant action of the tee-square and set square over them. These instruments also collect the spare lead and transmit it over the paper to produce a dirty sheet. The latter should be cleaned down, by a careful application of the rubber, after the whole drawing has been completed with the lightly drawn details. The drawing is then "lined in". *Before this is attempted the pencil should be sharpened and the squares cleaned.* He should commence lining-in at the top of the paper, working from left to right and gradually towards the bottom. Any printed matter is added *after* the lining-in has been completed. Some notes on lettering are given on pp. 37-42. When setting out the drawing sufficient space should be left for any titles and sub-titles. A piece of clean paper below the hand will prevent the drawing from becoming soiled during printing. Finally, the four thick lines of the border are drawn to complete the drawing.

METHODS OF REPRESENTATION.—A student attending a complete course of instruction will be taught in his geometry class several methods of representing on paper certain geometrical solids (such as cubes, prisms, pyramids, etc.) and consideration will there be given to the practical application of solid geometry to building problems. Hence, it is only necessary to make brief reference here to these methods which are: (1) Orthographic projection, (2) isometric projection, (3) oblique projection, (4) axonometric projection and (5) perspective.

1. *Orthographic Projection.*—This is the form of representation which

is chiefly used. It is, for example, the method adopted for working drawings comprising plans, elevations and sections of buildings.

A *plan* is the view presented when looking vertically down on an object. *Projectors* are perpendiculars; if these be drawn from the corners of an object to points on a horizontal flat surface (called a *plane*) and if these points be connected by lines, the resulting figure is known as a *projection* and is the plan of the object. If, for example, the object is a building plot, the plan will show its true shape as its boundaries will be of true length and correctly related. A plan of a room will show its true shape and the correct positions, etc., of the door, windows and any fireplace. Working drawings include a separate plan of each floor of a building, and the following terms are used: "Basement Plan", "Ground Floor Plan", "First Floor Plan", etc. Examples of plans are shown on pp. 55 and 119.

An *elevation* is the view obtained when looking in a horizontal direction towards the object. It is the projection on its vertical plane. All vertical lines are of true length. Thus, an elevation of a house, when developed from the plan, will show the true shape, dimensions and position in a wall of the door and windows, and will include the roof, chimney-stacks, etc. Terms applied to a building such as "Front Elevation", "Back Elevation", "End Elevation", "North Elevation", etc., are self explanatory. Examples of elevations are shown on pp. 57 and 146.

A *section* is the true shape of an object presented after it has been cut through (or assumed to have been divided) by a plane, and the portion between the observer and the plane removed. If the cutting is vertical, a *vertical section* results (as at C, Fig. 158). That called a *horizontal section* is produced by a horizontal cut; a ground floor, etc., plan of a building, which shows the thickness of the walls, etc., is really a horizontal section. Sometimes the dividing plane is indicated on the plan or elevation and distinguished by letters, and the section is similarly lettered (see Fig. 10). A further distinction is made between *longitudinal section* (*e.g.*, Fig. 99) and *cross* or *transverse section* (*e.g.*, Fig. 62), according to the positions of the actual or imaginary dividing planes. Sometimes a view shows an elevation combined with a section; such is called a *sectional elevation*.

A simple example incorporating a plan, elevations and section is shown in Fig. 10. The object is a pressed brick which, as stated on p. 15, has usually two frogs. The plan is first drawn to scale (see p. 36), the external dimensions being assumed to be 215 mm by 102·5 mm. The frog is then indicated, as shown. The cutting plane AB is drawn. The vertical section ("Section AB") is next developed and is a cross section; if the plane had been in the direction of the length, a longitudinal section would have been required. The width of the section is, of course, 102·5 mm and its height is assumed to be 65 mm. The two frogs must be shown. Finally, the cut surface is *cross-hatched*, *i.e.*, diagonal lines ($45°$) are drawn at close intervals as shown (see p. 44). The front elevation is developed by projecting

vertical lines from the plan and horizontal lines from the section. The
end elevation is then developed. The correct position of the end elevation
in relation to the front elevation must be carefully noted. As shown, the
end elevation is that of the brick when viewed in the direction of the

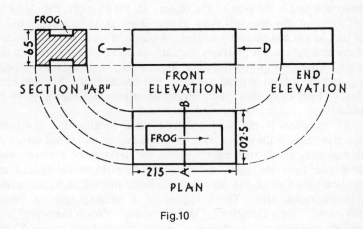

Fig.10

arrow C. If viewed in the direction of arrow D, the end view would be
shown on the left of the front elevation. Actually, as both ends of the
brick are the same, this is not an important matter in this case, but when
the end views differ it is essential that they be represented in the correct
relative position. In actual practice the broken concentric quadrant curves
are not drawn; they have been indicated in the figure to show the
development more clearly. The frogs could be shown by broken lines in
both elevations, but these have been omitted for the sake of simplicity.

    2. *Isometric Projection.*—In orthographic projection, as illustrated in
Fig. 10, three separate drawings are required to show the plan and the two

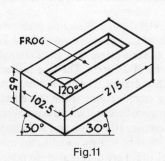

Fig.11

elevations. When isometric projection
is employed, these three views are em-
bodied in a single drawing. Thus, an
isometric drawing of the same brick is
shown in Fig. 11. A 30° set square is
used to draw the length and width and
lines parallel to them. In building drawing the height, length and width are
drawn to scale to the actual dimensions.
The drawing gives a distorted shape as
the angle between any two adjacent
sides is either 120° or 60°, instead of
90°. Nevertheless, this method of representation is most useful and is

often employed in either drawing to scale or sketching details of construction. Figs. 22 and 36 are examples of isometric drawings to scale, and an isometric freehand sketch is shown in Fig. 132.

3. *Oblique Projection.*—Fig. 12 is a drawing by oblique projection of the pressed brick. One of the vertical faces (the end face in this case) is assumed to be at right angles to the line of sight and is drawn true to shape and scale. The adjacent vertical face is drawn obliquely, usually with the 45° set square, although any angle may be adopted. In order to reduce the distortion, the dimensions of the inclined lines are sometimes halved. This is not so often used as the isometric method. Fig. 2 is an obliquely projected sketch.

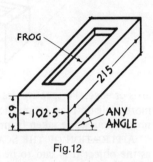

Fig.12

4. *Axonometric Projection* (see Fig. 13).—This resembles isometric projection in that both the adjacent vertical faces are inclined. There is,

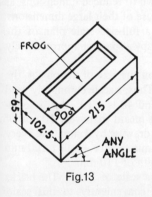

Fig.13

however, an important difference between the two, for, whereas the plan of the isometric drawing is distorted, that axonometrically drawn is of true shape. Observe in Fig. 13 (which is that of the pressed brick) that the sides of the top are at right angles. When presenting an object by this method, the plan is drawn true to scale, set at *any* convenient angle, and the elevations are then projected from it. The angle at which the plan is drawn varies in accordance with its shape and any special requirements—such as an important portion requiring emphasis—the aim being to provide the maximum information. This method is often employed.

5. *Perspective.*—In a perspective drawing the object is represented as it appears to the observer. Hence, to conform to the impression produced upon the eye, horizontal lines which are actually parallel are drawn converging towards a distant point. Also, the heights of objects are shown to diminish as the distance from the observer increases. The principles of perspective are beyond the scope of this book, but some idea of the features of this form of representation may be obtained by reference to the simple example illustrated in Fig. 14. The horizontal lines converge towards two points, one on either side of the object (a pressed brick), and it will be seen that the only true dimension is the figured height of the

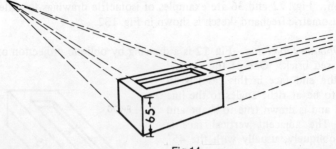

Fig.14

arris or edge. Perspective drawings serve a very useful purpose as they are more realistic than geometrical drawings, but correct measurements cannot, of course, be taken from them.

APPLICATION OF THE SCALE.—When a drawing is made the same size as the object it is said to be "drawn to full size". For example, certain purpose-made brick arches (see p. 137) are drawn to full size to enable the brick manufacturer to obtain the correct shape, number, etc., of the voussoirs and for assistance to the bricklayer in "setting out" (see p. 145).

Most brickwork details are, however, drawn to reduced dimensions, as it is not necessary, nor is it practicable because of their large dimensions, to draw them to full size. For instance, a full-size scale plan of the portion of the wall at K in Fig. 37 would occupy a space of approximately 1 100 mm by 350 mm.

The extent of the reduction depends upon the size of the object, the purpose of the drawing, size of sheet, etc. Thus, a scale commonly used for bonding such as is shown in Figs. 47 and 48 is 1:10; this is sometimes abbreviated to "one tenth". By this is meant that every 10 mm of actual length of the object is shown on the drawing by 1 mm, and every portion of 10 mm by the same fraction of 1 mm. Hence a wall 1 100 mm long would be represented on paper by a length of 110 mm.

Sometimes bonding details are drawn to a scale of 1:10. The bricks shown in Figs. 23 and 24 can be drawn conveniently to this scale. Occasionally details, such as a section through a window sill, are drawn to "one fifth full size" (i.e., 1:5) and "half full size" (1:2). Before a house can be built, a "plan" of it must be submitted, in duplicate, to the local authority for approval. This may also be referred to as a "general working drawing" or a "contract plan"; such includes plans of the several floors, elevations and at least one vertical section. It is usually drawn to a scale which is expressed as "1:100" or "100 mm to 1 mm". Less frequently a scale of "1:50" or "50 mm to 1 mm" is selected for such a drawing. Quite commonly a "one twentieth elevation" of the building or portion thereof (such as the main entrance) is required; as implied, this scale is 1:20.

It will be seen from the foregoing that a scale drawing is proportionate to the actual object. This ratio of reduction is called the *representative fraction*, and the scale is often referred to by such a fraction. Thus, the representative fraction of the 1 : 20 scale is $\dfrac{1 \text{ mm}}{20 \text{ mm}} = \dfrac{1}{20}$

Each drawing must have its scale clearly indicated on it, students should not, therefore, omit this from their class or homework sheets. This may be shown either by (*a*) a printed statement such as "Scale: 1 : 20" or (*b*) a portion of the scale, accurately drawn with a sharp pencil in a convenient position (often at the bottom of the paper) in a manner similar to that shown in Fig. 47; if the latter, measurements not figured are scaled from the drawing with the aid of dividers.

DIMENSIONS.—Drawings should be fully and clearly dimensioned. *This is most important.* The figures must be distinct; special care being taken when printing the figures 3 and 5. Two methods of indicating dimensions are shown in Fig. 17. The dimension lines should be lightly drawn and terminated against short thin lines which are continuous with the ends of the portion of the drawing concerned (see also Fig. 10). Ambiguity arises when the short terminal lines are omitted, as in the example "I" immediately below the title of Fig. 16. If a figured dimension does not agree with the scaled dimension (as occasionally happens in practice when an alteration is made to a working drawing), the figures must be taken as correct and either underlined or followed by the letters "N.T.S." (meaning "not to scale"). Figures are again referred to on p. 40.

PRINTING OR LETTERING.—A drawing is not complete without a printed title or heading, sub-titles, etc. Good lettering improves a drawing and, conversely, the appearance of a sheet is spoilt by bad lettering. Lettering must be distinct, and the letters must be well spaced and of pleasing form. That used for working drawings, class sheets and homework should be simple and easily formed in a reasonable time. An elaborate style of printing is now rarely called for; indeed, the practice in many drawing offices is to spend as little time as possible on lettering, and hence it is often produced by means of the stencil; the latter is a plate with perforated letters over which ink is brushed or the pencil applied.

A recommended plain type of lettering which, after a little practice, is easy to do is shown in Fig. 15. The student should study this carefully. Each letter is shown within a square in order that the proportions may be better appreciated and to help comparison. He should note that B, E, F, J, K, L, P, R and S are half letters (occupying half width of square), C, D, G, H, N, T, U, X, Y and Z are three-quarter letters, and A, M, O, Q, V and W are full letters. He should observe especially that O and Q are complete circles and C, D and G are three-quarter circles. Figures are also shown. The sloping or italic is another good style of lettering; the letters are inclined at an angle of approximately $10°$; most beginners find this more difficult than the upright version.

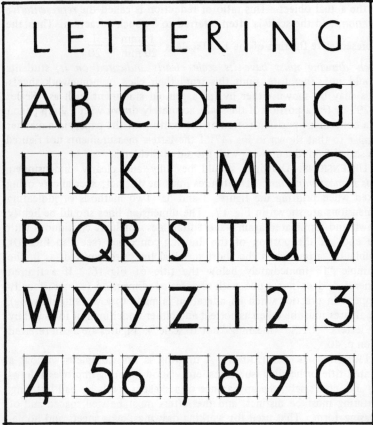

Fig.15

Many students pay too little attention to printing, with the result that their drawings are spoilt by hurriedly formed letters which are ugly in the extreme. In order to show examples of bad lettering Fig. 16 has been prepared, consisting of letters *reproduced from actual homework sheets.* Unfortunately, these are not by any means isolated examples. Such crudity is to be deprecated. The following few observations are made on these examples as most of the defects will be self-evident.

The first letter B, very popular with students, is too wide (compare with that in Fig. 15); such excessive width is also often given to letters E, F, K, P, R and S. On the other hand, C, D, G, O and Q are usually too narrow. Letters with flourishes and curly cues (see especially the first S) cannot be too strongly condemned. Regarding the printing at "2", apart from the badly spaced ill-formed letters, capitals should not be mixed with the lower case (as "and"). The space between each of the finicky lettered words of the title in "3" is excessive. Capital I's must not be dotted as shown in "4"; the first letter of each word should not, as shown, be higher than the rest; it is unnecessary to draw attention to the small n's mixed with the badly shaped capitals and to the wrongly placed

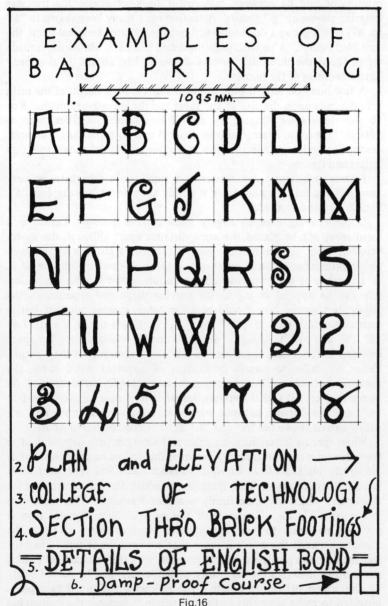

EXAMPLES OF BAD PRINTING

1. ← 1095 MM. →

A B B C D D E
E F G J K M M
N O P Q R S S
T U W W Y 2 2
3 4 5 6 7 8 8

2. PLAN and ELEVATION →
3. COLLEGE OF TECHNOLOGY
4. SECTION THR'O BRICK FOOTINGS
5. DETAILS OF ENGLISH BOND
6. Damp-Proof Course →

Fig.16

apostrophe. The placing of a title between two bold lines, as in "5", is undesirable and a single line only, as in underlining, is less common than formerly; the pair of short lines at the ends are inexcusable; if serifs (short strokes as at "T" and "H") are used they should be applied throughout and not occasionally as shown at "5". As stated below, printing should be between *faint* guide lines, otherwise the irregular lettering shown at "6" results. Attention has already been drawn to "1" (p. 37) which shows a dimension without the required terminal lines; the scribbled figured "3" is hardly distinguished from a 5. Reference is made on p. 42 to the three ugly arrows shown in Fig. 16 and to the fancy bottom corners of the border.

A few hints on lettering are given in Fig. 17. The height of the main title depends upon the size of the sheet and the space available, but 8 or 10 mm letters are suitable for an A2 size sheet. Sub-titles, such as "Plan", "Elevation", etc., may be from 3 mm to 6 mm high. General descriptive and brief specification notes are usually of 3 mm to 4 mm letters and figures.

Letters and figures, no matter how small, should be between *very faint* top and bottom guide lines, if untidy and uneven lettering (see "6", Fig. 16) is to be avoided.

Good lettering depends largely upon correct spacing. Letters in a word must not be placed the same distance apart although the spaces between them should *appear* equal; otherwise a letter is either given undue prominence, due to an excessive space on one or both sides of it, or a portion of the word may appear unduly crowded. No mechanical rule can be applied owing to the varying shape and sequence of the letters, but special care should be taken when spacing adjacent letters such as A and V (see "5", "6" and "7", Fig. 17), A and W, L and T (see "8", "9" and "10"), R and I, P and A, O and W, W and Y, etc. The space between letters must, therefore, be adjusted according to their shapes. Hence, in order to obtain interspaces of apparent equal areas, the distance between adjacent letters having *upright strokes must be increased* (see "3"), that between *round letters must be decreased* (see "4") and the distance between a letter having a *vertical stroke and one with a curved stroke* (as "N" and "G" at "1") *must be intermediate.*

When spacing letters forming titles and sub-titles, it is helpful if, after the guide lines have been *faintly* drawn at the desired height apart, points are *lightly* marked off at an equal distance apart and *very faint* short vertical lines are drawn from these points which serve as centre lines for the letters which are then firmly pencilled freehand. This method is shown at "2", Fig. 17, but with the vertical lines stronger than is normally necessary to meet reproduction requirements; note that the distance between the words is twice that between the letters. When the student becomes proficient he may dispense with the vertical lines (which also help to maintain the verticality of the letters) and be guided solely by the scaled off centre points. The following additional example is provided to make clear this method of spacing. Suppose the student has completed a sheet of brickwork details and he is about to start lettering it. Commencing with the title, which is assumed to be "BRICKWORK", he will faintly draw the horizontal guide lines at 10 mm apart and mark off from the *centre line* of the sheet four equal spaces (say, 25 mm) on

Fig.17

each side, erect the short faint vertical lines and then proceed to print the letters with half the width of each on both sides of the upright. Later he will become aware of the need to make slight adjustment in the spacing of the centres, especially when it is relatively small and there is a big variation in the shapes of adjacent letters; thus, in the title "LETTERING" in Fig. 15 the space between the centres of "R" and "I" is slightly less than the average and that between "N" and "G" is somewhat greater.

The description in Fig. 17 consists solely of capital letters. Some prefer to adopt the lower case (small letters). Horizontal guide lines (which were subsequently removed) were used for the dimension figures shown in the top left corner.

ARROWS.—These should be neatly drawn (preferably aided by the tee-square or set square) and carefully finished with *small* heads (see Fig. 17). A drawing is completely marred by large-headed arrows which sprawl at random over the sheet. Three bad examples are shown in Fig. 16. Incidentally, unlike that shown at "4", Fig. 16, an arrow head should point towards the detail concerned.

BORDER.—This completes the sheet and should preferably be a single heavy line drawn to leave about a 12 mm wide margin. Finicking corners, such as are indicated at the bottom of Fig. 16, should be avoided.

SUMMARY.—In general, each sheet of drawings produced in class or homework should:—

1. Consist of neat and accurate details, drawn lightly at first and subsequently lined in (p. 32) and arranged with the elevation over and projected from the plan, etc. (p. 33).

2. Be carefully set out to ensure a reasonable balance, *i.e.*, details should be suitably spaced to ensure a uniform covering of the sheet and the avoidance of local overcrowding and large blank spaces.

3. Be cross-hatched and lettered after the scale drawing has been completed, to avoid soiling the sheet (p. 32). Lettering and figuring should be well done as described. Scrawled cross-hatching must be avoided.

4. Have the scale or scales clearly indicated (p. 37).

5. Be numbered, dated and signed. Usually the number is placed in the top right-hand corner and the student's name with the date underneath is printed in the bottom right-hand corner.

SKETCHING.—In addition to preparing drawings to scale, students are required to make freehand sketches of constructional details, etc. Many of the sketches made by the teacher on the blackboard are copied by the student. Sketches direct from constructional models are sometimes called for. Later in the course of his work he may be required to make sketches of building sites, portions of buildings in course of construction, etc., for the purpose of progress reports, existing buildings requiring alterations and repairs, and the like. He is also strongly recommended to make sketch details of work in course of erection and of completed buildings, a one-metre rule (see Fig. 83) being used for obtaining dimensions; such sketches should be filed for future reference. Sketching should therefore be regarded as an essential accomplishment.

Sketches are made with the pencil and occasionally in ink. For the former a well-conditioned H.B. pencil of good quality is best. The note-book or pad (p. 31) should be of good surfaced *plain* paper. It is recommended that from the outset no mechanical aid, such as a scale, ruler, set square, lined or squared paper, etc., should be employed. When one or other of these aids is resorted to the mechanical appearance of such sketches is usually unsatisfactory, and, what is more important, such assistance, if continued, results in an imperfectly trained eye, hand and sense of proportion.

Sketches should be neat, well-proportioned and workmanlike. They should be of a reasonably large size; puny sketches are strongly condemned. Each freehand line should be drawn freely from end to end with a single stroke; many students cultivate the bad habit of sketching each line by a series of short strokes. The beginner should practise simple exercises such as sketching:— horizontal and vertical lines of varying thickness which are afterwards checked with the scale and squares; bisecting and dividing lines into a given number of equal parts; lines inclined at $30°$, $45°$ and $60°$; curved lines, such as arcs and circles. Assiduously practising these and similar exercises will gradually increase his confidence and technique.

When sketching from the blackboard and models, the student should observe with close concentration each detail and thoroughly understand it before commencing to sketch; this will help the memory. Merely copying lines serves little useful purpose. It is a common fault with students, when sketching from the blackboard, to make frequent reference to the board—at least one glance per line sketched; a preliminary careful study will obviate this. Any figuring must be *clearly* indicated and cross-hatching *carefully* sketched; many sketches are marred by scrawled hatching.

INKING-IN, TRACING AND COLOURING.—A first year student is not usually required to ink-in, trace and colour drawings (although any spare time devoted to it will result in a general improvement in his drawing technique), and the following brief notes are for reference purposes.

Waterproofed Indian ink (which is jet black) is required for inking-in drawings and making tracings; such is obtainable in bottles ready for use. Before inking-in a drawing the student should practise ruling inked lines of varying thickness (regulated by the screw) with the pen. The pen, charged with ink from the quill (attached to the top of the bottle), is held almost vertically with the fixed blade (as distinct from that which is hinged) touching the tee-square or set square. After each charging of the pen the outside of the blade should be wiped dry with a soft rag, otherwise the ink will be transmitted to the edge of the square and an inked smudge on the paper will result.

The pencilled drawing is cleaned down with a rubber before inking-in is commenced. Horizontal lines of the required thickness are usually inked-in first, followed by the verticals; there is thereby less tendency for smudges to occur at the intersections. Hatching and dimension lines should be relatively thin. On completion, the pen should be thoroughly cleaned and the blade tension relieved by a turn of the screw.

Until proficiency has been gained, lettering should be pencilled as already described. This is then inked-in. A Heath "Telephone Pen" or similar broad-pointed nib is recommended for the style of printing illustrated in Figs. 15 and 17; a fine pointed pen-nib, such as a Gillett No. "303", is suitable for forming arrow heads, sketching, etc.

A tracing of a drawing is made when a number of copies is required. Tracing paper and cloth, which is transparent and obtainable in rolls, are used for this purpose; the cloth, also known as tracing linen, is stronger than the paper and is capable of withstanding much handling without damage. The tracing paper or cloth is pinned and well stretched over the original drawing; the longer it remains stretched before tracing is commenced the better. Tracing on paper is done in either ink or pencil, and in ink only on cloth. The latter has one side glazed and one unglazed. Tracing is usually done on the unglazed side and, to assist the ink to flow readily, the "chalk bag" (a piece of boiled linen containing powdered chalk) is applied; if the chalk is well rubbed in, the cloth is stretched in the process and is therefore better conditioned.

Both paper and linen copies, called prints, are obtained from tracings in a printing machine. *Blue prints* are of paper with white lines on a blue ground; *black-on-white prints* are of paper or linen and are white sheets with black lines. Briefly, in one type of machine, prints are produced in the following manner: The tracing is placed face downwards on a glass cylinder, a sheet of sensitized paper or cloth is stretched over the tracing (with the sensitive side next to the tracing) and a canvas cover is tightly stretched over them. An electric lamp is passed down the cylinder at the required speed; the sensitized paper is removed, placed in a tray for development, washed, dried and its edges trimmed. The washing process causes these prints to shrink and hence the drawings on them are not true to scale. So-called *true-to-scale prints* can now be produced which, as implied, are not affected by shrinkage, but such are relatively expensive.

Working drawings are often coloured. Various portions of the plans, elevations and sections are coloured according to the materials of which they are composed. Whilst established office practice and individual preference may influence the colours used, the following are those commonly adopted for the materials stated: Brickwork, red produced by mixing crimson lake and vermilion; masonry, burnt umber; concrete, Prussian blue; carpentry or undressed timber, yellow ochre; joinery or dressed woodwork, burnt sienna; slating, Payne's grey or green obtained by an admixture of Prussian blue and yellow ochre; roof tiling, as for brickwork but with an increase in the vermilion content. A denser colour is used for indicating materials in section than in plan or elevation.

Bottled inks in at least a dozen different colours are obtainable; water colours are also sold in tubes, cakes and sticks. The colours are mixed in either saucers, palettes or tiles (divided into compartments). Sable brushes in various sizes are used for applying the colours.

The sheet or print to be coloured is stretched taut and pinned to the board, cleaned and preferably washed, *i.e.*, clean water is applied with a large brush (size No. 9 or 10) to each plan, elevation, etc.; pre-watering assists the colour to flow freely and prevents a patchy appearance; a clean double sheet of blotting paper should be applied immediately after each portion has been washed, and this should be also used to prevent the hand from touching and soiling the drawing during the colouring operation. Large light coloured washes are first applied, followed by the darker colours. At each dip of the brush the colour in the saucer should be well stirred and a full brush of the pigment collected. The colour should be kept flowing during the application. Large washes are commenced at the top and gradually worked from side to side with quick broad sweeps, finishing in one of the bottom corners; the colour should be allowed to dry naturally, the blotter not being used for this purpose. The brush should be well washed in a glass of water between each change of colour. The tendency to lay on the colours too thickly must be avoided.

CHAPTER THREE

BONDING OF WALLS

Bonding; sizes of bricks; terms; heading, stretching, English and Flemish bonds; stopped ends.

BOND is the interlacement of bricks produced when they lap (project beyond) those immediately above and below them. If a wall was constructed with bricks arranged in such a manner that the vertical joints were continuous from top to bottom it would have little strength. But the strength and stability of a wall are considerably increased if it is built, as it should be, of bricks arranged in accordance with the several forms described on the following pages in each of which the vertical joints are staggered. Reference should be made to Fig. 18 which shows the

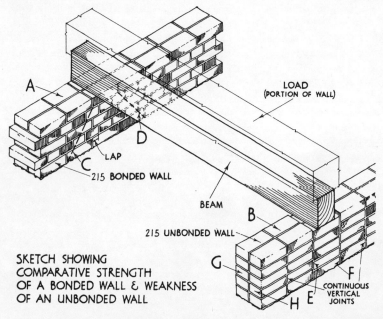

SKETCH SHOWING
COMPARATIVE STRENGTH
OF A BONDED WALL & WEAKNESS
OF AN UNBONDED WALL

Fig.18

difference between bonded and unbonded walls. A portion of a 215 mm thick unbonded wall is shown at B and part of a bonded wall of the same thickness is shown at A. These two walls support a wood beam which carries a load in the form of a wall. In the unbonded wall B the bricks are shown built one above the other with continuous vertical joints. Half of the total load is thus concentrated on the portion of the wall between the vertical joints E and F and therefore there is a tendency for this portion to drop as indicated. Furthermore, the two vertical sections G and H would tend to separate as they are not bonded together. Compare this with the bonded wall at A which shows the overlapping of the bricks both longitudinally (note the face) and transversely (observe the end). As a result the load transmitted to this bonded wall is distributed over a relatively large area, as indicated within the broken lines C and D.

In a soundly constructed wall, therefore, the bricks are properly bonded to form, together with the mortar, a keyed homogeneous structure. As far as possible *continuous vertical joints* must be avoided.

Various bonds are described on pp. 54-62, 115-118, etc.

SIZES OF BRICKS.—The maintenance of correct bond is facilitated during the construction of a wall if the size of the bricks is uniform. Otherwise time is wasted if a consignment contains bricks of varying sizes which necessitate their sorting out by the bricklayer. As stated on p. 12, clay shrinks when it dries; some clays shrink more than others. Accordingly, allowance is made for this shrinkage in the moulding process of manufacture.

The following brick sizes appear in the British Standard Specification, No. 3921, for "Bricks and Blocks of Fired Brickearth, Clay or Shale"[1] :— length 215 mm; width, 102·5 mm; depth or thickness, 65 mm. The length of a brick should be twice its width plus the thickness of one vertical joint in order that the proper bond may be maintained (see Fig. 19). Fig. 20 is an elevation of a portion of a wall showing bricks of the above standard maximum size arranged in English bond (see p. 56). Observe that both the bed or horizontal joints and the cross or vertical joints are 10 mm thick. Certain buildings, especially those of a domestic character (such as houses), have a more attractive appearance if the walls are faced with 50 mm thick bricks instead of the thicker standard bricks; such thin bricks are, however, only used in first-class work because of their relatively high cost.

TERMS.—Before making a study of the various types of bonds the following definitions of terms which have a general application to brickwork should be memorized:—

Arris.—An edge of a brick (see Fig. 19).

Bed.—The lower (215 mm by 102·5 mm) surface of a brick when placed in position (Fig. 19).

Header.—The end (102·5 mm by 65 mm) surface of a brick (Fig. 19).

Stretcher.—The side (or 215 mm by 65 mm) surface of a brick (Fig. 19).

Face.—A surface of a brick such as the *header face* (102·5 mm by 65 mm) and *stretcher face* (215 mm by 65 mm) as indicated in Fig. 19; the exposed surface of a wall, such as that shown in Fig. 20, is known as its *face* appearance.

[1] Included by permission of the British Standards Institution.

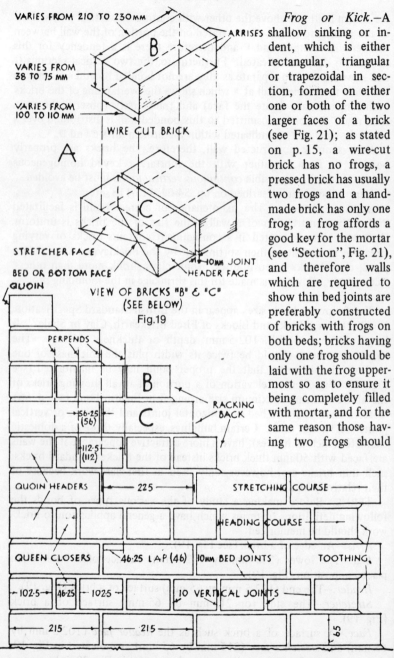

VARIES FROM 210 TO 230 MM

ARRISES

VARIES FROM 38 TO 75 MM

VARIES FROM 100 TO 110 MM

WIRE CUT BRICK

STRETCHER FACE

BED OR BOTTOM FACE

QUOIN

10 MM JOINT

HEADER FACE

VIEW OF BRICKS "B" & "C"
(SEE BELOW)
Fig.19

PERPENDS

RACKING BACK

56·25 (56)

112·5 (112)

QUOIN HEADERS

225

STRETCHING COURSE

HEADING COURSE

QUEEN CLOSERS

46·25 LAP (46)

10 MM BED JOINTS

TOOTHING

102·5 46·25 102·5

10 VERTICAL JOINTS

215

215

65

ELEVATION OF PORTION OF WALL IN ENGLISH BOND
Fig.20

Frog or Kick.—A shallow sinking or indent, which is either rectangular, triangular or trapezoidal in section, formed on either one or both of the two larger faces of a brick (see Fig. 21); as stated on p. 15, a wire-cut brick has no frogs, a pressed brick has usually two frogs and a hand-made brick has only one frog; a frog affords a good key for the mortar (see "Section", Fig. 21), and therefore walls which are required to show thin bed joints are preferably constructed of bricks with frogs on both beds; bricks having only one frog should be laid with the frog upper-most so as to ensure it being completely filled with mortar, and for the same reason those having two frogs should have their lower ones filled with mortar before being laid in position (see p. 109).

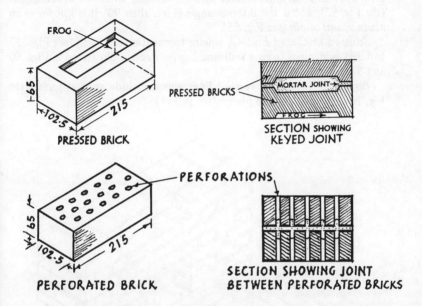

Fig.21

Course.—A complete layer of bricks; a *heading course* consists of headers and a *stretching course* comprises stretchers (see J and K, Fig. 37); a *brick-on-edge course* consists of bricks placed on their 215 mm by 65 mm faces (see A and B, Fig. 161, and B and J, Fig. 167) and a *brick-on-end* or *soldier course* is composed of bricks laid on their 102·5 mm by 65 mm faces (see Fig. 123, and N and O, Fig. 169).

Continuous Vertical Joints or Straight Joints.—Vertical joints which come immediately over each other in two or more consecutive courses (see B, Fig. 18); although these are sometimes unavoidable (as in Flemish bond shown in Fig. 39), they should never appear on the face of brick-work (see "English Bond" on p. 56).

Bed Joints.—Mortar joints, parallel to the beds of the bricks, and therefore horizontal in general walling; the thickness varies from 3 mm (often specified for glazed brickwork) to 10 mm; the 10 mm joints shown in Fig. 20 are generally adopted in good-class facing work.

Cross or Vertical Joints.—As implied, these are between the ends of bricks in general walling; the thickness equals the difference between the length of a brick and twice its width, which, in the example shown in Fig. 20, is 10 mm.

Collar Joints.—Internal longitudinal vertical mortar joints in walls exceeding 102·5 mm in thickness, *i.e.*, the middle long joint shown in the plan of the stretching course at J, Fig. 37.

Quoin.—A corner or external angle of a wall; those shown in Figs. 50 and 51 are *square* or *right-angled quoins*; a quoin formed when two walls meet at an internal angle greater than 90° is called an *obtuse squint quoin* (see Fig. 52), and if the internal angle is less than 90° it is known as an *acute squint quoin* (see Fig. 53).

Stopped or Closed End.—A square termination to a wall (see Figs. 37 and 39) as distinct from a wall which is returned as illustrated in Figs. 50 and 51.

Perpends.—Imaginary vertical lines which include vertical joints (see Fig. 20); these should be *plumb* (see p. 111).

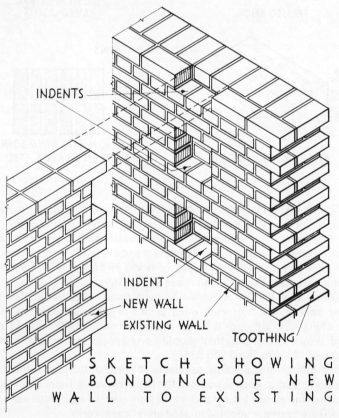

INDENTS

INDENT

NEW WALL

EXISTING WALL

TOOTHING

SKETCH SHOWING
BONDING OF NEW
WALL TO EXISTING

Fig.22

Lap.—The horizontal distance which one brick projects beyond a vertical joint in the course immediately above or below it (Fig. 20); it varies from approximately a ¼- to a ½-brick.

Racking Back.—The stepped arrangement formed during the construction of a wall when one portion is built to a greater height than that adjoining (see Figs. 20 and 100, p. 110). In order to avoid unequal settlement no part of a wall during its construction should rise more than 900 mm above another.

Toothing.—Each alternate course at the end of a wall projects as shown in Figs. 20 and 39 (front elevation); thus, adequate bond is provided between it and the new portion if the wall is continued horizontally at a later date.

Indents.—Sinkings left or formed in each alternate course of a wall into which a new wall is toothed and adequately connected (see Fig. 22). The width of the indents is equal to the thickness of the new wall and the depth should be at least ¼-brick. Usually the indents are formed three (as shown) or four courses high with a similar distance between each.

Bat.—A portion of an ordinary brick with the cut made across the *width* of the brick; the cut is made with the bolster (Fig. 84) and, if necessary, dressed with the scutch (Fig. 89). Four different sizes are shown at E, F, G and H, Fig. 23. Applications are illustrated in the

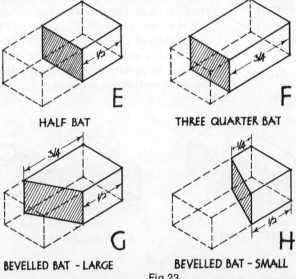

HALF BAT   THREE QUARTER BAT

BEVELLED BAT - LARGE   BEVELLED BAT - SMALL

Fig.23

following: *Half Bat* (E) at F, Fig. 39. *Three-quarter Bat* (F) at K, Fig. 37, *Bevelled Bat* (G) at H, Fig. 57 and *Bevelled Bat* (H) at E, Fig. 56.

Closer.—A portion of an ordinary brick with the cut made *longitudinally* and usually having one uncut stretcher face. Seven forms are shown at J, V and K, Fig. 24, and N, O and P, Fig. 26.

The *Queen Closer* (J, Fig. 24) is usually placed next to the first brick in a heading course (see J, Fig. 37). Sometimes the abbreviated or three-quarter queen closer V is required, as shown at Q, Fig. 37. The queen closer K is more often used than J as it is easier to cut by first splitting it centrally across its width and then subdividing each half; as shown at L, Fig. 38, however, this generally produces a ¼-brick wide continuous vertical joint.

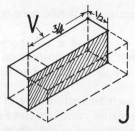

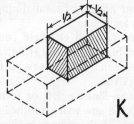

QUEEN CLOSER –HALF   **QUEEN CLOSER –QUARTER**

Fig.24

The *King Closer* (Fig. 25) is formed by removing a corner and leaving

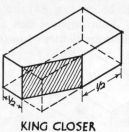

KING CLOSER

Fig.25

half-header and half-stretcher faces. Applications of king closers are shown at D, E and F, Fig. 56, and G, H and J, Fig. 57.

The *Bevelled Closer* (N, Fig. 26) has one stretcher face bevelled (splayed or slanted) and is shown in each of E, K, L and M, Fig. 56.

The *Mitred Closers* (O and P, Fig. 26) are only used in exceptional cases where they are required to be mitred (joined at an angle), *i.e.*, quoins of certain bay windows.

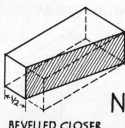

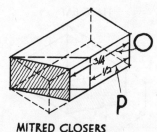

BEVELLED CLOSER   **MITRED CLOSERS**

Fig.26

Special Shaped Bricks.—These are called *specials* or *purpose-mades* as they are moulded to shape and used for special purposes. Some of the larger brick manufacturers keep stocks of these shaped bricks which are made by machinery (pressed or wire-cut) and are known as *standard specials.* Wherever possible, a selection should be made from these as non-standard specials are more costly because they have to be moulded by hand in moulds which have to be made specially to the required shape. Furthermore, standard specials are normally readily available, whereas delivery of non-standard bricks may be delayed. The use of these standard specials for faced work has resulted in a saving of time of the bricklayer, as formerly he was required to cut ordinary bricks accurately

to the shape required. For common work, or where the brickwork is to
be covered with plaster, the bricks are still cut
to shape by use of the bolster, etc. The following are only a few of these special bricks:—

Bullnose.—These are used for copings (see
D, Fig. 167) or in such positions where
rounded corners are preferred to sharp arrises
as at piers (see Q, Fig. 114), door and window
openings, etc. A brick with only one rounded
edge is called a *single bullnose* (see Q, Fig.
114). A *double bullnose* (Fig. 27) has two

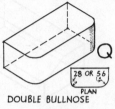

DOUBLE BULLNOSE

Fig. 27

rounded edges (see D, Fig. 167); the radius of the quadrant curve varies
from 28 to 56 mm.

It is difficult to neatly cut a mitre at the intersection between two
bullnose arrises; special *returns*
containing mitres are therefore

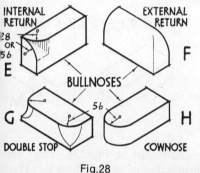

Fig. 28

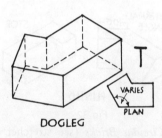

Fig. 29

useful. That at E, Fig. 28, shows an internal return; similar right and left-
handed returns on bed, edge and end are also available. An external return
is shown at F. A *stop* is required to provide a satisfactory finish when a
bullnose edge is continued by a square arris, as at the base of a pier or door
opening; a double stop is
shown at G; single stops are
also made. That shown at H,
sometimes called a *cownose*,
suitable for copings and ends
of ½-brick walls.

Dog-leg or Angle (see Fig.
29). These bricks are used
to ensure a satisfactory bond
at quoins which depart from
a right angle and are to be
preferred to the mitred
closers (Fig. 26); the angle

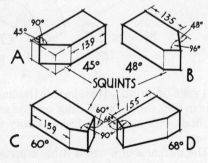

Fig. 30

and lengths of faces forming the dog-leg vary.

Squint Bricks (see Fig. 30) are specials used in the construction of
acute and abtuse squint quoins and are applied in Fig. 52.

Plinth Bricks.—One or more courses of splayed bricks are adopted at

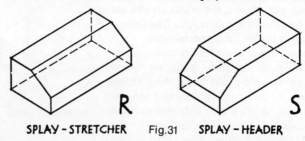

SPLAY – STRETCHER   Fig.31   **SPLAY – HEADER**

plinths (see p. 177). A *splay-stretcher* is shown at R, Fig. 31 (see also P, Fig. 169) and a *splay-header* at S; the amount of splay varies. A dog-leg internal angle splay plinth is shown at R, Fig. 32, and a *stop* at S. Right and left-handed plinth internal returns, like the bullnose brick E, Fig. 28, and external returns are also available.

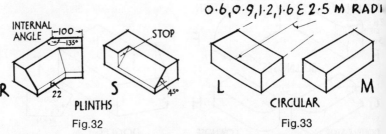

Fig.32   Fig.33

Circular Bricks (see stretcher L and header M, Fig. 33).—These are used for circular work, as in the construction of bay windows (see Figs. 154 and 155), tall chimneys, etc.

Coping Bricks.—A few standard shapes are shown at N, O and P, Fig. 34. Bullnose bricks are used for the same purpose. See also Fig. 167.

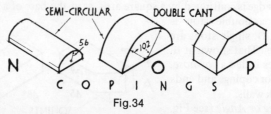

Fig.34

TYPES OF BOND.—These include Heading, Stretching, English, Flemish, Garden Wall, Cross, Dutch, Brick-on-edge and Facing Bonds. The last five are dealt with in Chapter Eight. Cavity walls are described in Chapter Eleven.

The thickness of a wall is either expressed in inches or in terms of the length of a brick, thus: 102·5 mm or ½-brick, 215 mm or 1-brick, 328 mm or 1½-brick, 440 mm or 2-brick, etc. It should be pointed out that large modern buildings are usually of steel-framed or reinforced concrete construction which provides for the support of heavy loads (on floors, etc.) by the use of either steelwork or reinforced concrete (the latter consisting of concrete and steel bars or other reinforcement), and therefore walls which exceed two bricks in thickness are now rarely required. As explained in Chapter Eleven, cavity walls are extensively used in lieu of solid external walls.

A bond is usually identified by the appearance of the external face of the wall, and it is this face appearance which is referred to in the following description of bonds. Thus the expression "alternate courses of headers" refers to the arrangement of the bricks on the face, even if the headers in each course are backed by stretchers.

It should be noted that the joints in most of the following details are indicated by single lines, the thickness not being shown. Students are not recommended to show the joints by double lines (as in the plan in Fig. 165), for, unless they are very accurately drawn, accumulative errors are likely to occur, resulting in the bond being shown incorrectly. Drawing is further facilitated if, as shown in the examples, the dimensions of a brick are assumed to be 225 mm by 112·5 mm by 75 mm.

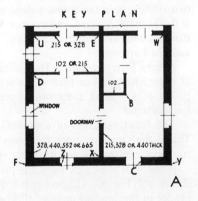

KEY PLAN

Fig. 35

Heading Bond.—Each course of a wall consists of headers only. It is used chiefly in the construction of footings (see Fig. 61) and walls which are sharply curved, where the long faces of stretchers would unduly break the line of the curve (see p. 155).

Fig. 35 is a key plan of a portion of a building and it is assumed that the following details of bonding are referred to this plan.

Stretching Bond.—An isometric drawing of a portion of walling, such at at B, Fig. 35, is shown in Fig. 36. This shows three courses of the two ½-brick thick walls at the corner with a detached fourth course to indicate the arrangement of the bricks at alternate courses. It will be observed that the first or quoin bricks alternate as stretchers and headers in adjacent courses. Both walls are therefore well bonded at the corners and a "break joint" equal to ½-brick lap is produced by a quoin stretcher appearing as a header on the return face. The break joint at the stopped end (see below) of a ½-brick wall is effected by placing a half bat at

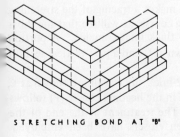

STRETCHING BOND AT "B"

Fig. 36

the end of each alternate course. This bond is suitable for ½-brick walls, such as are required for division walls (as above), cavity walls (see Chapter Eleven), chimney-stacks (see Chapter Fourteen) and sleeper walls (built as intermediate supports to ground floor wood joists). Low division walls which are not required to support loads may be built with the bricks placed on edge and in stretching bond; the thickness is thus reduced to 65 mm.

ENGLISH BOND

English bond consists of *alternate courses* of headers and stretchers. It is the strongest bond as the bricks are well lapped and, with a few exceptions stated below, there are no continuous vertical joints. Observe in the following details: (1) In each *heading course a queen closer is placed next to the quoin header* and the remaining bricks are headers; (2) every alternate header in a course comes centrally over the joint between two stretchers in the course below, giving an approximate lap of ¼-brick; and (3) there are no continuous vertical joints, excepting at certain stopped ends and particularly where queen closers of the form K, Fig. 24, and not J are used.

Square Stopped Ends.—The following shows the treatment at the end of a detached wall or that at the stopped end (called a *square jamb*—see p. 76) of a wall at a doorway opening, such as at C, Fig. 35, built in English bond.

The front elevation of a portion of the wall is shown at G, Fig. 37. This is the same for every thickness of wall. The stretching and heading courses are lettered R and P respectively.

If the wall is 1-brick thick the plans of the alternate courses will be as shown at J, Fig. 37. Observe that a queen closer is placed next to the first header in the heading course; this produces the necessary lap of ¼-brick. A heading course should never *commence* with a queen closer as in this position it would be liable to displacement. The stretching course has been indicated by broken lines on the plan of the heading course; this shows that none of the joints is continuous.

Assuming that the external wall at C, Fig. 35, is 1½-brick thick, the plans of successive courses will be as shown at K, Fig. 47. The end of each heading course (P) is formed of two three-quarter bats (see F, Fig. 23) next to which are placed two queen closers similar to that at V, Fig. 24. The end of each stretching course (R) is built of three stretchers. If after drawing these two courses, the student makes a tracing of the stretching course and transposes it over the heading course, he will see that the short ¼-brick portions of joints indicated by thick lines coincide. A portion of the end elevation of this wall is shown at G and a part vertical section through this wall is also given at G.

The plans of alternate courses of a 2-brick thick wall are shown at L, Fig. 38. The arrangement of the bricks in the heading course (P) follows the rule, *i.e.*, "header-closer-headers". The treatment at the end of the stretching course (R) shows that queen closers have been employed.

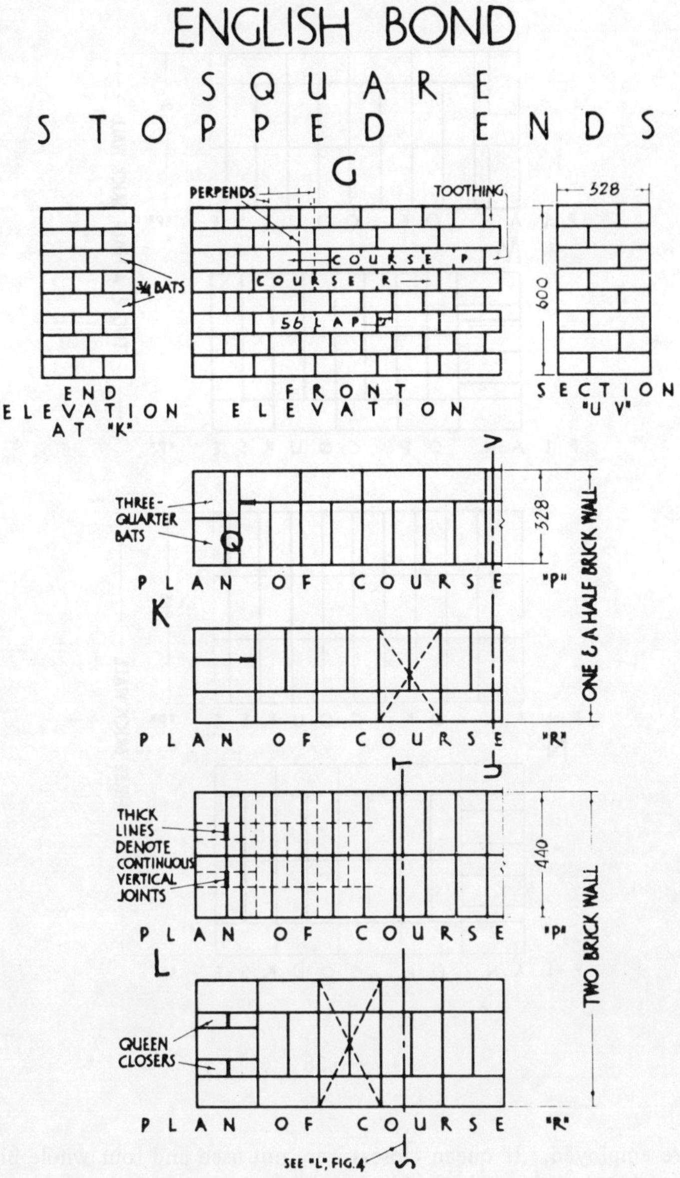

ENGLISH BOND
SQUARE
STOPPED ENDS

Fig.37

These are quarter bricks (see K, Fig. 24), which, as explained on p. 51, are often used as they are easily cut. Part of the stretching course has been indicated by broken lines on the heading course and the short thick lines denote the straight joints which result. These short continuous vertical joints would, of course, be avoided if full queen closers (J, Fig. 24)

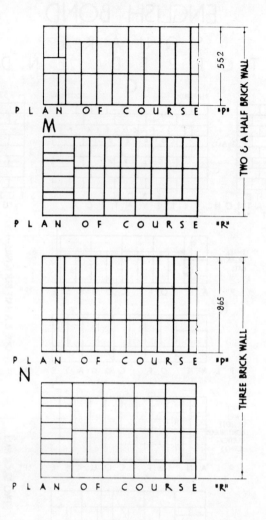

PLAN OF COURSE "P"

M

PLAN OF COURSE "R"

PLAN OF COURSE "P"

N

PLAN OF COURSE "R"

TWO & A HALF BRICK WALL

THREE BRICK WALL

552

865

Fig.38

were employed. If queen closers were not used and four whole bricks were placed at the end of each stretching course, the joint between the two inner bricks would coincide with the longitudinal joint in the heading course and thus a 1-brick continuous vertical joint would result.

The alternate course plans of a 2½-brick thick wall (which nowadays is very rarely called for) are shown at M, Fig. 38.

Special attention should be taken in the construction of stopped ends of walls as these are often required to take concentrated loads from lintels, etc. (see Figs. 124, 129, 130 and 131).

To summarize, the following should be noted in connection with English bond:—

1. The bond consists of alternate courses of headers and stretchers.

2. A queen closer always adjoins the first header and this produces an approximate lap of a ¼-brick.

3. Each alternate header is centrally over a vertical joint.

4. The absence of continuous joints (except at certain stopped ends).

5. At least every alternate transverse joint (those at right angles to the face of the wall) is continuous from face to face; a 1½-brick wall consists of units comprising a stretcher backed with two headers, or vice versa (see broken lines at K, Fig. 37); a stretcher course of a 2-brick wall is formed of units having a stretcher on each face with two headers in the middle (see broken lines at L, Fig. 38).

Students at examinations frequently make the mistake of showing non-continuous transverse joints.

6. Walls of an *even* number of *half* bricks in thickness present the same appearance on both faces, *i.e.*, a course consisting of stretchers on the front elevation will also show stretchers on the back elevation (see J, Fig. 37, and L, Fig. 38).

7. Walls of an *odd* number of half bricks in thickness will show *each* course consisting of headers on one face and stretchers on the other (see K, Fig. 37, and M, Fig. 38).

8. The middle portion of each of the thicker walls consists entirely of headers (see L and M, Fig. 38 and p. 159).

Note.—A scale of 1 : 10 is generally used when detailing brick bonding. Students are recommended to commence with the heading course followed by the stretching course immediately below it. A tracing of the latter course transposed over the heading course will emphasize that there are no continuous vertical joints (except short portions at certain ends). The brick units must be carefully scaled and measurements *lightly* marked with a *sharp* pointed pencil (see p. 32), otherwise errors will accumulate. Mere copying of lines should be avoided and the student should imagine that each brick is being placed in position as he draws it. If the student appreciates that a queen closer is *always* placed next to the quoin header (and never appears in the stretching course) he should not have much difficulty in memorizing the details.

The external walls of some buildings if built of solid brickwork may be 1½-brick thick, and the division walls either 102·5 or 215 mm thick. Other types of buildings may have thicker walls, but, as already explained, walls exceeding two bricks in thickness are now rarely employed. Most houses are built with external cavity walls — see Chap. XI.

FLEMISH BOND

There are two kinds of Flemish bond, *i.e.*, (1) Double Flemish and (2) Single Flemish.

1. *Double Flemish Bond.*—The front elevation of a portion of wall built in Flemish bond is shown at ·D, Fig. 39, and, as indicated, it comprises *alternate* headers and stretchers in *each* course. In double Flemish bond this characteristic appearance is the same on *both* faces. It will be seen that each header comes centrally over a stretcher, and, unlike English bond, no header comes over a vertical face joint. It is not so strong as English bond because of the large number of short continuous joints which occur in the longitudinal joints (see pp. 61-62). Some consider that Flemish bond has a more pleasing appearance and is more economical than English bond.

Whilst there is a difference of opinion concerning the appearance of Flemish bond, it is accepted that where a fair or uniform face is required on *both* sides of a 215 mm wall this is more readily obtained if Flemish and not English bond is used. The reason for this is that the stretcher faces of bricks often vary in length on account of the unequal shrinkage which may occur during the burning process, and thus the combined length of two headers plus the thickness of a vertical joint often exceeds the length of a stretcher. Consequently, when a 1-brick wall is built in English bond one face is fair but the opposite face often shows each heading course set back slightly in relation to the stretching course. This irregularity is not so pronounced if the wall is constructed in Flemish bond, as each course consists of alternate headers and stretchers, and therefore the slight set-back of the short headers is

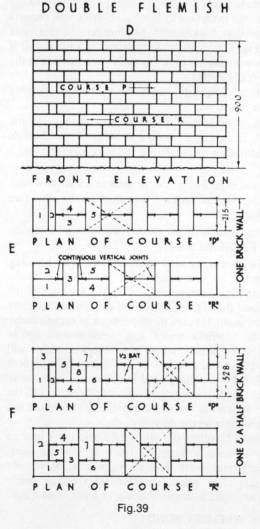

DOUBLE FLEMISH

D

FRONT ELEVATION

E PLAN OF COURSE "P"

CONTINUOUS VERTICAL JOINTS

PLAN OF COURSE "R"

F PLAN OF COURSE "P"

PLAN OF COURSE "R"

Fig.39

better distributed and is considered to improve the surface texture or character of the work.

Square Stopped Ends. The plans of two successive courses at the end of a 1-brick wall built in double Flemish bond are shown at E, Fig. 39. As in English bond, a queen closer is placed next to the quoin header and thus a lap of approximately ¼-brick is provided. The short (56 mm) thick portions of

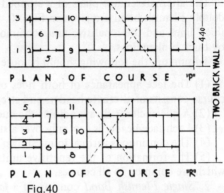

Fig.40

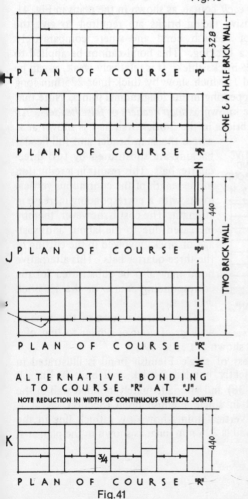

Fig.41

the longitudinal joints are continuous and are the cause of the relative weakness of this bond. It will be seen that the front and back elevations must be the same. Attention is drawn to the units (each consisting of a header and two adjacent stretchers) of which *every* course is comprised and which are indicated within the broken diagonal lines.

Plans of alternate courses at the end of a 1½-brick wall are shown at F, Fig. 39. The first header and adjacent queen closer are backed by a three-quarter bat. Each of the units common to all courses, and indicated within the broken diagonal lines, is square and made up of four bricks enclosing a half bat. Bricks damaged in course of transit, etc., may be formed into these half bats and to this extent a saving in cost results which cannot be effected in English bond. Note the joints indicated by short many continuous vertical thick lines.

The alternate course plans of a stopped end of a 2-brick wall built in double Flemish bond are given in Fig. 40. Straight joints are shown by thick lines and the repetitive units common to all courses are indicated by thick broken lines.

To sum up, the following should be noted in double Flemish bond:—

(1) The face appearance of both sides of a wall is the same and *each* course consists of alternate headers and stretchers.

(2) A queen closer always adjoins the quoin header.

(3) Each face header is centrally over a stretcher.

(4) The continuous vertical joints shown by thick lines.

(5) The formation of the repetitive units within broken diagonal lines which are common to all courses.

2. *Single Flemish Bond* consists of a *facing of Flemish bond* with a *backing of English bond* in *each* course, as shown in the plans in Fig. 41. It is adopted where expensive facing bricks are required to give the characteristic appearance of Flemish bond and where comparatively cheaper bricks are used as a backing. This bond cannot be applied to walls which are less than 1½-bricks thick. It is relatively weak, as can be seen on reference to H and J, which show by thick lines 225 mm long continuous vertical joints appearing in the longitudinal joints. Note that half bats are used which are known as *snap headers* or *false headers*. An alternative arrangement of bricks in the 2-brick wall at J is shown at K where the snap header and full header backing are substituted by two three-quarter bats. This results in a reduction in the length of the continuous vertical joints with a corresponding increase in strength. The cost is, however, thereby increased due to the labour and wastage of bricks involved in the cutting of the three-quarter bats. This alternative bond may also be substituted for the corresponding course of the 1½-brick wall at H.

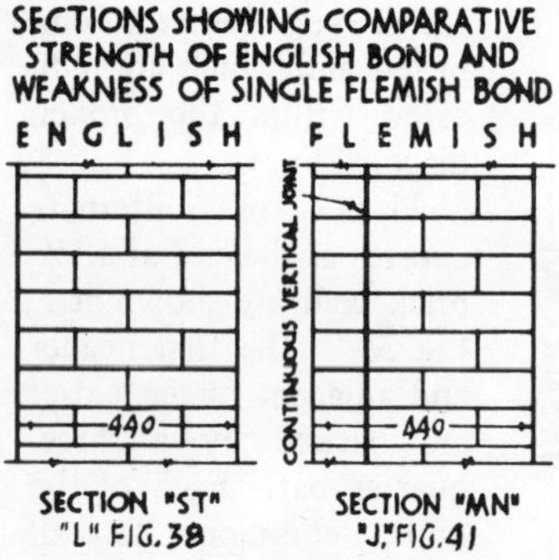

SECTIONS SHOWING COMPARATIVE
STRENGTH OF ENGLISH BOND AND
WEAKNESS OF SINGLE FLEMISH BOND

ENGLISH   FLEMISH

SECTION "ST"   SECTION "MN"
"L" FIG. 38   "J" FIG. 41

Fig. 42

The front elevation of this type of wall is, of course, similar to that of a double Flemish bonded wall shown at D, Fig. 39.

The comparative weakness of single Flemish bond is illustrated in Fig. 42. This shows a perfectly bonded 2-brick wall built in English bond (Section ST at L, Fig. 38) and an inadequately bonded wall of the same thickness constructed in single Flemish bond (Section MN at J, Fig. 41). The continuous vertical joint shown by a thick line in the section through the latter wall is 225 mm long, as shown in the plan at J, Fig. 41.

CHAPTER FOUR

JUNCTIONS AND QUOINS

½ to 1, 1 to 1 and 1 to 1½-brick right-angled junctions in English and Flemish bonds; squint junctions; right-angled quoins to 1, 1½ and 2-brick walls in English and Flemish bonds; obtuse and acute squint-angled quoins.

JUNCTIONS

THESE are classified into (1) right-angled junctions and (2) squint junctions.

1. RIGHT-ANGLED OR SQUARE JUNCTIONS.—There are two forms of right-angled junctions, *i.e.*, (*a*) tee-junctions and (*b*) cross-junctions or intersections.

(a) *Tee - junctions.*—A tee-junction is a connection between two walls which on plan is in the form of the letter T. Several such connections are shown at D, U, W and X in the key plan, Fig. 35.

Plans of tee-junctions between walls built in English bond are shown at A, B and C, Fig. 43.

That at A is an enlargement of the junction at D, Fig. 35. It shows that one of the courses of the ½-brick internal division wall enters the stretching course of the 1-brick external main wall, giving a ½-brick lap, and the alternate course of the division wall butts against the heading course of the main wall. The courses lettered P and R may be assumed to be those indicated in

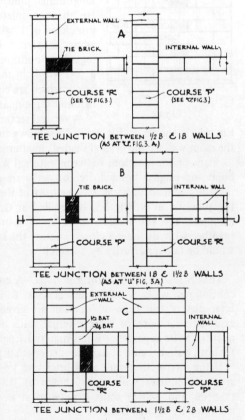

TEE JUNCTION BETWEEN ½B & 1B WALLS
(AS AT 'U' FIG. 3. A)

TEE JUNCTION BETWEEN 1B & 1½B WALLS
(AS AT 'U' FIG. 3A)

TEE JUNCTION BETWEEN 1½B & 2B WALLS

Fig. 43

the elevation at G, Fig. 37; similar references are also made in the following details.

If the tee-junction at U, Fig. 35, is between a 1½-brick external wall and a 1-brick internal wall, the bonding at alternate courses will be as shown at B, Fig. 43. The alternate courses at C show the bonding if the external and internal walls are 2-brick and 1½-brick thick respectively. The following should be noted in connection with details B and C: (1) Each heading course of the internal wall is bonded into the stretching course of the main or external wall, the first header or tie brick (shown shaded) giving a ¼-brick lap and being adjacent to a queen closer; (2) each stretching course of the division wall butts against headers in the external wall.

Note.—The student when drawing these details is advised to commence with the bonded course (*i.e.*, course P at B), and, after drawing the outline of the junction, he should fill in the tie brick or first header

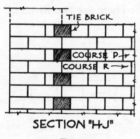

SECTION "HJ"

Fig. 44

(see B) in the internal wall, followed by the queen closer which gives the position of the longitudinal joint in the main wall. Both walls are then completed in accordance with the principles of English bond stated in the previous chapter. Compliance with the rule regarding continuous transverse joints (see p. 59) will help the student to arrange the cut bricks which are sometimes necessary, *i.e.*, the half and three-quarter bats shown at C, Fig. 43. A vertical section HJ through the walls at B,

Fig. 43, is shown in Fig. 44. This shows the division wall well tied to the main wall by the bricks (shaded) in alternate courses.

Plans of tee-junctions between external walls built in double Flemish bond and English bonded division walls are given in Fig. 45. That at F may be assumed to be an enlargement of the junction at W, Fig. 35, and the junction at X, Fig. 35, is detailed at G, Fig. 45. As in the above examples, the key header has a lap of ¼-brick and half of this header, together with the queen closer, occupy the space in the main wall which would be taken normally by a stretcher.

(b) *Cross Junctions or Intersections.*—A cross junction consists of two continuous walls which intersect (see E in the key plan, Fig. 35). Examples of this type of junction are given at D and E, Fig. 46. It is assumed that both of these internal walls are to be plastered. Consequently, as its appearance is not material, English bond would be adopted for both walls because of its greater strength in preference to Flemish bond.

If the intersecting walls are 1-brick and 1½-brick thick, the bonding of alternate courses will be as shown at D. An intersection between 1½-brick and 2-brick walls is detailed at E, the alternate course being indicated by broken lines.

Note.—(1) One of the courses is continuous and the course at right angles butts against it; (2) these continuous courses alternate; and (3) a key header (shown shaded) forms a ¼-brick lap at each side of the non-continuous course.

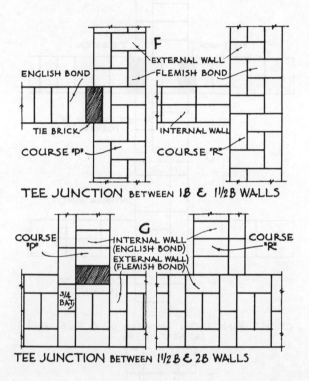

TEE JUNCTION BETWEEN 1B & 1½B WALLS

TEE JUNCTION BETWEEN 1½B & 2B WALLS

Fig.45

The above are only a few examples of several methods of bonding at junctions. The arrangement of the bricks depends largely upon the relative position of the cross and main walls. The details given in Figs. 43, 45 and 46 show that the junctions occur with at least one of the faces of the entering course of each division or cross wall coinciding with a continuous transverse joint in the main wall. In actual practice the required dimensions of a building do not always allow of this and in such cases variations from the bonding shown have to be made. The essential requirements are the avoidance of continuous vertical joints with the employment of the minimum number of broken bricks.

2. SQUINT OR OBLIQUE JUNCTIONS are not often called for.

Some typical examples of squint junctions indicating English bond are shown in Fig. 47.

Details A and B show alternate courses of 1-brick and 1½-brick squint walls connected at an angle of 45° to a 1½-brick wall, and those at C and

D indicate an angle of 60° between the walls. It should be noted that:
(1) The heading course of the squint wall is bonded into the stretching

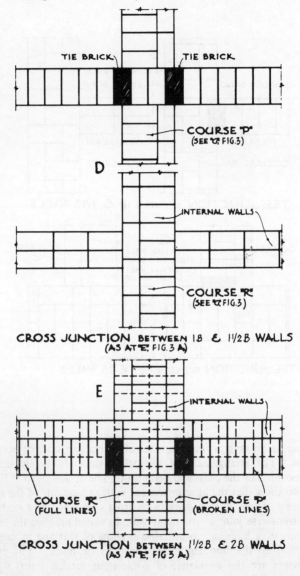

TIE BRICK   TIE BRICK

COURSE "P"
(SEE "G" FIG.3)

D

INTERNAL WALLS

COURSE "R"
(SEE "G" FIG.3)

CROSS JUNCTION BETWEEN 1B & 1½B WALLS
(AS AT "E", FIG. 3 A)

E

INTERNAL WALLS

COURSE "R"   COURSE "P"
(FULL LINES)   (BROKEN LINES)

CROSS JUNCTION BETWEEN 1½B & 2B WALLS
(AS AT "E", FIG 3 A)

Fig.46

course of the main wall; (2) the alternate stretching course of the squint
wall butts against the heading course of the main wall; and (3) the first
brick at J in this stretching course is a three-quarter bevelled bat (somewhat similar to G, Fig. 23).

Fig.47

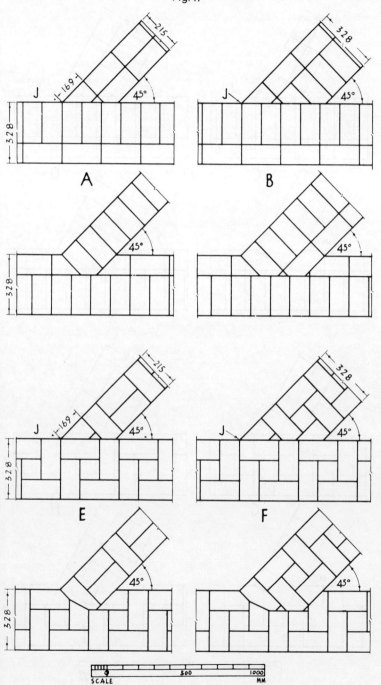

SCALE 0 — 500 — 1000 MM

67

Fig.48

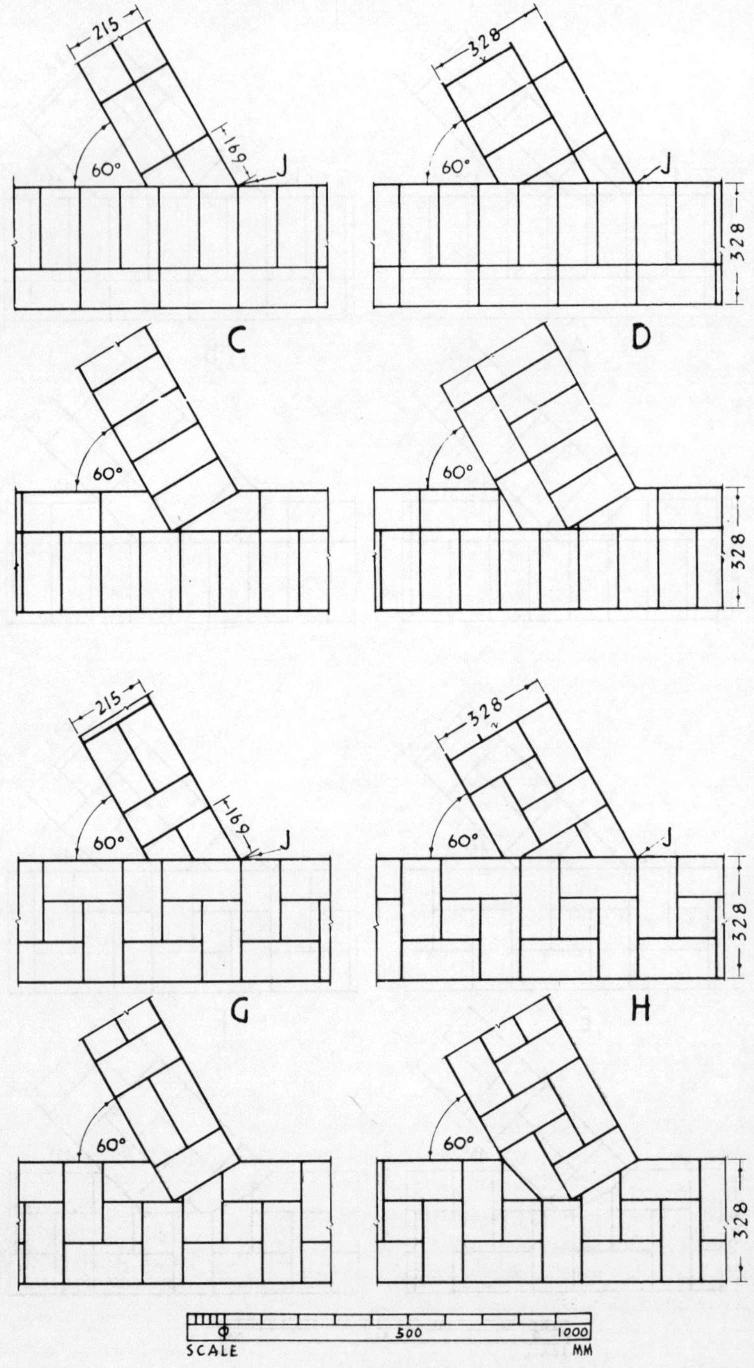

C

D

G

H

SCALE
500
1000
MM

68

For comparative purposes and convenience in setting out, the angle between the walls in each detail has been made to coincide at J with the continuous transverse joint of the main wall. In practice, both the position and size of this angle vary.

Squint junctions in double Flemish bond are detailed in Fig. 48. The angles and thickness of walls are similar to the above. It will be observed that, for convenience, the three-quarter bevelled bat in each of the squint walls coincides with the through transverse joint of the main wall at J, and the first bonding brick in the alternate course of each squint wall is a header on face.

In this class of work the amount of cutting necessary to avoid continuous vertical joints should be kept to a minimum, the cut bricks should be as large as possible, and awkward shapes of bricks difficult to cut should be restricted.

QUOINS, CORNERS OR EXTERNAL ANGLES

There are two forms of quoins, *i.e.* (1) right-angled quoins and (2) squint quoins.

1. RIGHT-ANGLED OR SQUARE QUOINS.—As is implied, a right-angled quoin is formed by two walls which meet at 90°.   Examples of right-angled quoins are shown at F and Y, Fig. 35.

An isometric sketch of a square quoin indicating 1-brick walls in English bond is shown in Fig. 49; the quoin between two 1½-brick walls is shown in the sketch, Fig. 61. Plans of alternate courses of right-angled quoins formed by walls built in English bond are shown detailed in Fig. 50; these may be considered as alternative details of the quoin F, Fig. 35. The plans

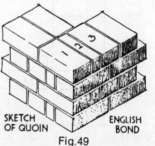

SKETCH OF QUOIN   ENGLISH BOND

Fig.49

of successive courses at A show 1-brick walls, those at B show 1½-brick walls and two-brick walls are shown at C, Fig. 50. Note:—

(1) At the same level, the heading course on one face of the quoin is returned by a stretching course.

(2) When the wall is an *even* number of half-bricks in thickness the brick figured 3 is a *header* projecting ¼-brick (see A and C, Fig. 50 and Fig. 49).

(3) When the wall is an *odd* number of half-bricks thick, the brick figured 3 is a *stretcher* projecting ¼-brick (see B, Fig. 10).

(4) At the ¼-brick projection (or "quarter bond") of number 3 brick the transverse joint is continuous (see M at B, Fig. 50).

(5) In the 1 and 2-brick quoins the heading course of one wall is continuous to the front of the return face (see H and K) and that in the 1½-brick quoin is continuous to the back of the stretching face; the return stretching course in each case butts against the heading course.

(6) There are no continuous vertical joints.

Fig.50

ENGLISH BOND

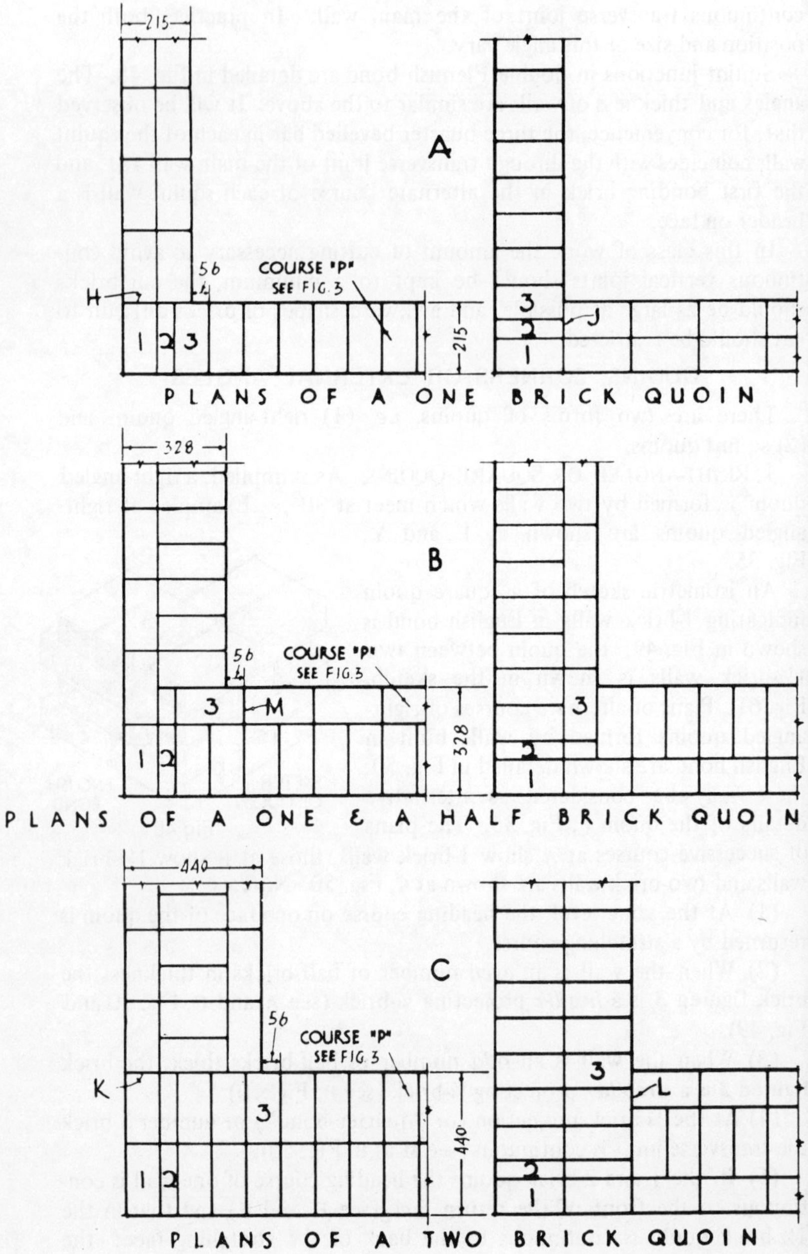

215

A

56
4

COURSE "P"
SEE FIG.3

H

215

3
2
1

J

1 2 3

PLANS OF A ONE BRICK QUOIN

328

B

56
4

COURSE "P"
SEE FIG.3

3 M

328

3

1 2

2
1

PLANS OF A ONE & A HALF BRICK QUOIN

440

C

56

COURSE "P"
SEE FIG.3

K

3

440

3

L

1 2

2
1

PLANS OF A TWO BRICK QUOIN

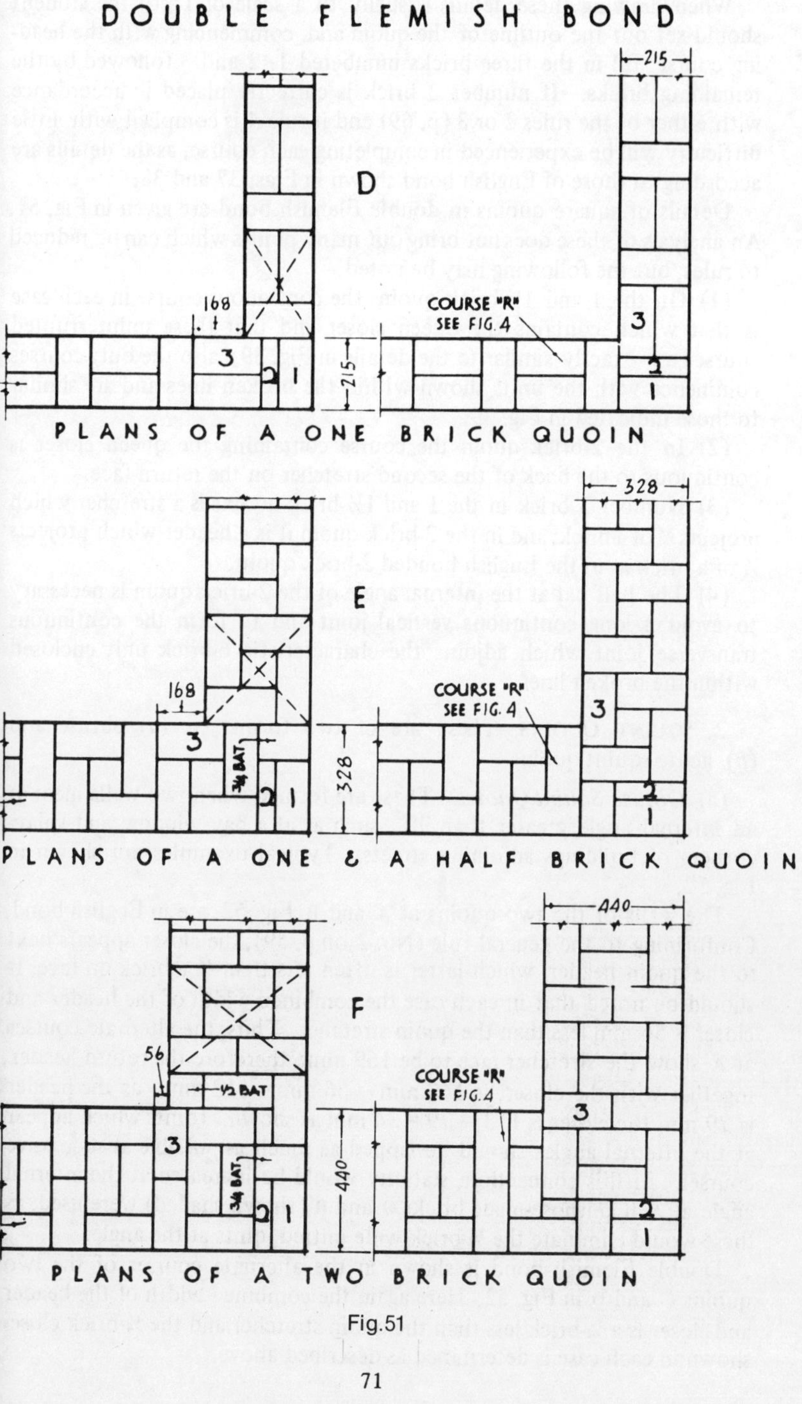

DOUBLE FLEMISH BOND

PLANS OF A ONE BRICK QUOIN

D

COURSE "R" SEE FIG.4

215

168

215

3 2 1

PLANS OF A ONE & A HALF BRICK QUOIN

E

COURSE "R" SEE FIG.4

328

168

3/4 BAT

3 2 1

PLANS OF A TWO BRICK QUOIN

F

COURSE "R" SEE FIG.4

440

56

1/2 BAT

3/4 BAT

3 2 1

Fig.51

71

When drawing these details (usually to a scale of 1:10) the student should set out the outline of the quoin and, commencing with the heading course, fill in the three bricks numbered 1, 2 and 3 followed by the remaining bricks. If number 3 brick is correctly placed in accordance with either of the rules 2 or 3 (p. 69) and if rule 4 is complied with, little difficulty will be experienced in completing each course, as the details are according to those of English bond shown in Figs. 37 and 38.

Details of square quoins in double Flemish bond are given in Fig. 51. An analysis of these does not bring out many points which can be reduced to rules, but the following may be noted:—

(1) On the 1 and 1½-brick quoins the continuous course in each case is that which contains the queen closer and that these uninterrupted courses are exactly similar to the details in Fig. 39; also the butt courses commence with the units shown within the broken lines and are similar to those indicated in Fig. 39.

(2) In the 2-brick quoin the course containing the queen closer is continuous to the back of the second stretcher on the return face.

(3) Number 3 brick in the 1 and 1½-brick quoins is a stretcher which projects ¾ of a brick, and in the 2-brick quoin it is a header which projects ¼ of a brick as in the English bonded 2-brick quoin.

(4) The half bat at the internal angle of the 2-brick quoin is necessary to avoid a long continuous vertical joint and to form the continuous transverse joint which adjoins the characteristic 6-brick unit enclosed within the broken lines.

2. SQUINT QUOINS.—These are of two forms, i.e. (a) obtuse and (b) acute squint quoins.

(a) *Obtuse Squint Quoins.*—These are formed when two walls meet at an internal angle greater than 90°, such as at a bay window and splay-corners of buildings adjoining streets. Typical examples are shown in Fig. 52.

The walls of the two quoins at A and B, Fig. 52, are in English bond. Conforming to the general rule (No. 2 on p. 59), the closer appears next to the quoin header, which latter is often less than ½ a brick on face. It should be noted that in each case the combined width of the header and closer is 56 mm less than the quoin stretcher. Thus, the alternate courses at A show the stretcher face to be 169 mm; therefore the return header, together with the closer, is 169 mm − 56 mm = 113 mm; as the header is 79 mm the closer is 113 − 79 = 34 mm as shown. Joints which appear at the internal angles should be lapped as much as possible at successive courses. In this connection, stability would be increased at the internal angle at A if purpose-made bricks Q and R (shown shaded) were used, as these would eliminate the ½-brick wide mitred joints at the angle.

Double Flemish bond is shown in the alternate courses of the two quoins C and D in Fig. 52. Here again the combined width of the header and closer is a ¼-brick less than the quoin stretcher and the ¼-brick closer shown in each case is determined as described above.

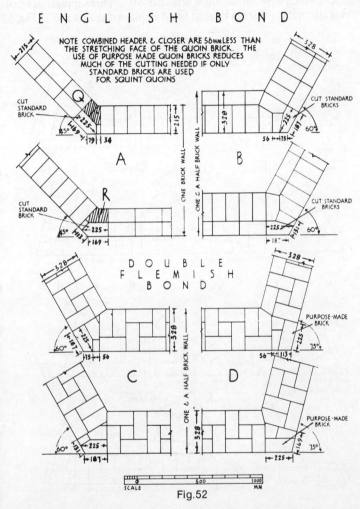

Fig.52

At the above quoins A and B the quoin bricks are ordinary bricks which have been cut to shape. It is now general for faced work to employ purpose-made (see p. 53) quoin bricks, and most of the larger manufacturers stock special squint bricks for this purpose. Four of several such standard special bricks are shown in Fig. 30. Purpose-made quoin bricks are shown at D, Fig. 52. A much better appearance is thus obtained than when ordinary standard bricks are cut to shape with the bolster and scutch-dressed (p. 51). In the absence of purpose-made bricks, wire-cuts only should be shaped, as those with frogs produce ugly joints if the margins are removed.

An obtuse squint quoin of a cavity wall is shown in Fig. 153.

(b) *Acute Squint Quoins* are necessary at corners of buildings abutting on streets which meet at an angle less than 90°. Three typical examples showing alternate courses in English bond are shown at F,G and H,Fig. 53.

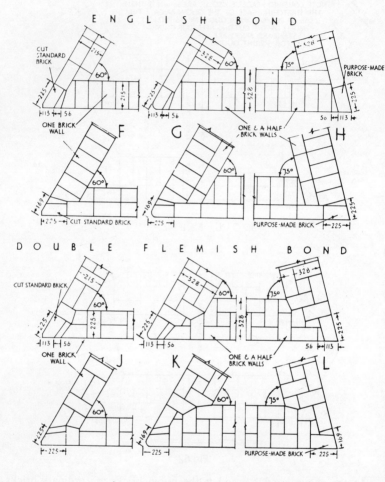

Fig.53

The rules of bonding (see on p. 59–62) which influence the face appearance have been complied with. Several expedients may be adopted to dispense with the sharp arrises at very acute quoins, and which arrises are readily damaged, difficult to cut (if standard bricks are used) and may cause injury to persons coming in contact with them. Thus at F the corner is removed (or, preferably, purposely moulded to the shape shown) and bullnoses are used as shown at G. A simple and effective alternative is shown at N, Fig. 54, where a birdsmouthed appearance is obtained by the use of ordinary bricks which require little cutting and which cut surfaces are not exposed.

Three examples of acute squint quoins showing alternate courses in double Flemish bond are given at J, K and L, Fig. 53. It will be seen that

Fig.54

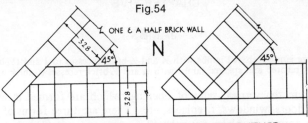

ALTERNATE COURSES SHOWING BIRDSMOUTHED
ACUTE SQUINT QUOIN IN ENGLISH BOND

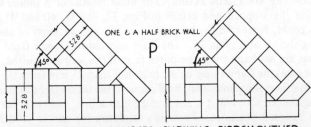

ALTERNATE COURSES SHOWING BIRDSMOUTHED
ACUTE SQUINT QUOIN IN DOUBLE FLEMISH BOND

the bonding complies with the face appearance illustrated in Fig. 39. The corners at J and K are shaped for the reasons stated on p. 74. A birds-mouthed acute squint quoin in this bond is shown at P, Fig. 54.

The above are only a few examples of squint quoins. There are several alternatives. The aim should be to obtain the maximum lap with the minimum of cutting. Whilst the correct face appearance is not necessary if the walls are to be plastered, the principles of sound bonding should be observed and continuous vertical joints avoided.

CHAPTER FIVE

JAMBS

Square jambs; rebated jambs with ¼ and ½-brick recesses to 1 and 1½-brick walls; rebated and splayed jambs with ¼ and ½-brick recesses to thick walls.

JAMBS are the vertical sides of openings which are formed in walls to receive doors, windows, fireplaces, etc. There are three forms of jambs, *i.e.* (1) square or plain, (2) rebated or recessed and (3) rebated and splayed.

1. SQUARE OR PLAIN JAMBS –The bond treatment is similar to that shown in the stopped end details in Figs. 37, 38, 39, 40 and 41; such details could, for example, be applied to the square jamb of the door opening shown at C, Fig. 35. The door or window frames fixed in the openings are set back from the outer face of the wall as required. Thus, in some cases the frames may be set back less than 25 mm from the front, whilst in others the frames may be flush with the inside faces of the walls. Although often adopted, it is not sound construction, especially for buildings in exposed positions. There is a tendency for rain to be driven in between the frames and the brickwork, and dampness is thereby caused. This is avoided if the frames are fixed in recesses as described below.

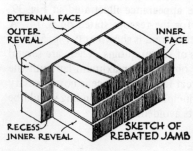

EXTERNAL FACE
OUTER REVEAL
INNER FACE
RECESS
INNER REVEAL
SKETCH OF REBATED JAMB

Fig.55

2. REBATED OR RECESSED JAMBS.—A sketch of a rebated jamb, showing English bond, is given in Fig. 55. As shown it consists of (*a*) an *outer* face or *reveal,* (*b*) a *recess* and (*c*) an *inner reveal.* As is implied, the outer reveal is that portion of the jamb which is seen from the outside; it may be ½-brick (see Figs. 55, 56 and 57) or it may be 1-brick (see Figs. 58 and 59). The recess varies in depth from ¼-brick or less (suitable for external doors and certain windows, such as fixed lights or those having hinged sashes which open outwards) to ½-brick (sometimes used for windows with sashes which slide vertically). Those with ¼-brick recesses are shown at D, E and F, Fig. 56, G, H and J, Fig. 57 and Fig. 58; ½-brick recesses are indicated at K, L and M, Fig. 56, N, O and P, Fig. 57 and Fig. 59. The object of a recess is to accommodate the door or window frame (see F, Fig. 56). The protection afforded by the outer "nib" of brickwork assists in preventing

the access of wind and rain into a building between the frame and adjacent brickwork. Additional protection is afforded when the frames are bedded in mortar (*i.e.*, mortar is trowelled in between the frame and brickwork) and pointed (*i.e.*, a neat triangular fillet of cement mortar or mastic is formed round the outside of the frame next to the brickwork); there are several proprietary mastics available (e.g. "Seelastik").

An elevation of a portion of a wall in English bond with an opening is shown at A, Fig. 56, and alternative plans showing the bonding are given below it. These details may be applied, for example, at the windows indicated in the key plan, Fig. 35. The same treatment is provided at door openings having rebated jambs.

The plans at D, E and F, Fig. 56, show ½-brick wide outer reveals and ¼-brick deep recesses. One course of each wall is shown on the left of the centre line of the opening and the alternate course is shown on the right.

In the plan at D, the correct face appearance of "header-closer-header" (see p. 56) is obtained by using a small bevelled bat (H, Fig. 23) and a king closer (Fig. 25) in course T. In the alternate course U a three-quarter bat (F, Fig. 23) is employed at the back.

In this and most of the plans which follow the joints of the brickwork above and below the opening are indicated by broken lines, alternate courses being indicated on each side of the centre line. *Consideration should always be given to the size of the bricks to be used and the desired thickness of joints when deciding upon the sizes of door and window openings. The width of an external opening should be a multiple of 1 brick for English bond in order to maintain vertical perpends and the normal face appearance of the bond above and below the opening.* Thus, for English bond, the size of the opening may be 215 mm (or length of brick used), 430 mm, 645 mm, 860 mm, etc., plus the combined thickness of the vertical joints. It will be noted in Fig. 56 that the width of the opening is 685 mm [*i.e.* $(3 \times 215) + (4 \times 10)$]. The figured dimensions on working drawings should include the thickness of the joints (see Figs. 133 and 136). It is also important that the length of walling between openings should be a multiple of a brick (for stretching, English and English garden wall—see Fig. 101—bonds) plus the combined thickness of vertical joints. *These dimensions must be carefully set out when the brickwork has reached the ground level* (see p. 113). The carrying out of these precautions will involve some thought and the expenditure of a little time, but the results obtained are well worth while. *Otherwise the appearance will be unsatisfactory because of defects such as broken perpends, unbalanced treatment at jambs of openings (i.e., a stretcher at one side and a header or bat in the same course at the other), and the presence of closers, etc., in the brickwork above and below openings.*

In the plan at E, Fig. 56, a small bevelled bat and a king closer are also provided, as at D. In the alternate course, as shown on the right, two bevelled closers (N, Fig. 26) are needed in order to avoid a continuous

FLEMISH BOND

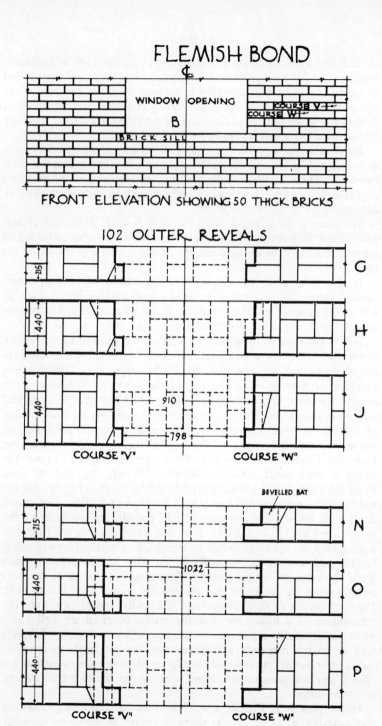

FRONT ELEVATION SHOWING 50 THICK BRICKS

102 OUTER REVEALS

WINDOW OPENING

B

BRICK SILL

COURSE V

COURSE W

G

H

J

910

798

COURSE "V"   COURSE "W"

BEVELLED BAT

N

1022

O

P

COURSE "V"   COURSE "W"

Fig.56

ENGLISH BOND

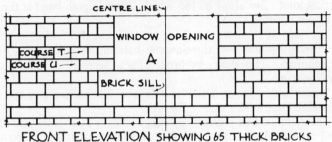

CENTRE LINE

WINDOW OPENING

COURSE T

COURSE U

A

BRICK SILL

FRONT ELEVATION SHOWING 65 THICK BRICKS

102 OUTER REVEALS

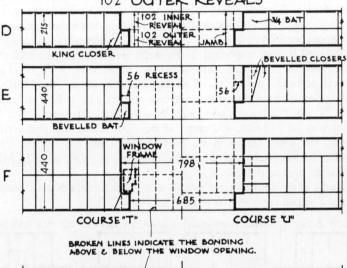

D

215

102 INNER REVEAL

102 OUTER REVEAL JAMB

¾ BAT

KING CLOSER

E

440

56 RECESS

56

BEVELLED CLOSERS

BEVELLED BAT

F

440

WINDOW FRAME

798

685

COURSE "T"

COURSE "U"

BROKEN LINES INDICATE THE BONDING ABOVE & BELOW THE WINDOW OPENING.

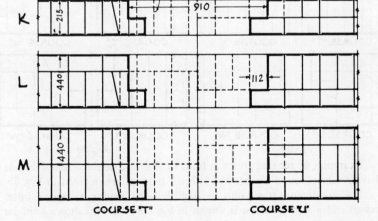

K

215

910

L

440

112

M

440

COURSE "T"

COURSE "U"

Fig. 57

vertical joint. See also Fig. 165 which shows English bond at the jambs of a door opening.

The plan at F shows the above treatment at the heading course. In the alternate course two three-quarter bats and two closers (V, Fig. 24) are required. This shows by broken lines the relative position of the window frame.

Jambs with ½-brick outer reveals and ½-brick recesses are shown in English bond at K, L and M, Fig. 56.

The treatment at jambs of openings in walls built in double Flemish bond when ½-brick outer reveals and ¼-brick recesses are required is shown in Fig. 57. The part elevation at B shows 50 mm thick bricks. Plans of alternative courses are shown below. These should be carefully studied. It will be seen that either king, queen or bevelled closers, etc., are employed in order to prevent straight joints and to obtain the correct face appearance on both sides of each wall. The internal face appearance of the wall is only important if the walls are not to be plastered. To ensure the maintenance of the normal face appearance of the bond and vertical perpends the width of an external opening in a wall built in double Flemish bond should be a multiple of 1 brick (as in English bond— see p.77) up to 2 bricks and a multiple of 1½ brick afterwards; thus the width may be 215 mm, 430 mm, 748 mm, 1065 mm, etc., plus vertical joints; the width shown in the examples G, H and J is 798 mm. The distance between openings should be 533 mm and múltiples of 1½ brick thereafter, plus vertical joints.

Jambs with ½-brick outer reveals and ½-brick recesses are shown in double Flemish bond at N, O and P, Fig. 57.

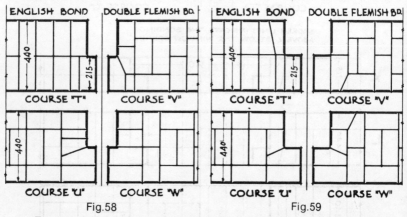

ENGLISH BOND | DOUBLE FLEMISH BD. | ENGLISH BOND | DOUBLE FLEMISH BD.

COURSE "T"   COURSE "V"   COURSE "T"   COURSE "V"

COURSE "U"   COURSE "W"   COURSE "U"   COURSE "W"

Fig.58   Fig.59

Examples of rebated jambs in both English and double Flemish bonds having 1-brick outer reveals and ¼-brick recesses are detailed in Fig. 58.

The treatment at a jamb in English bond having a 1-brick outer reveal and a 1-brick recess is shown in Fig. 59; this also shows a similar jamb of an opening in a double Flemish bonded wall.

3. REBATED AND SPLAYED JAMBS.—These are detailed in Fig. 60. As

shown, such a jamb (if of a window opening) consists of a square outer reveal, a recess and a 45° or 60° splayed inner reveal of obtuse squint quoin form (see pp. 72 and 73). These jambs are only applied to door and window openings in thick walls either as an architectural feature or to disperse the light entering a building. As thick walls are rarely employed in modern construction, it follows that these jambs are not now so often required.

The examples shown in Fig. 60 are only suitable for window openings. Those at A, B, C and D have ¼-brick recesses, and are therefore suited for

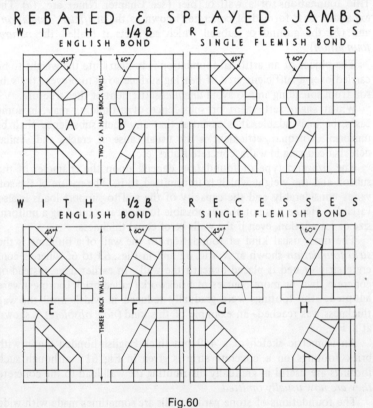

Fig.60

solid framed windows, whilst the remainder have ½-brick recesses for the reception of box framed windows (having vertical sliding sashes).

The suggested bonding of alternate courses in both English and single Flemish bonds is typical only, there being several different arrangements of the bricks. The internal face appearance is only important if the walls are not to be plastered. The bond should be as strong as possible on account of the additional stresses which are transmitted from lintels or arches (see Chapter Ten), and therefore continuous vertical joints should be avoided and the cut bricks should be as large as possible.

CHAPTER SIX

FOUNDATIONS

Foundations for ½, 1, 1½ and 2-brick walls; horizontal damp proof courses;
surface concrete; temporary timbering to shallow trenches.

THE foundations of a wall or pier (see Chapter Nine) are: (a) The
expanded base formed of concrete (known as the *artificial foundation*),
and (b) the ground or subsoil which supports it (called the *natural
foundation*).

The object of an artificial foundation is to distribute the weight to be
carried over a sufficient area of bearing surface so as to prevent the subsoil from spreading and to avoid *unequal* settlement of the structure.

Whilst slight settlement or subsidence of a building may, in some
cases, be unavoidable, it is essential that any such subsidence shall be
uniform. Unequal settlement is the usual cause of cracks and similar
defects occurring in walls, concrete floors, etc.

The size and type of foundation depend upon the character of the
subsoil and the weight which is transmitted to it. The nature of the soil
varies considerably and the capacity of the soil to support loads is also
variable. Hence it is not always possible to adopt in a building a uniform
size of foundation, even if the walls be of equal thickness.

The most usual kind of foundation for the wall of a building is the
strip foundation shown at A, Fig. 62 and in Figs. 63 to 65 where a concrete strip or bed is placed beneath the wall. In earlier days, instead of
concrete, two or more courses of brickwork (called brick footings) were
adopted; the footings were gradually reduced in width until the wall
thickness was reached—an example of this kind (*now obsolete*) is shown
at B, Fig. 62.

An isometric sketch of a 440 mm thick English bonded quoin with
brick footings on a concrete strip is given in Fig. 61; although such
footings are useful in gradually distributing the wall load to the concrete
they are now usually omitted.

The foundations of stone garden walls are sometimes made with wide
slabs of stone.

Buildings must conform to the Building Regulations and the following
summarises the main provisions of these in respect of foundations.

The foundation shall be:—

(1) Constructed to sustain the dead and imposed loads and to transmit these to the ground in such a way that the pressure on it will not
cause settlement which would impair the stability of the building or
adjoining structures.

(2) Taken sufficiently deep to guard the building against damage by
swelling or shrinking of the subsoil (see pp. 84 and 86).

82

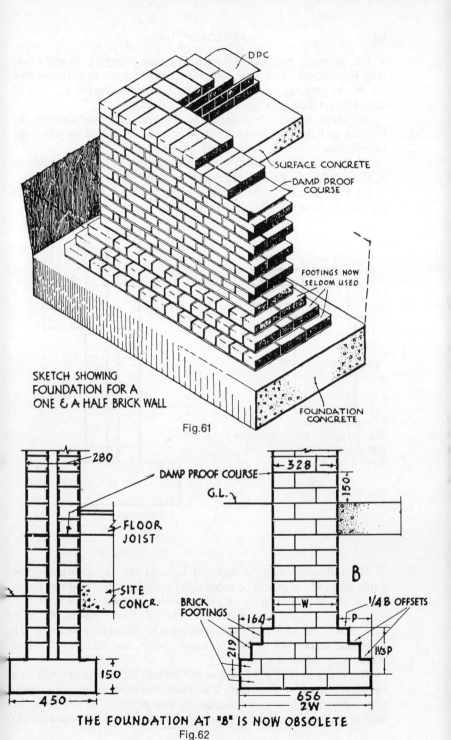

DPC

SURFACE CONCRETE

DAMP PROOF COURSE

FOOTINGS NOW SELDOM USED

FOUNDATION CONCRETE

SKETCH SHOWING
FOUNDATION FOR A
ONE & A HALF BRICK WALL

Fig.61

280

DAMP PROOF COURSE

FLOOR JOIST

SITE CONCR.

150

450

328

150

G.L.

B

W

164

219

1/4 B OFFSETS

P

1/3 P

BRICK FOOTINGS

656
2W

THE FOUNDATION AT "B" IS NOW OBSOLETE

Fig.62

For domestic buildings not exceeding four storeys in height where strip foundation's using plain concrete (1 kg of cement to not more than 0·1 m³ of fine aggregate and 0·2 m³ of coarse aggregate—*i.e.* 1 : 3 : 6 concrete) are used the Regulations are satisfied if:—

(*a*) There is no wide variation in the type of subsoil beneath the building and there is no weaker type of soil below that on which the foundations rest which would affect stability.

(*b*) The foundation width is not less than that given in the Table on p. 85 according to the load and type of subsoil.

(*c*) The thickness of the concrete is not less than its projection from the base of the wall or footing and in no case less than 150 mm.

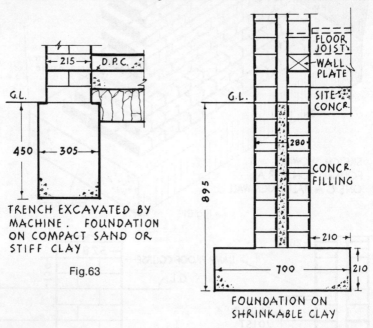

TRENCH EXCAVATED BY
MACHINE . FOUNDATION
ON COMPACT SAND OR
STIFF CLAY

Fig.63

FOUNDATION ON
SHRINKABLE CLAY

Fig.64

The following examples illustrate some of the requirements of the Table on p. 85; it should be noted that for the average two-storey house the wall load is not likely to exceed 40 kN per metre length of wall (*i.e.* in such cases the width is obtained from sub-column 3 in column 4 of the table). Foundations must be placed at sufficient depth to remain unaffected by frost damage; hence, the minimum depth in this country is 460 mm.

The detail at A, Fig. 62, shows the normal 280 mm cavity wall to a building erected on firm clay. The Table therefore requires a foundation width of 450 mm; the foundation thus projects 165 mm from the base of the wall and in order to comply with (c) above the concrete strip

Type of subsoil	Condition of subsoil	Field test applicable	Minimum width (mm) for total load in kilonewtons per lineal metre of load bearing walling of not more than					
			20 kN/m	30 kN/m	40 kN/m	50 kN/m	60 kN/m	70 kN/m
Rock	Not inferior to sandstone, limestone or firm rock	Requires at least mechanically operated pick for excavation	In each case equal to width of wall					
Gravel, sand	Compact	Requires a pick for excavation	250	300	400	500	600	650
Clay, sandy clay	Stiff	Cannot be moulded with the fingers and requires a pick for its removal	250	300	400	500	600	650
Clay, sandy clay	Firm	Can be moulded by substantial pressure with the fingers and can be excavated with a spade	300	350	450	600	750	850
Sand, silty sand, clayey sand	Loose	Can be excavated with a spade. A 50 mm wood peg can be easily driven	400	600	When the load exceeds 30 kN/m per mm length of foundations in these subsoils have to be specially designed (e.g. wider and thicker strips which may require steel reinforcement).			
Silt, clay, sandy clay, silty clay	Soft	Fairly easily moulded in the fingers and readily excavated	450	650				
Silt, clay, sandy clay, silty clay	Very soft	Natural sample in winter conditions exudes between fingers when squeezed in fist	600	850				

Note. The unit of force is the newton (N) and 1 N=1 unit of mass (1 kg)×1 unit of acceleration=1 kg×1 m/second². As the earth's gravitational acceleration is 9.806 65 m/s² then the force exerted by the earth's gravity on a mass of 1 kg=1×9.806 65 N. The latter factor can be taken as 10; hence in the Table the load of 20 kN/m, for example, can be written also as 2 kg/m because a force of 10 N has a mass of 1 kg.

must be 150 mm thick. Such foundation could be excavated by hand or machine; for shallow foundations which are to be cut by hand the minimum width in which a man can conveniently work is about 450 mm.

The detail in Fig. 63 shows the much narrower foundation which can only be formed by a machine excavator; it is suitable in compact sand or stiff clay subsoils where the load is only 30 kN/m length of wall.

Some clay subsoils expand and contract according to the water content, this shrinkage movement decreases as the depth of the foundation increases; therefore in such soils the foundation must start at a depth sometimes as much as 1·2 or 1·5 m below ground level. An example of this kind is shown in Fig. 64 where the subsoil is of soft shrinkable clay; the foundation is 700 mm wide and starts at a depth of 895 mm.

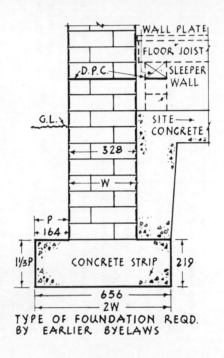

Fig.65

The foundation shown in Fig. 65 is of a type demanded by earlier byelaws; the foundation was made twice as wide as the wall and its thickness one and one-third that of its projection from the wall face or footing. *This type is now obsolete but this general rule is a useful one to follow.*

It is essential that all brickwork from the top of the concrete strip to the underside of the damp proof course (see p. 87) be built of sound, hard and well burnt bricks; engineering type bricks are often specified for this purpose.

The position of the ground floor is indicated by broken lines in Fig. 64. Briefly, a wood floor consists of *joists* spaced at about 400 mm centres to which *floor boards* (about 25 mm thick) are nailed. In good class work it is a common practice to support the ends of the

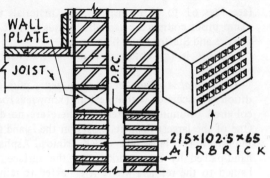

Fig.66

joists on a continuous wood member called a *wall plate*; the latter must be level and is "bedded" on the wall or damp proof course (see below), *i.e.*, the bricklayer spreads a layer of mortar upon which the wall plate is placed. In cheaper work the wall plate is omitted. Instead of building the floor joists into the wall as at Fig. 64 a more expensive and better method is to build a *sleeper wall* inside the main wall as shown in Fig. 65 by the construction in broken lines. The sleeper wall is a ½-brick thick, parallel and about 60 mm from the outer wall. Intermediate supports to ground floor joists are often provided by constructing ½-brick sleeper walls at a maximum distance apart of about 1·8 m. The sleeper walls are constructed on the site concrete (see p. 90) or on 150 mm thick concrete foundations. These walls must be *honeycombed, i.e.*, bricks are omitted during the construction of the wall, and through the holes so formed air passes and circulates under the wood floor. Adequate ventilation under all wood joisted floors must be provided, otherwise the timber is liable to become affected with a disease called *dry rot*. Hence it is necessary to fix air bricks in the external walls at about 1·8 m apart. An air brick is shown in Fig. 66; it is made of clay, in several sizes, and is perforated, as shown. A vertical section through a portion of an outer wall indicating the air brick in position, etc., is also shown. Wood floors are also supported on offsets and corbels (see pp. 123-125).

A foundation of a pier is shown in Fig. 117.

DAMP PROOF COURSES

Brickwork below the ground level will draw moisture from the ground and may impart it from one course to another for a considerable height. The amount of water absorbed depends upon the soil (if waterlogged or otherwise), the porosity (pore space) of the bricks, quality of the mortar and workmanship, etc.

To prevent this subsoil water rising and causing dampness in a wall, a continuous horizontal layer of an impermeable material is provided. This is called a *horizontal damp proof course* and the Building Regulations require it to be placed at a level not less than 150 mm above the ground (see Figs. 61 to 65 inclusive). The materials used to form horizontal damp proof courses are asphalt, fibrous asphalt felt, slates, lead, copper, plastics and Staffordshire blue bricks.

Asphalt is (*a*) obtained from natural deposits and (*b*) produced artificially.

(a) *Natural Asphalt* occurs in either a pure (or moderately so) condition or associated with limestone (known as *rock asphalt*). It is a black coloured bituminous material. There are no deposits in this country. One of the largest deposits exists on the Island of Trinidad, British West Indies. It is a large lake called Trinidad Asphalt Lake. The asphalt is hand-picked by men working on the surface, loaded into trucks and hauled to the refiners where it is heated to remove the water, screened and poured into barrels which are then exported to this country. Rock asphalt is obtained from deposits found in France (Seyssel), Switzerland (Val de Travers), etc. This is limestone which is impregnated with asphalt. This stone is ground to a powder and, as it is deficient in asphalt, a certain amount of Trinidad Lake asphalt is mixed with the powdered asphalt-limestone in a heated tank; sand is also added. The material is then poured into moulds and 50 kg flat blocks of asphalt are thereby formed.

These blocks are received on the site, when they are reheated and applied in the following manner: Wood battens are fixed horizontally along both faces of the wall with their top edges usually 12 mm above the top of the course of the wall which is to receive the asphalt. The heated material is placed on the wall between the battens and finished off to a level surface by means of hand floats which are similar to that shown at E, Fig. 173. The asphalt is kept back slightly from the external face of the wall so that it may be pointed with cement mortar after the wall has been completed. This covers the dark line of the asphalt and assists in preventing the asphalt from being squeezed out and discolouring the brickwork, especially if it is subjected to intense action of the sun.

This natural asphalt forms an excellent (but relatively expensive) damp proof course, it being very durable, tough and elastic.

(b) *Artificial Asphalt* is a cheap and inferior substitute for the natural product. It is composed of a mixture of *tar* (a black, thick, oily, strong-smelling liquid obtained as a by-product from coal used in the manufacture of gas), sand and crushed chalk. It is liable to deteriorate and become brittle, and therefore when used as a damp proof course cracks may appear through which water may penetrate.

Fibrous Asphalt Felt.—This damp proof course is now more extensively used than any other. There are several varieties, but that chiefly employed consists of a tough felt or hessian base which is impregnated with and covered by asphalt. It is obtained in rolls 23 m long and from a ½ to 4-bricks wide.

Briefly, it is produced in the following manner: The felt is passed in a continuous stretched sheet through a machine and successively (1) heated as it travels over and under steam-heated rollers, (2) impregnated with hot asphalt as it passes through a tank containing the liquid, (3) cooled as it traverses rollers, (4) passed through a second tank containing hot asphalt and surface coatings of the liquid applied to each side of the sheet, (5) on leaving the tank the sheet is sprayed on the upper surface with grains of sand or talc (to prevent the sheet from sticking together when coiled up), (6) passed between rollers to embed the particles of sand, etc., and coiled over rollers, (7) automatically cut into 23 m lengths, and (8) finally wound into coils by a winding machine.

This damp proof course is very easy to handle and, provided it is obtained from a reputable manufacturer, forms a very reliable damp-resisting material. In laying it in position, a thin layer of mortar is spread on the brickwork and the damp proof course is bedded on it. It should be lapped 75 mm where joints occur, and lapped full width at all cross-ings and angles. The next course of brickwork is bedded on mortar spread over the asphalt felt. The damp proof course should be pointed in cement mortar.

Some of the cheaper varieties are practically worthless on account of their thinness and the inferior quality of the jute and asphalt.

Another excellent but more expensive damp proof material consists of a continuous core of light lead covered both sides with asphalt and coated with talc. It is made in two or three grades of varying widths and in rolls which are 7 m long.

Slates.—These form a most efficient damp proof course. They are not now extensively used for this purpose although they are still employed on important buildings and in districts where the slates are prepared.

Slate is a hard, fine-grained rock which is either quarried or mined in Wales, the Lake District and in Cornwall. The blocks of slate are sawn by a machine into slabs and the latter are split into slates. This splitting operation is easily performed by hand labour owing to the laminated character of the slate; a wide chisel is driven by means of a hammer or mallet into an end of the slab until it splits. The thickness varies but should not be less than 4 mm; the length and width of roofing slates also vary; those used for damp proof courses should extend the full thickness of the wall and their length should be at least 215 mm.

A slate damp proof course must consist of two layers of slates, laid broken-jointed, with three layers of cement mortar composed of 1 part Portland cement and 3 parts sand. Thus: A layer of mortar is spread over the brickwork, upon which the first layer of slates is bedded with butt joints. More mortar is spread over these slates and the second layer of slates is laid in position so as to form a half-lap bond with the first course. The next course of brickwork is then bedded in cement mortar on this top layer of slates, after which the damp proof course is neatly pointed with cement mortar.

Lead.—This is an excellent damp-proofing material, but because of its relatively high cost it is not often used for this purpose. The sheet lead is produced from ore which is roasted in a furnace to remove impurities, further refined in pans from which the liquid is cast into bars called *pigs*, the latter are melted, cast into slabs and passed backwards and forwards between rollers until the desired thickness is obtained. Lead is specified by a number corresponding to its weight when it used to be expressed in lbs. per sq. ft. That used for damp proof courses varies from No. 4 to No. 8 lead. It is lapped as described for fibrous asphalt felt; it must be embedded in *lime* mortar and not cement mortar, as the latter may act upon the lead and destroy it. The surfaces of the lead should be well scratched to give a key for the mortar.

Copper.—This is a very durable and effective damp proof material. It is not commonly used as it is expensive. It is obtained in sheets that are cut into strips, the width of which equals the thickness of the wall. It should preferably be 0·45 mm thick. It is lapped as described above, and bedded in lime or cement mortar.

Plastic.—This is made of black polythene, 0·5 or 1 mm thick, in the usual walling widths and in roll lengths of 30 m.

Staffordshire Blue Bricks.—These dark-coloured bricks are practically impermeable and when built in two to four courses in cement mortar form a very efficient damp proof course. Their colour is not acceptable for general application, but they are still used occasionally.

Horizontal damp proof courses should be provided under copings (see p. 174).

Damp proof material (usually asphalt of 20 mm thickness) is also applied to basement, etc., walls to prevent dampness; this application is known as *vertical damp proofing*. It is also provided within the thickness of basement concrete floors. Such work is beyond the scope of this book.

SURFACE OR SITE CONCRETE

The Building Regulations state that the area of a building below wood floors next to the ground must be covered with an impervious material in order to exclude dampness. The Regulations are met if 100 mm thickness of cement concrete is provided on a bed of broken bricks, stone, etc.

Surface concrete (or site concrete) is shown in Figs. 61-65 (inclusive). The Regulations require that such concrete shall consist of not less than 50 kg (1-bag) of cement to 0·1 m^3 of fine aggregate (sand) and 0·2 m^3 of coarse aggregate (broken brick or stone, gravel, etc.), and its top shall not be lower than the level of the adjoining ground.

Vegetable soil or turf covering a site should be removed as a preliminary operation. The excavated material may be spread over that portion of the site set apart for the garden, and the turf may be stacked (as rotted turf is a valuable manure) or used subsequently for making lawns. The depth of soil varies from 150 to 230 mm and the site concrete is laid on the exposed surface. The concrete should be laid and levelled off (see "one-course work" described on p. 183), it being *spade finished, i.e.*, well surfaced with the back of the shovel (see p. 184). As already stated (p. 87), sleeper walls are sometimes constructed on the surface concrete.

Besides excluding dampness, surface concrete prevents the growth of vegetable matter and the admission through the floors of ground air.

TEMPORARY TIMBERING TO SHALLOW TRENCHES

The sides of trenches excavated in certain soils to receive wall foundations must be temporarily supported. Otherwise the sides may collapse and possibly cause injury to the workmen and damage to the work.

Wood members are used for such temporary supports. The timbering of the excavations is done by the labourers as the work proceeds. The sizes and arrangement of the various timbers are influenced by the nature of the soil and the depth of the cutting. There are many different kinds of soil, but for convenience they may be divided into: (1) *Hard* (including rock and exceptionally hard chalk), (2) *Firm* (including hard chalk and dense gravel), (3) *Moderately Firm* (including soft chalk, loose gravel and compact clay), (4) *Loose* (including dry sand, soft clay, ordinary loamy soil and made-up ground such as earth which has been tipped on to low-lying ground and levelled off), and (5) *Loose and Waterlogged* loamy soil and sand.

Terms.—The following are the various members which are used in trench timbering:—

Poling Boards.—Members placed vertically next to the sides of the excavation or sheeting (see below): sizes vary from 175 by 32 mm to 225 by 38 mm and are from 0·6 to 1·2 m long.

Wallings, Wales, Waling Pieces or Planks.—Members placed horizontally next to the earth or poling boards; various sizes are 100 mm by 75 mm, 100 mm by 100 mm, 150 mm by 100 mm, 175 mm by 75 mm, etc., and from 2·4 to 4·25 m long.

Sheeting.—Members placed horizontally next to the earth; of similar sizes to poling boards but from 2·4 to 4·25 m long.

Struts.—Short pieces of timber driven down between poling boards or walings at a minimum distance of 1·8 m centres; are from 75 to 100 mm (or even larger for wide trenches) square, or they may be short ends of scaffold poles which are from 75 to 125 mm diameter.

In addition, *wedges* are required to tighten struts, etc. These are small pieces of wood, preferably hardwood such as oak, and of triangular section. They are also called *pages*.

Whilst the above poling boards, walings, etc., are generally of spruce, in practice old but sound scaffold poles, putlogs (horizontal members of scaffolding), floor joists and wood which is unsuitable for better work are employed.

The following description is applied to trenches, excavated in various soils, such as are required to receive a foundation which is 1·2 m wide and 1 m deep.

1. HARD GROUND —No timbering would be required for the sides of the trench would be self-supporting.

2. FIRM GROUND (see Fig. 67).—There would be little likelihood of the sides of a shallow trench caving in if left unsupported for a short time as hard chalk, for example, will retain a 3 m high vertical face until weather conditions cause it to crumble. It is, however, sometimes necessary to provide as shown a light support in the form of a pair of poling boards strutted apart at a *minimum* distance of 1·8 m centres. This distance is necessary to allow ample working space for the men engaged in constructing the foundation. Usually it is sufficient to use one central strut to each pair of poling boards (as shown at B), but occasionally it is advisable to use two struts (see C).

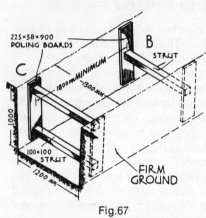

Fig. 67

The struts are slightly longer than the horizontal distance between the boards and they are driven down until they are tight and more or less horizontal. The sides of the trench are given a slight batter from the top inwards to facilitate this operation and to reduce the tendency for the members to become loose when the earth shrinks, as it does on the removal of moisture. Care should be taken not to overdrive the struts and disturb the earth behind the boards.

Sometimes wedges are used to tighten the struts. Thus, a wedge is driven down between an end of a strut and the adjacent poling board. This is only necessary at one end of each strut. Struts which in time become slack are easily tightened by driving the wedges down as required.

3. MODERATELY FIRM GROUND.—If the soil is generally firm but inclined to be loose in patches the timbering may consist of the simple arrangement shown at D, Fig. 68. Otherwise the trench may require a temporary support as shown at E, Fig. 68.

The wide walings at D provide a continuous support, three struts being used per 4·25 m length of waling. Wedges may be driven in between the ends of the struts as described above.

The arrangement at E shows poling boards held in position by walings which are strutted. The poling boards are placed at a distance apart varying with the circumstances; in the sketch they are shown at 450 mm centres, but this distance may be reduced to 300 mm or increased to 900 mm. The timbering is fixed in easy stages, for it is not advisable in this kind of soil to defer it until a length of trench is excavated equal to that of the walings, as a portion of the unsupported excavation may collapse. The following procedure is therefore adopted: A short length is

excavated sufficient to enable the labourer to insert and temporarily
strut a pair of poling boards (thus resembling B or C, Fig. 67). This is
repeated until sufficient poling boards have been placed which can be
spanned by the walings. A waling is then placed along each side and
strutted against the boards as shown at E, Fig. 68, after which the temporary struts are removed. An example of the temporary strutting
referred to above is shown by the broken lines at F. It is often necessary
to drive wedges or pages down between the waling and boards which
have become loose. An example of this is shown in Fig. 68.

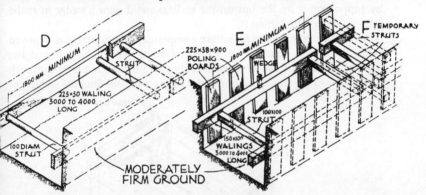

Fig.68

4. LOOSE EARTH.—The timbering required is somewhat similar to
that shown in Fig. 69, except that the sheets are sometimes placed about
25 mm apart, and is described below.

5. LOOSE AND WATERLOGGED GROUND (see G, Fig.69).—Horizontal
sheeting must be provided here for, unlike the soils referred to in the
above first three classes, it is not possible to excavate in loose soil
(especially if waterlogged) for several feet in depth before resorting to
timbering. The sides of the trenches dug in this soil begin to fall before
300 mm depth has been reached, and hence the need for *horizontal*
boards or *sheets*. The following is the sequence of operations: The
excavation is made to a depth slightly in excess of the width of the
sheeting to be used, when a sheet is placed against each side of the trench
and two or more struts are driven between. The excavation is continued
for 230 mm depth or so, and a second pair of sheets is placed tight up
against the bottom edges of the first pair and strutted. The timbering at
the end of a section at this stage is shown at H. This operation is
repeated until four sets of sheets have been temporarily strutted or the
required depth has been reached, when poling boards are placed at a
minimum distance apart of 1·8 m centres and strutted, as shown in the
sketch, and the temporary struts removed.

The timbering of trenches in loose soil, such as sand, which is waterlogged, is rendered difficult if water and the sand which accompanies it
escape between the boards. If measures are not taken to prevent the

escape of this silt, the members would become loose and ultimately collapse. Hence any open joints, such as those between the ends of sheets in adjacent sections, are stemmed by packing wads of grass, canvas, etc.

The fixing of large-sized heavy struts (such as are required for wide trenches) is facilitated if they are provided with *lips*. A lip is a piece of wood, 25 to 38 mm thick, which is nailed at one end of a strut on its top edge; the lip projects about 50 mm beyond the end of the strut. A strut is provided with two lips, one at each end. Such a strut is fixed simply by supporting it by the lips on the walings and driving a wedge in at the side of one end to tighten it.

When the foundations have been completed, the timbering is removed gradually as the construction of the wall proceeds, and when it has reached a height of two or three courses above the ground level the earth is returned to the trench on both sides of the wall and rammed solid.

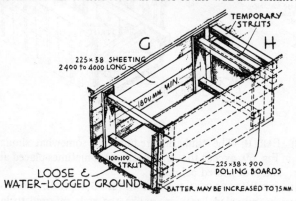

Fig.69

Note.—The examples illustrated in Figs. 67, 68 and 69 should only be taken as typical. The nature of the soil and the general conditions are so variable that the spacing and arrangement of the timbers can only be decided upon the site. Very often the general system of timbering on work in progress has to be departed from on account of the local variations in the character of the soil. The sizes of the timbers vary; any sound members approximately of the sizes given may be used. Many buildings are erected with foundations of such little depth that the shallow trenches formed to receive them do not require any temporary timbering.

CHAPTER SEVEN

TOOLS, SETTING OUT AND CONSTRUCTION

Tools used by the bricklayer and bricklayer's labourer; setting out trenches and walls, profiles. Construction of foundations and walls; hints on brick-laying; setting out openings in faced work.

TOOLS.—The tools used by the bricklayer's labourer are: Picks, crowbars, shovels, spades, rammers, hod and rake.

Those in common use by the bricklayer include: Brick trowel, plumb-rule, straight-edge, gauge-rod, line and pins or line bobbins, tingles, squares, spirit level, vertical level, one-metre rule, chisels, club hammer and brick hammer. Additional tools employed for special purposes are: Scutch, bevel, saw, rubbing stone, pointing trowel, frenchman, jointer, pointing rule and hawk.

The following are brief particulars of these tools:—

Picks.—Each consists of a steel head (with pointed ends, or one end pointed and the other chisel-edged) and wood shaft. Used when excavating for breaking up hard soils, loosening gravel, etc.

Crowbars.—These are steel rods, 1·2 to 1·5 m long, having either pointed, chiselled or forked ends. Employed for breaking up rock or hard ground at excavations, and levering heavy objects, such as blocks of stone, beams, etc.

Shovels and Spades. — Various types include: *Shovel* having a 250 or 300 mm square steel blade and a T or D-shaped wood shaft, and used for moving light soil; *navvy shovel.* with 300 mm wide and pointed blade, used for general purposes; *spade* having a 400 mm wide blade and used for excavating ordinary soil; *grafting tool,* similar to the spade but with a narrower and longer blade, and used for digging stiff clay.

Rammers or beaters are either entirely of wood or a wood handle with a 3 to 6 kg metal head; both are shown in Fig. 9. Used for ramming bottom of trenches to make them firm, consolidating filled-in material, concrete, etc.

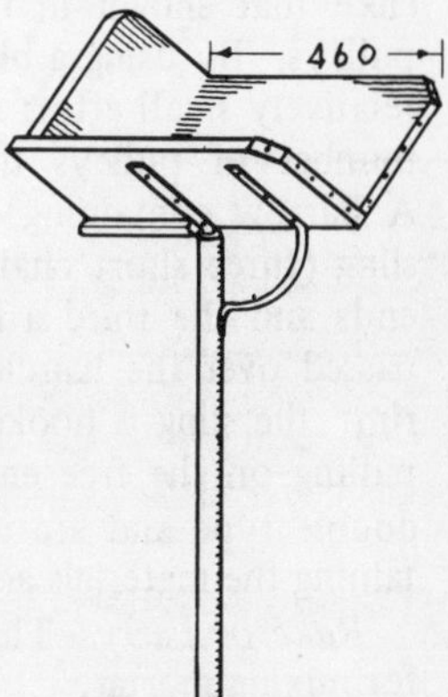

HOD
Fig.70

Hod.—A three-sided wood (as in Fig. 70) or metal box of several sizes fixed to a wood pole. Used on small contracts for carrying bricks (from 9 to 12) and mortar (approximately 0·014 m³).

In addition to the hod, a *gin wheel* (or "jenny wheel") is used on small jobs. As shown in Fig. 71, this is a grooved pulley or wheel supported by a frame which is lashed (roped) to the scaffold, etc. A long rope, to which a metal hook is secured, is passed over the pulley. A bucket containing mortar, etc., is raised by slipping the handle over the rope hook and pulling on the free end of the rope. A clutch or holdfast clip, as shown, is sometimes provided; this grips the rope if the pull is released, and thus any load being lifted is suspended and prevented from running down.

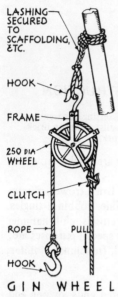

LASHING SECURED TO SCAFFOLDING, ETC.

HOOK

FRAME

250 DIA WHEEL

CLUTCH

ROPE   PULL

HOOK

GIN WHEEL

Fig. 71

Slings or *lashings* are useful accessories for lifting skips (trays) of bricks, rubbish baskets, etc. The simplest of several types of slings is a piece of rope with its ends spliced together, or a continuous metal chain. A sling after being hitched or hooked to the skip, etc., is slipped over the jenny hook and lifted.

Lifting appliances used on large contracts include (a) *barrow lifts* and (b) *hoists*. (a) Briefly, a barrow lift consists of a *block and tackle* and a sling; the simplest of several forms of block and tackle has two blocks or frames, one above the other, and each with a pulley or sheave; the top block is hooked to the scaffold and the lower is free; the rope is fastened to the top block and, after being passed under the lower pulley is threaded over the top pulley (like that shown in Fig. 71). Each block may contain two or three pulleys. By using a block and tackle, a large weight may be lifted by a relatively small effort or pull on the free end of the rope; the larger the number of pulleys the smaller the effort required to lift the load. A barrow containing concrete, etc. is hoisted by fixing a three-legged sling (three short chains, attached to a ring, two of which have ringed ends and the third a hooked end) to the barrow; the ringed ends are passed over the handles, and the hooked end is engaged on the wheel rim; the sling is hooked to the lower block, and the barrow is raised by pulling on the free end of the rope. (b) Hoists are of the single and double type and are operated by diesel or petrol engines; hoppers containing the materials are thereby raised to any desired height.

Rake or Larry.—This has a metal blade fixed to a long handle; used for mixing mortar.

Wood or steel barrows are employed for removing excavated material, wheeling and depositing concrete, etc. Rubbish baskets, made of mild steel, are used for removing brick chippings, etc.

Trowels.—The *brick trowel* (Fig. 72) has a steel blade 250 to 330 mm long, and shank (having a pointed and jagged tang) to which a conveniently shaped wood handle is fixed. It is the principal tool of the bricklayer, as it is used for lifting mortar from the mortar board (p. 107) and spreading it on the wall, forming joints, "rough" cutting bricks (to form closers and bats), etc. It is obtainable "handed", *i.e.*, right and left-handed to suit individual requirements. A long trowel, when loaded with mortar, imposes a greater strain on the wrist than does a short trowel, and therefore a 250 mm or smaller trowel is at first usually preferred by the young apprentice. If considered to be too pointed, the point may be cut off by applying a chisel and hammer and

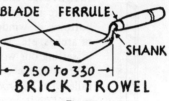

BLADE   FERRULE

SHANK

250 to 330

BRICK TROWEL

Fig.72

rounding it off on the rubbing stone (see p. 101). For laying facing bricks, preference is given to a trowel with a 175 to 230 mm blade.

   The *pointing trowel* is similar to but smaller than the brick trowel, it being obtainable in various sizes, common lengths being 75 to 150 mm. It is used for jointing or pointing (see p. 179).

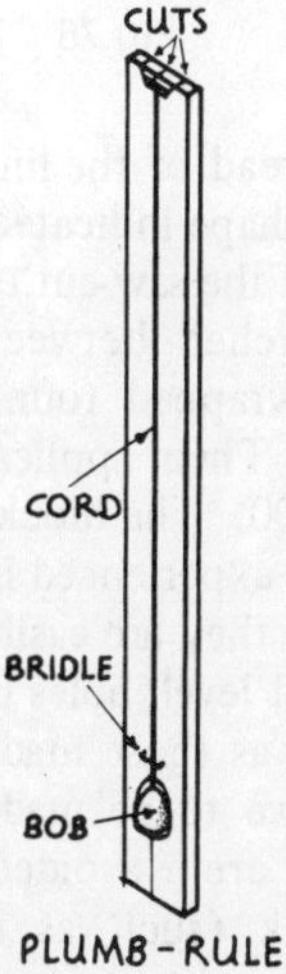

CUTS

CORD

BRIDLE

BOB

PLUMB-RULE

Fig.73

   Plumb-rule (Fig. 73).–This is a dressed piece of wood, 1·3 to 1·8 m long, 100 to 125 mm wide and 12 to 25 mm thick, holed near the bottom to permit slight movement of a pear-shaped lead *plumb-bob* which is suspended by a length of whipcord fixed to the top of the rule. The long edges of the rule must be parallel. A centre or *gauge line* is cut down its face and extends the full length. Three short saw-cuts are made down its top edge, one coinciding with the gauge line and one inclined on each side; the cord is passed down the middle cut and wound round the side cuts two or three times. The plumb-bob weighs from 1·3 to 1·8 kg, and the hole is slightly larger than the bob. Excessive swinging of the line and bob is prevented by the copper wire *bridle* or *guard*, which is bent over the line and fixed just above the hole. As implied, the plumb-rule is used for plumbing (obtaining and maintaining a vertical face) a wall (see p. 110). See also vertical level on p. 99.

   Straight-edge (Fig. 74).–This is a dressed piece of wood, 0·9 to 1 m long, 75 mm wide and 12 or 19 mm thick; both long edges must be

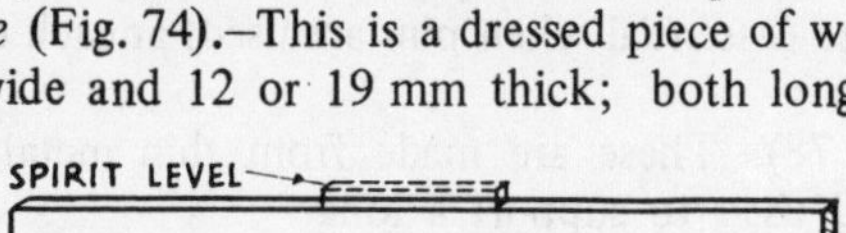

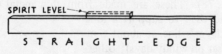

SPIRIT LEVEL

S T R A I G H T - E D G E

Fig.74

straight and parallel. It is employed for testing brickwork, especially at quoins, and checking the alignment of individual bricks before plumbing; it is also used in conjunction with the spirit level (see p. 99). For special purposes, such as for "levelling pegs" (see p. 104), the straight-edge may be up to 4·25 m long.

Gauge-rod or Gauge-staff (Fig. 75).—Similar to but longer than the straight-edge and upon which the bed joints or course lines are marked; courses conforming with the tops and bottoms of window sills, string courses, springing points of arches, etc., are specially indicated. Used at the quoins in setting our work and ensuring the maintenance of the courses at the correct level (see p. 110). A longer rod, called a *storey-rod*, has the height of each floor or storey marked on it, in addition to the course lines.

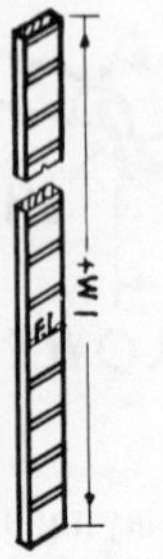

GAUGE-ROD

Fig.75

Line and Pins (Fig. 76).—A *bricklayer's line*, made of nylon and at least 30 m long, is wound round two steel pins having thin blades, long shanks and large heads; the line is wound clockwise on one pin and anti-clockwise on the other to assist in the maintenance of a taut line when in use. Employed to ensure the correct alignment of courses (see p. 111).

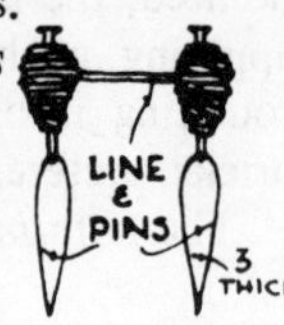

Fig.76

Line Bobbins or Blocks (Fig. 77).—These are used instead of the line and pins. Two hardwood blocks are made to the size and shape indicated.

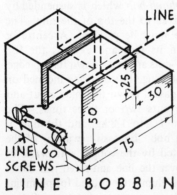

LINE BOBBIN

Fig.77

The line is passed down the saw-cut of each block when stretched between opposite quoins and wrapped round the projecting screws. Their application is shown in Fig. 100. The blocks are preferred (by those experienced in their use) to the pins, as they are easily adjusted to the required level, holes in the mortar joints (such as those made by pins and which have to be made good subsequently) are avoided, damage to faced work (such as is caused when pins are driven into joints, the mortar in which has set) is prevented, and time is saved as unwrapping the line (essential when pins are used) at each course lift is not required.

Tingles (Fig. 78).—These are made from thin metal (brass, copper, zinc or tin) and used to support a long length of bricklayer's line at about 6 m intervals (or closer on windy days); otherwise the line will sag (see also p. 111 and Fig. 100).

Squares.—The joiner's *try square* (Fig. 79), consisting of a 150 to 300 mm steel blade and wood stock, is used by the

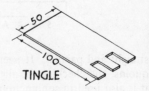

TINGLE

Fig.78

bricklayer for testing perpends, etc. The bricklayer's square, used for marking bricks preparatory to cutting and for setting angles from the face of a wall (as required for window openings), is similar in shape but

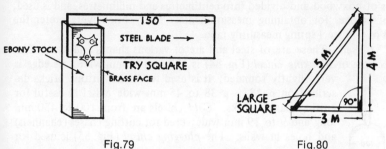

Fig.79

Fig.80

entirely of steel; the blade is sometimes divided into metres and millimetres, and as such is useful for obtaining measurements. The *large square* (Fig. 80), made of wood, is used for setting out right angles, as at quoins; the size varies and may be double that shown.

Spirit Level (Fig. 81).—Used for levelling bricks at quoins, etc., and in conjunction with the straight-edge for obtaining horizontal surfaces. Consists of a hardwood case, in the central recess of which is fixed a glass tube filled with alcohol, save for a small bubble

SPIRIT LEVEL

Fig.81

of air, and having a slightly concave lower surface. A horizontal or level surface is denoted when the spirit level placed on it (or on the middle of the straight-edge when applied on its edge—see Figs. 74 and 97) shows the bubble in the centre.

Vertical or Upright Level (Fig. 82).—This is 75 to 100 mm wide, 19 to 32 mm thick, 1 to 1·5 m long and made of metal or hardwood. It has a spirit level (A) fitted in the centre of one edge for levelling instead of that shown in Fig. 81, and at least one and sometimes two small spirit tubes (B and C) fixed at right angles to its length. It is used instead of the plumb-rule for plumbing purposes, a vertical

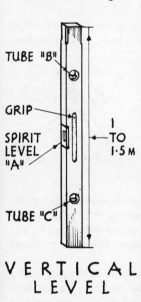

VERTICAL LEVEL

Fig.82

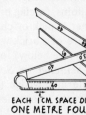

EACH 1 CM. SPACE DIVIDED INTO 10 MM.
ONE METRE FOUR-FOLD RULE

Fig.83

surface being indicated when the bubble in a small tube is in the centre of its run (see p. 110).

One-metre Rule.—The four-fold rule shown in Fig. 83 is one type; it is of boxwood and divided into centimetres and millimetres, and is used, of course, for obtaining measurements. Many bricklayers prefer the 3 or 5 m steel spring measuring tape.

Chisels.—These are of steel and are of various shapes and sizes. The *bolster* or *blocking chisel* (Fig. 84) is 100 to 125 mm wide; its edge is very slightly rounded; it is used for "fair" cutting bricks described on p. 135; a 38 to 45 mm wide chisel is useful for cutting glazed bricks. *Cold* chisels are from 100 to 450 mm long and 9 to 19 mm wide; used for cutting chases (channels) and holes in walls. The *plugging chisel* (Fig. 85) is used for

BOLSTER

Fig.84

PLUGGING CHISEL

250

Fig.85

65

225

PITCHING TOOL

Fig.86

"raking out" joints for lead flashings and cutting small holes to receive wood plugs to which woodwork is fixed by the joiner. The *pitching tool* (Fig. 86), although a mason's tool, is a very useful chisel for cutting hard bricks and stone templets. Drills of various sizes and shaped steel ends are also used for forming neat holes in brickwork required for plugging, etc.

Club or Lump Hammer (Fig. 87).—The steel head weights from 0·9 kg to 1·8 kg and the wood handle is 150 to 230 mm long; used in conjunction with the bolster, chisels, etc.

CLUB HAMMER
100

Fig.87

BRICK HAMMER
280

Fig.88

S C U T C H
300
WEDGE
BLADE

Fig.89

Brick Hammer (Fig. 88).—One end of the steel head is square (for plumbing quoins, forcing bricks tightly when bedding, striking nails, etc.) and the other is pick or chisel-shaped (which cutting end is used to trim the rough face of a brick when split by the bolster). It is often preferred to the scutch (see below) for dressing firebricks.

Scutch, Scutcher or Scotch.—Consists of a hard steel blade, and a wood handle and wedge (Fig. 89). When the cutting edge has been dulled, the wedge is loosened and the blade is removed, reversed, replaced and rewedged. Used for "fair" cutting bricks, *i.e.*, dressing cut surfaces of bricks after they have been split with the bolster, and for this purpose it has largely superseded the brick hammer except for trimming firebricks.

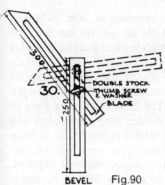

BEVEL   Fig.90

Bevel (Fig. 90).–The slotted steel blade can be secured to the wood stock at any desired angle by tightening the thumb screw; used for setting out angles, such as on bricks which are to be cut to shape (see p. 143).

Saw or Bow Saw (Fig. 91).–The narrow steel saw blade (or twisted wire) is fitted into the wood handles; about 3 m of strong string is wound round the upper ends of the wood sides, and a short wood lever is passed between it; the string is twisted by means of the lever, and this tightens the blade to the required tension; unwinding of the string is prevented, as the lever is restrained by the wood bar. Used for sawing rubbers (p. 144), etc.

Rubbing Stone.–This is a slab of hard grit sandstone or carborundum upon which cut faces of bricks are rubbed (after water has been applied) to a true surface.

Frenchman.–Is a discarded table knife, the blade of which is cut to a point and then bent 10 mm at right angles; used, together with the pointing rule (see below), for struck and cut jointing (p. 179) and tuck pointing (p. 182).

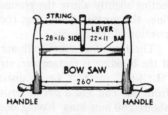

Fig.91

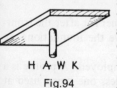

JOINTER

Fig.92

Jointer (Fig. 92).–This has a 50 to 150 mm long blade with either a flat, grooved, concave or convex edge; used for jointing and pointing brickwork (p. 178).

Pointing Rule (Fig. 93).–Is a dressed piece of 75 to 100 mm by 25 mm wood of varying length, having a bevelled (sloping) edge with 10 mm cork (preferably) or wood distance pieces fixed on the bevelled side. Used in conjunction with the frenchman and jointers for pointing and jointing.

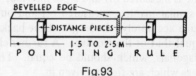

Fig.93

H A W K

Fig.94

Hawk or Hand Board.–Is a 200 or 230 mm square board, 12 to 25 mm thick, to which a handle is fixed (Fig. 94), and usually made on the job; the bricklayer uses it to hold a small quantity of mortar whilst engaged in pointing brickwork (see p. 182).

SETTING OUT

Before actual building operations are commenced, the walls and trenches to receive the foundations must be *set out* on the site, the exact positions of the corners, division walls, etc., being indicated. This is also known as *pegging out* or *lining out*.

The first line to be set out is generally that of the main frontage of the building. Its relative position must be carefully fixed and its length accurately measured by means of a tape. The latter is a narrow band of linen or steel, usually 10 to 20 m long, divided into centimetres and millimetres, and coiled within a flat circular leather-covered box. A linen tape is used for general purposes, but as this is apt to stretch, it is necessary to employ a steel tape when accurate measurements are required. A wood *peg* (a piece of wood, usually 50 mm by 50 mm by about 600 mm long and having one end pointed) is driven firmly into and projecting slightly above the ground at each end of the measured front wall line, the centre of the pegs (or nails driven into them) indicating the position of the corners.

The lines of all other walls are measured off from this front line. Thus, if the building is rectangular, right angles are set off from it by using the "3 : 4 : 5" method, *i.e.*, a distance of 12 m is measured along the line from one end and a *pin* or *arrow* (of wrought iron resembling a skewer, about 230 mm long, having one end pointed and the other bent ring-shaped) is inserted; a tape is held at each end of this length, the 9 m division on one of the tapes is then held at the 15 m division of the other, both tapes are stretched and a pin is inserted at the intersection. The 9 m side line thus set off is at right angles to the frontage line as, in a right-angled triangle, the sum of the squares on the two sides containing the 90° angle equals the sum on the hypotenuse, *i.e.* $12^2 + 9^2 = 15^2$. The large wood square shown in Fig. 80 is also used for setting out and checking right angles (see also Fig. 96). The required length of the side line is measured off and a pin inserted. The opposite side line is set out in a similar manner, measured off and pinned. If this setting out has been done accurately, the length of the back line between the two pins should equal that of the frontage. A further check is obtained by measuring the diagonals, which should be equal. The two pins are then replaced by pegs which are firmly driven in.

After the building has been set out in this manner (or after the frontage only has been set out), the trenches to receive the foundations are set out. There are several methods of doing this.

The best method is that in which *profiles* are employed. A profile is a temporary guide. There are two forms of profiles, one being used at corners and the other at division walls. A sketch of a corner profile is shown at B, Fig. 95. It consists of two boards (usually pieces of floor boarding) nailed to three wood pegs or stakes which are well driven in. A division profile, shown at C, has only one board fixed to two driven pegs.

An application of profiles is shown in Fig. 95. The key plan of a

building is shown by broken lines at A, and the several profiles are indicated by full lines at the corners and opposite the division walls. Enlarge-
ments of these profiles are given in the plan G and sketches B and C.
A profile is fixed at each corner (see A and G), with the boards parallel to
and at 610 to 915 mm from the outer trench lines. The profiles are carefully set out from the frontage, etc., pegs previously inserted (see above),
a steel tape being used for accurate measurements; the setting out is
checked by taking diagonal measurements between opposite corner pegs
of the corner profiles. The division profiles, such as E at C and at G, are
fixed in true alignment. Permanent divisions are marked on each board

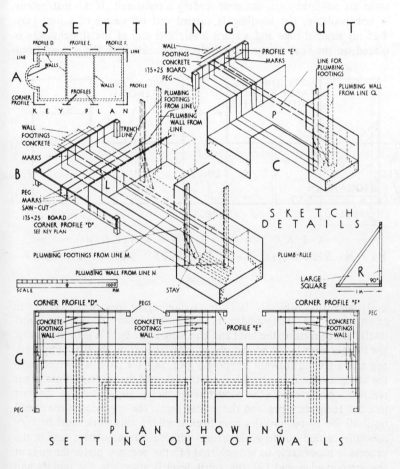

Fig. 95

indicating the width of the concrete bed (which is the same as that of the
trench), brick footings (assuming that these are to be provided) and the
thickness of the wall—see B, C and G. Saw cuts, about 12 mm deep, are

made down these marks in the top edge of each board to receive the ends of the *ranging lines* of stout cord.

In good practice, the corner pegs of the corner profiles are driven down until their tops are at "ground floor level", *i.e.*, level with the top of the ground floor decided upon. This is achieved on large and important work by the use of a surveying instrument, known as a *dumpy level,* and a *levelling staff* (divided into mm, cm and metres); one of the corner pegs is driven down until its top is at ground floor level; the staff is held vertically on this peg and the "reading" taken, *i.e.*, the height on the staff is observed through the telescope (which is horizontal) of the dumpy level; the staff is now placed in turn on the other corner pegs and these are adjusted until the same reading is registered. If this instrument is not available, the levelling is carried out by means of a long (say 4·25 m) straight-edge and a spirit level; one end of the straight-edge is placed on the first corner peg (made to coincide with the ground floor

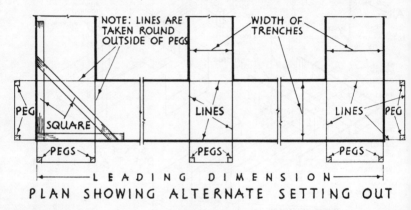

PLAN SHOWING ALTERNATE SETTING OUT

Fig.96

level) and the other is laid on a temporary peg which is driven down until the straight-edge is horizontal (indicated by the spirit level); after reversing the level and checking if the bubble is in the centre, the straight-edge is moved and placed with its *ends* on the first temporary peg and a second forward temporary peg, and the latter is lowered until the straight-edge is level; this is continued until the second corner peg is reached and levelled (the straight-edge being supported on the last inserted temporary peg and the corner peg); the operation is continued until all the corner profiles have been levelled; this work must be *very carefully* carried out to avoid errors—which are accumulative—and in the process it is advisable to arrange that (1) the pegs are under the ends of the straight-edge and (2) the spirit level is always in the middle and applied on the same edge of the straight-edge.

The position and correct alignment of the trenches, footings and walls are obtained by plumbing down from lines which are stretched in turn between opposite profiles. Thus, assuming that the trenches have been lined out and excavated, and the concrete has been placed in position (see p. 27), the bottom course of footings would be aligned in the following manner: One end of a line (see M at B and P at C, Fig. 95) is passed down the saw-cut and wrapped round the board, and after the line has been stretched taut the opposite end is fixed in a similar manner. The plumb-rule, sometimes stayed as shown (the wood stay being nailed to the rule), is held by one hand against the line near one end of the trench, and when vertical a mark is made by the point of the trowel in a little mortar trowelled on the concrete bed. A brick is laid temporarily on this mortar with the outer face in line with the mark; the plumbing of this face is checked. Another brick is laid in a similar manner at the other end. A bricklayer's line, with pins, is fixed between and level with the top of the bricks. The bottom course of footings is then built, commencing at the corners, the position of each being found by plumbing down at the intersection of the two lines (see L at B). The remaining courses of footings are constructed, the second course being measured back from the first and the top course from the second. Similarly, the wall is set off correctly by plumbing down from lines N at B and Q at C.

Sometimes, instead of a corner profile, two profiles like E shown at G placed at right angles to each other, are used at each corner. Profiles for division walls are often dispensed with, the right-angled intersections being then checked by the use of the large square (see Fig. 80).

Whilst profiles are preferably adopted to ensure accuracy in setting out, their use is by no means general. In the absence of profiles, the lines are pegged out as shown in Fig. 96, the dimensions being taken to the outside faces of the pegs and the lines stretched taut between them before being fastened. After the trenches have been excavated and the concrete foundation formed, the position of the quoins, etc., is set out on the concrete bed.

The setting out of circular walls is described on p. 157.

CONSTRUCTION OF WALLS AND FOUNDATION

The trenches for the foundations are excavated to the required depth. Digging must be continued until a good bottom has been reached, the depth rarely exceeds 1 m if the soil is firm and a basement is not required. The bottom of each trench must be level. Loose patches are consolidated by application of the rammer. It is sometimes necessary to remove patches of loose soil at the bottom of trenches and replace with concrete. Any necessary trench timbering is fixed as described on pp. 91-94.

CONCRETE BED.—The concrete bed is now formed to the desired thickness. Assuming that the ground floor level has been decided upon and the corner pegs of the corner profiles have been levelled accordingly (see p. 103), the following procedure is carried out to ensure that the "bed joint of the brickwork is in course with the ground floor level." Commencing at one corner, the gauge-rod (Fig. 75) is levelled by means of a straight-edge and spirit level on to a peg previously inserted at the corner in the bottom of the trench. This is illustrated in Fig. 97, where it is assumed that the top of the concrete is to be eight courses below the proposed level of the ground floor. If the trench peg B is at the correct level, the levelled straight-edge (supported on the corner profile peg A) will coincide with the *bottom* of the eighth course marked on the rod as shown; if not, the peg must be adjusted. The top of the peg, after being levelled, must project above the trench bottom by an amount equal to the required thickness of the concrete bed; if the height of the exposed peg is found to be inadequate, the trench must be deepened by skimming off the soil.

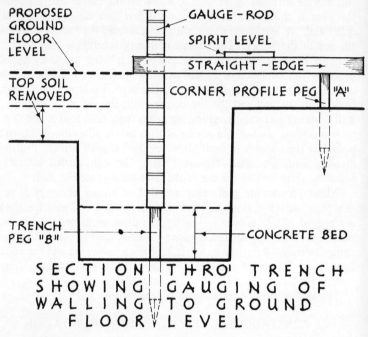

SECTION THRO' TRENCH SHOWING GAUGING OF WALLING TO GROUND FLOOR LEVEL

Fig.97

After each trench corner peg has been levelled in this manner, intermediate pegs are driven in at convenient intervals (say 1·8 m) along the bottom of each trench. The tops must be level throughout, and to ensure this three *boning rods* of the same height are used. A boning rod is shown in Fig. 98; it is made of two pieces of 50 to 75 mm by 25 mm timber, the head being nailed at right angles to the blade. A longitudinal section through a trench showing the application of boning rods is shown in Fig. 99. The three rods are held vertically on the pegs, one on each corner peg and the third on the intermediate pegs in turn. The foreman, holding a

BONING ROD

Fig.98

rod on peg at A, "sights through" to the rod held by an assistant on the peg at D until he can just see the top edges of both heads. At the same time the third boning rod is held on one of the intermediate pegs; if this peg is at the correct level, the head of the third rod will coincide with the "line of sight" (which is horizontal), as indicated by rod B; otherwise, if as shown at C, the head appears above the line of sight, the peg must be driven down until the top edge of its head agrees with the other two when sighting through.

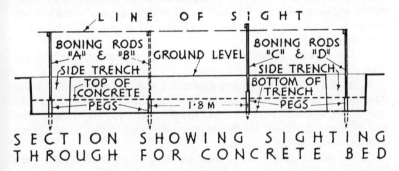

SECTION SHOWING SIGHTING THROUGH FOR CONCRETE BED

Fig.99

When all of the pegs have been dealt with in this manner, concreting can be commenced. The concrete is wheeled and carefully deposited in the trenches to peg-top height. In good work, the concrete is consolidated by tamping, rammers (Fig. 9) being used for this purpose. For comparatively thin beds of concrete, the back of the shovel is often applied to consolidate and bring the concrete level with the pegs; such a surface is said to be *spade-finished*. By another method, the concrete is levelled by means of a *strike-board* as described on pp. 183 and 184. The trench pegs must be removed as the concreting is completed, otherwise they may become affected with *dry rot* (a disease which attacks timber) which may spread to ground floor joists, etc. and cause serious damage.

WALLS.—Construction of the walls is then proceeded with when the concrete has sufficiently set to permit the work being carried out without causing damage to the concrete.

The following general observations should be noted:—

1. Before actually commencing building, the bricklayer will arrange for an adequate supply of bricks and mortar being available in convenient positions adjacent (about 600 mm) to the work. The bricks should be neatly stacked by the labourer; if thrown into a heap they may be chipped or otherwise damaged, and unnecessary time is spent by the bricklayer in sorting them out. The mortar is placed by the labourer on a *mortar board* or *spot* (of wood and about 600 mm square) which is supported on a brick at each corner to raise it above the ground (or scaffold), otherwise the bricklayer may injure his hand by contacting the

ground when lifting mortar from the board with the trowel. If the brick-layer is right-handed, the bricks are on his left (as in the laying operation he picks them up with his left hand) and the mortar board on his right (the trowel being in his right hand); if he is left-handed, the bricks will be on his right and the mortar on his left.

2. Porous bricks, especially in hot weather, should be well wetted before being laid to prevent them absorbing moisture from the mortar too quickly. Hard pressed bricks having smooth non-absorbent surfaces should not be watered, as this would render them difficult to lay; they would not have sufficient "suction" to keep them in place when laid, the mortar in the joints would tend to run and the bricks would be apt to *overhang* (slide forward).

3. The mortar should be of the correct consistency, neither too sloppy nor too stiff.

4. At the outset, the young apprentice will be taught to lay bricks right for his hand; if right-handed, he will stand with his left side to the face of the wall and work from left to right; the opposite to this applies to a left-handed person. He should practise picking up mortar and bricks with the least possible motions.

5. He will be taught the correct handling of the brick trowel when lifting mortar from the board and *spreading* it. When gripping the trowel, the thumb should be on top of the ferrule and the four fingers under the handle. When taking a trowelful of mortar from the board, a portion is chopped with the vertical blade, moved forward from the heap, made into a neat pat with a backward and forward movement of the trowel, and then collected cleanly on the blade when passed sharply under it from the back towards the front of the board.

The mortar is now spread on the wall. This operation of spreading or "laying the bed of mortar" is a most important one, and much practice is required before the apprentice will be able to perform it properly and expeditiously. The mortar is spread on the last completed course for several bricks ahead, the trowel being passed backwards and forwards until a solid bed of uniform thickness is obtained; this is facilitated if the point of the trowel is pressed in the mortar and drawn in a zigzag fashion along the centre of the layer. Only sufficient mortar should be laid to ensure a solid bed; if applied too thinly, the pressure on the brick will be inadequate to form a solid joint; if too thick, time will be wasted in knocking or tapping the brick down to the correct level and the brick may be damaged in the process. As the apprentice becomes proficient he should be able to lift sufficient mortar on his trowel which will serve to lay three or four bricks, although this depends upon the mortar (cement mortar, for example, sets or stiffens more quickly than lime mortar).

6. The bricks must be laid immediately the mortar has been spread, as delay will result in the latter becoming too stiff. A brick when picked up is gripped by the hand, with the palm on top at the middle, the thumb at the front face and the four fingers at the back. It is firmly and evenly pressed down on the mortar; if the bed has been spread correctly, a few

taps only with the trowel on the brick will be necessary to line it in place (see p. 111), although an experienced bricklayer frequently accomplishes this by hand pressure alone. The apprentice should stand close to the wall, with his head vertically over the brick being laid.

7. Pressure on the brick squeezes some of the mortar out beyond the face of the wall. This is cut off, collected on the trowel and returned to the mortar board; smearing the brickwork with the mortar must be avoided and, therefore, during this operation the trowel must be held with the blade almost at right angles to the wall face, as it is pushed forward from end to end, with the edge of the blade near its widest part scraping the brickwork at the joint. *In inferior work, this mortar cut off from the bed is "buttered" on the outer vertical arris of the brick to form the vertical or cross joint, and as this is the only mortar applied, it follows that such vertical joints are inadequately filled.*

8. The vertical or cross joint should be formed with mortar picked up with the trowel from the mortar board at the same time as the brick. The blade is held almost vertically, and at an angle to the end of the brick on which the mortar is applied, as the apprentice draws the trowel towards himself; the joint is then made of uniform thickness by pressing the inside of the blade against the mortar. During this operation the brick is kept in position by the free hand.

9. Correct collar jointing (see p. 49) must be practised, *i.e.*, sufficient pressure must be applied to squeeze the mortar on to all the inside faces of adjacent bricks (of a wall exceeding ½-brick thickness) to ensure solid bed, collar and cross joints, and, incidentally, a saving of time. The common practice of attempting to accomplish this by applying mortar on top of the bricks after being laid and "flushing off" (trowelling off the mortar which has not passed down the joints) is most unsatisfactory; actually, very little of this mortar penetrates the joints unless water is added and the mortar is carefully pushed down with the edge of the trowel; *as a result of such scamped work, spaces are left in the joints through which dampness may penetrate, and the strength of the wall is considerably reduced.*

10. Cross and bed joints should be 10 mm thick (see p. 49). In "tight joint work" (that with thinner joints) bricklayers are apt to tip the edges only with mortar, especially at cross joints, as otherwise even joints can only be obtained with difficulty; spaces are thus left.

11. Hand-made bricks, having only one frog (p. 15), should be laid with the frogs uppermost to ensure that they will be completely filled with mortar. Machine-pressed bricks, having two frogs (p. 15), should have the "lower" frogs filled with mortar before being laid in position. Care must be taken that certain rough textured or rustic bricks are laid on their proper beds; it is not uncommon to see such bricks laid upside-down. Any slightly mis-shapen bricks used for facings and which are to be struck-jointed (p. 179) should be laid hollow bed down and the "round" (convex) face outwards, otherwise the appearance will not be satisfactory.

12. When constructing external walls the corners (or quoins or *leads*) are first built to a height of several courses (see Figs. 20 and 100) and the walling between completed course by course. The accuracy of the whole work depends upon that of the corners and therefore great care should be taken to ensure that these are properly built. The position of each corner is determined by plumbing down from the wall lines as described on p. 105. A quoin is constructed in the following manner:—

Assuming that a portion of the wall has been completed and a quoin is to be continued, the straight-edge with spirit level is placed on the brickwork at the corner and "levelled length and width" (*i.e.*, in both directions) to check if the brick bed is square with the front and return vertical faces. The corner brick is laid with the apprentice standing well over the wall in order that he may see that both outer faces of the brick are in alignment with the brickwork below. The gauge-rod (Fig. 75) is used to ensure that the brick is laid at the correct height; for this purpose, the rod is held vertically against the brickwork, supported on a nail driven into a horizontal joint (or wood peg driven into the ground with its top level with the top of the first bed joint above ground level); the courses as constructed must correspond with the divisions on the rod. A short straight-edge is applied vertically against both faces of the corner brick to ensure that it is in alignment with the vertical faces of the brickwork below; any corrections are made; this will save adjustment when the plumb-rule is used (see below).

Several bricks are now laid in each direction. These must be horizontal, and to test this a short straight-edge and the spirit level are applied on top of the newly laid bricks. To check the faces of these bricks, which must be in alignment, the straight-edge is held in an inclined position with one end touching the top of the face of the corner brick and the other in contact with the face of a brick in the course below; any corrections are made by using the brick hammer or trowel handle.

After four or five courses of the quoin have been built in this manner, the plumb-rule or vertical level is applied to make certain that the faces of the quoin are truly vertical. If the plumb-rule is used, it is placed against one face at about 25 mm from the corner, kept in position by placing a foot against its outer edge, and controlled by one hand held near the top. The top of the rule is gradually brought towards the body until the bob swings slightly backwards and forwards in and out of the hole. If the cord coincides with the gauge-line (p. 97) marked down the middle of the rule, the face is plumb; otherwise adjustment must be made by using the handle of the trowel or brick hammer. The plumb-rule is next placed against the return face of the quoin (at about 25 mm from the corner) and any corrections made. If the vertical level (Fig. 82) is used (and many bricklayers prefer this), it is held in similar positions, verticality being assured if the bubble in the short tube (or both tubes, depending upon the type of level) is in the centre.

13. When both corners of a wall have been built in this manner to a height usually not exceeding 1 m, the courses of brickwork between are

constructed with the aid of either the line and pins (Fig. 76) or line bobbins (Fig. 77). If the former, one of the pins is inserted in and near the top of a vertical joint (usually the first cross joint or on the return face of the wall), and after the line has been stretched taut to prevent any sag, the second pin is pushed into the corresponding cross joint in the opposite quoin. The line should now be level with the top of the course to be built and 3 mm clear of the brickwork; if the quoins have been correctly built, the line will be horizontal.

If the line bobbins are used instead of the pins and line, one bobbin (with the line fastened round the screws and engaged in the saw-cut) is placed with the notched portion against the corner and line level with the course; at the opposite quoin the line is placed in the saw-cut of the second bobbin which is placed in a similar manner against the corner, and after being stretched taut, the line is finally secured at the screws; once the line has been fixed in this manner no further adjustment at the bobbins is required, for, after one course is completed, the bobbins are simply slid up the corners to the next. The application of line bobbins is shown in Fig. 100. An enlargement of the bobbin at B is shown and the bobbin at the opposite corner is indicated at C. As mentioned on p. 98, tingles are required at about 6 m centres if the line is a long one; when fixing a tingle, a brick (called a *tingle brick*) is laid plumb and to the gauge (guided by the brickwork below) in the course to be built; the tingle, placed flat on this brick, is weighted by a loose bat; the taut line is passed under the outer nibs and over the centre nib (see D, Fig. 100, and the enlarged sketch). The bricks are now laid as described on p. 109 to complete the course, care being taken that the top face edge of each brick is tapped level with the line, level from back to front, and 3 mm clear of the line; *the tendency to lay the bricks too close to the line must be avoided,* any overhang being corrected after frequent application of the plumb-rule or vertical level. If the bricks are of the hard, dense type (with little "suction") only *slight* pressure or tapping should be resorted to, otherwise the bed mortar will run and the bricks will tend to overhang.

14. When a break in the line occurs, it should be spliced and not tied with a knot; *a straight wall cannot be built if the line is full of knots.* To make a splice, a small loop is first formed (by untwisting and dividing the strands) at about 75 mm from one of the broken ends; the second broken portion is threaded through both it and a second loop,. made at about 38 mm from the first; a loop is made in the second portion at about 75 mm from its end, the first broken end is passed through it and both portions are pulled tight; the loose ends of the line are then cut off.

15. Perpends must be kept vertical. This is checked as the work proceeds by using the straight-edge and try-square (Fig. 79). The former is placed flat on the course being constructed, with its edge projecting slightly beyond the face. The stock of the square is set

against the underside of the straight-edge, with the edge of the
blade on the last formed vertical joint. If the work is satisfactory, the
blade will coincide with the joint in the course next but one to it (in

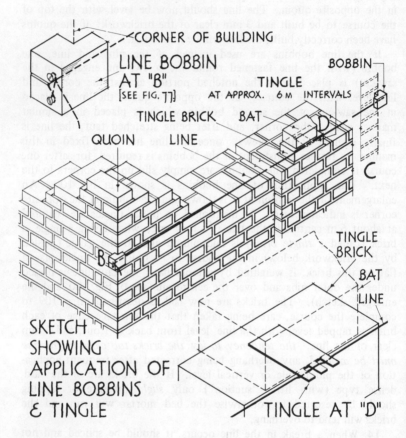

Fig.100

English, Flemish and certain other bonds). This procedure is sometimes
reversed, *i.e.*, the blade is placed coincident with a vertical joint in the
alternate course, a mark is made on top of the last formed course
against the blade, and this gives the position of the end of the brick
which is now laid in the course under construction.

16. It has been stated on p. 77 that (*a*) the width of openings and
the distance between each should be multiples of 1-brick in an English
bonded wall in order to avoid broken bond; (*b*) the width of openings

in a Flemish bonded wall should be multiples of 1½-brick plus 2-bricks and the distance between openings should be 1½-bricks and multiples of 1½-brick thereafter (see p. 80). *Such openings should be carefully set out when the brickwork has reached the ground level,* the distance from quoin to window, window to door, etc., being marked on the wall. As the work proceeds, the perpends at the cross joints above these marks must be maintained truly vertical. This will render unnecessary any adjustment to the bond when the sills are reached. The thickness of the vertical joints must, of course, be included when arriving at the above dimensions.

17. The height of door and window openings should have regard to the thickness of the bricks and bed joints, as *split courses above lintels and flat arches (and under ends of stone sills) must be avoided* (pp. 128 and 172). Window sills should also course with the brickwork to avoid splits. When setting out these heights, it is desirable at window jambs to start with stretchers immediately on the sills (Figs. 56, 57 and 141) and finish with stretchers directly under stone heads (Fig. 130); the number of courses from the start of the facings at the ground level (or 75 mm below it) should be worked down from the tops of the sills to ensure this. *These essentials must be borne in mind when marking off the gauge-rod* (p. 98) as all the various heights must conform to it (p. 110).

18. The plumbing of door and window reveals and the adjacent perpends should receive special attention. The square should also be applied horizontally to make sure that the reveals are being constructed at right angles to the face of the wall.

19. Brickwork must not be constructed during frosty weather, as frost interferes with the setting of the mortar and can do considerable damage. Brickwork carried out during the winter should be adequately protected before operations are ceased for the day. In this connection. tarpaulin or canvas sheets arranged to overhang the outer face of new work, and suitably weighted with planks, etc., on top of the wall, serve as a good protection against cold winds, etc.

20. The mortar board should be kept in a clean and tidy condition. If allowed to spread all over the board, the mortar will be difficult to lift cleanly and spread on the wall due to it drying and hardening too quickly. An occasional trim up is therefore required to keep it free from the edges of the board. Mortar droppings and small pieces of bricks should be periodically removed from the working space on the scaffold and elsewhere. The scaffold board adjoining the wall should be at least 65 mm away from the face to allow clearance for mortar droppings. When work is discontinued at the end of the day, or on account of bad weather, care should be taken to see that the scaffold board next to the face is removed and placed on top of the wall; failure to do this may result in the facings being spoilt (especially if they are rough textured bricks) due to rain splashing the dust and mortar droppings on the wall face.

21. Finally, the apprentice should take great care of his tools, keeping them clean and oiled, and the cutting edges of such tools as the brick hammer and chisels sharpened.

The setting out and construction of arches are described on pp. 142-148, and circular work on pp. 155, 157 and 158. A description of jointing and pointing of brickwork is given on pp. 178-183.

CHAPTER EIGHT

MISCELLANEOUS BONDS

Special bonds, including garden wall, cross, Dutch, brick-on-edge and facing bonds.

THE description of bonds which has been given on previous pages has been limited to those of English and Flemish. The following bonds will now be described: English and Flemish garden wall, cross, Dutch, brick-on-edge and facing bonds.

GARDEN WALL BOND.—This bond, as its name implies, is suitable for garden, division and similar walls which usually do not exceed 1-brick in thickness. On account of the slight variation in the lengths of bricks, it is difficult to construct a 1-brick thick wall in English bond if a fair or uniform face is required on both sides (see p. 60). As fewer headers are employed in garden wall bond than in either English or Flemish bonds, it is usually possible to select from the bricks available on the site sufficient of the longer bricks of uniform length as headers for a garden bonded wall, the remaining bricks being used as stretchers and built flush with both faces of the headers. Fair faces on both sides of a garden bonded wall are thus ensured. Whilst garden wall bond is not as strong as English bond (the transverse tie being inferior), it is sufficient for most dwarf walls and for those not required to withstand large stresses. As mentioned on p. 151, because of its good appearance garden wall bond is sometimes used for the construction of the outer leaves of cavity walls (Chapter Eleven).

There are two forms of this bond, *i.e.*, (*a*) English garden wall bond and (*b*) Flemish garden wall bond.

(*a*) *English Garden Wall Bond* (see Fig. 101).—This consists of one course of headers to three or five courses of stretchers. As in English bond, a queen closer is introduced next to the quoin header in the heading course. A header is placed at the quoin of each middle (or alternate) course of stretchers to give the necessary lap and face appearance of stretching bond (see also Fig. 36). The longitudinal vertical joint between each three (or five) successive stretching courses is continuous, and this causes the

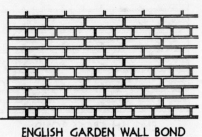

ENGLISH GARDEN WALL BOND

Fig.101

deficiency in transverse strength as stated above. This bond, because of

115

its economy, is frequently adopted in the construction of 1-brick thick external walls which are plastered or roughcasted on their outer faces.

The thickness of the bricks shown in Figs. 101-104 inclusive is 50 mm; thicker bricks may, of course, be employed.

(*b*) *Flemish Garden Wall Bond* (see Fig. 102).—This is also known as *Sussex* and *Scotch* bond. It consists of three or five stretchers to one

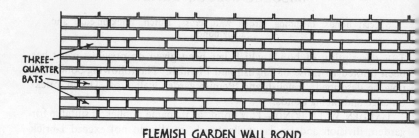

FLEMISH GARDEN WALL BOND

Fig.102

header in *each* course. A three-quarter bat is placed next to the quoin header in every alternate course, and a header is laid over the middle of each central stretcher. Because of its good appearance, this bond is also often used for facing cavity, etc., walls.

In a modified arrangement at the quoin of a Sussex bonded wall, a queen closer is placed next to the quoin header of each alternate course, and this is followed by a series of three stretchers and a header. Each alternating course comprises a quoin stretcher with a stretcher adjoining, followed by a series consisting of a header and three stretchers. Excepting at the quoin, the appearance is similar to the above, as each header is centrally over the middle stretcher.

MONK BOND is a variation of Flemish garden wall bond, *each* course consisting of a series comprising a header and two stretchers, the header coming centrally over the joint between a pair of stretchers.

ENGLISH CROSS BOND (see Fig. 103).—This is similar to English bond, in that it consists of alternate courses of headers and stretchers, with queen closers next to the quoin headers. Each *alternate stretching* course has, however, a header placed next to the quoin stretcher. This causes the stretchers to break joint in alternate courses.

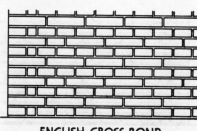

ENGLISH CROSS BOND

Fig.103

DUTCH BOND (see Fig. 104).—This is another modification of English bond. The bond consists of alternate courses of headers and stretchers, but *each stretching* course begins at the quoin with a three-quarter bat, and every *alternate stretch-ing* course has a header placed next to the quoin three-quarter bat. This has the effect of the stretchers breaking joint in alternate courses. The presence of the quoin three-quarter bats makes it unnecessary for queen closers to be placed next to the quoin headers as in English bond.

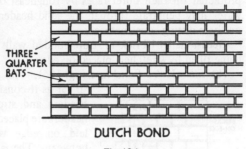

DUTCH BOND

Fig.104

BRICK-ON-EDGE BONDS.—These differ from normal bond in that at least alternate courses are a half-brick high, the bricks being laid on edge and not on bed. They are economical as, compared with English bond, considerably less bricks and mortar are required. Their strength is deficient, and the appearance is unsatisfactory on account of the large scale of the brick units and the light colour which is character-istic of the beds of most bricks. Only wire-cuts should be used, as bricks with frogs are unsuitable. These bonds are sometimes employed for garden and similar walling, and occasionally for walls of cheap one-storied cottages. The best known brick-on-edge bonds are (*a*) rat-trap bond and (*b*) Silverlock's bond.

(a) *Rat-trap Bond* (see Fig. 105).—All bricks are laid on edge, and as shown, are arranged to give a face appearance of Flemish bond. Each

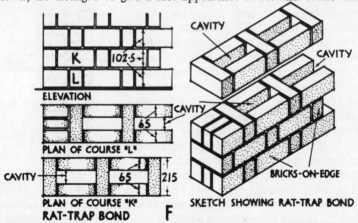

Fig.105

alternate course L commences with a three-quarter bat, followed by a header, and each alternate course K commences with a header, succeeded by a stretcher. As indicated on the plans, there is an 85 mm cavity between each pair of stretchers, except at the jambs, which are solid—see also sketch. A rat-trap bonded wall is considerably cheaper than the normal solid type. External walls of cottages built in this bond must be protected on their outer faces by roughcast or vertical tiling, otherwise water may penetrate through the solid headers and mortar which drops on them during construction.

Occasionally 1-brick rat-trap bonded walls are built solid, the cavity being filled by stretchers placed on edge.

(b) *Silverlock's Bond* (see Fig. 106).–This resembles English bond in

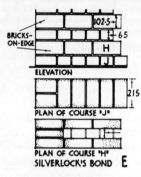

PLAN OF COURSE "H"
SILVERLOCK'S BOND E

Fig.106

so far as it consists of alternate courses of headers and stretchers, but, whereas the headers are placed on bed, the stretchers are laid on edge with a continuous cavity between. The jambs are solid, and a three-quarter bat at the beginning of each heading course gives the necessary bond. Whilst this is stronger than rat-trap bond, it is not so economical.

On the score of economy in materials and space, brick-on-edge stretching bond is frequently employed in the construction of 65 mm thick internal partition walls in lieu of ½-brick thick brick walls.

FACING BOND.–This is usually adopted for solid walls exceeding 1-brick in thickness which are faced with thin bricks and backed by thicker standard commons. The faced work is bonded to the backing in a series of blocks of a height which depends upon the difference in thickness between the two types of bricks.

Thus, in the vertical section through a portion of a 2-brick wall in Fig. 107, the height of four courses of 50 mm thick facings with their bed joints is shown to coincide with three courses of commons together with their bed joints, and the blocks of facings are alternately ½ and 1-brick thick. The facings may be built in either English, Flemish, or any of the bonds shown in Figs. 101, 102, 103 and 104 (with snap headers at the ½-brick thick blocks) and the backing is built in English bond. Some-

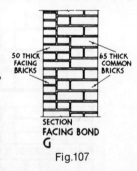

SECTION
FACING BOND
G

Fig.107

what similar construction may be applied to 1½-brick walls, with the backing to the alternating 1-brick thick facing blocks built in stretching bond.

A modified form of facing bond may be applied to 1-brick thick walls. Thus, the facings and commons would be built in ½-brick thick courses in stretching bond with facing heading courses at suitable intervals. For example, if the facing and backing bed joints coincide as shown in Fig. 107, such facing headers would appear at every fifth facing course.

Facing bond is not, of course, as strong as English bond, but the alternative would be to use thin bricks for the backings as well as the facings. This would add considerably to the cost, especially if the facings were only 50 mm thick.

CHAPTER NINE

PIERS, OFFSETS AND CORBELS

Detached and attached piers in English and Flemish bonds; offsets, corbels, oversailing courses and buttress cappings.

PIERS

THESE are provided to support concentrated loads from floors, roofs, arches, beams or lintels, etc., and to strengthen walls at intervals. There are two kinds, *i.e.*, (*a*) detached and (*b*) attached.

Fig. 108 is a key plan of a portion of a building showing the application of piers.

The materials and workmanship must be sound and consequently English bond is often adopted, bricks of the engineering class (see p. 17) are often specified and cement mortar is usually employed.

(a) *Detached Piers or Pillars or Columns.*— Alternative plans of the square pier shown at C, Fig. 108, are given at J, K and L, Fig. 109, and the corresponding part elevations are shown at D, E and F. It is only necessary to show one plan of each pier, as in every

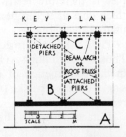

Fig.108

case the arrangement of the bricks in each course is the same. Thus, the 1-brick square pier has every alternate course constructed as shown at J with similar intermediate courses at right angles (see elevation D); the 1½-brick square pier has alternate courses as shown at K with similar adjacent courses having the stretcher face of two three-quarter bats at the front over the three headers (see E); each course in the 2-brick square pier, built in English bond, is as shown at L, but every alternate course is turned to the side (see elevation F). The only continuous vertical joints are those shown by thick lines at K.

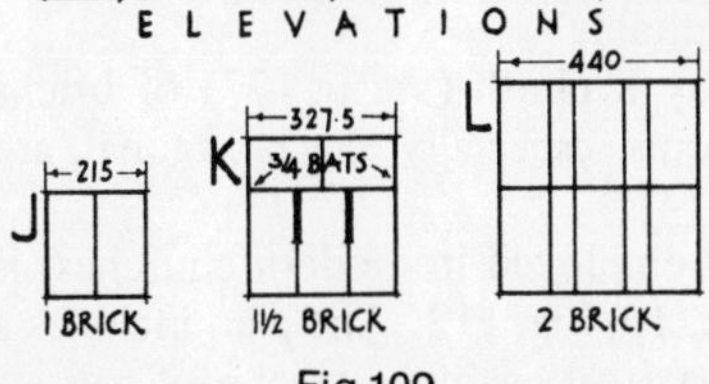

Fig.109

side (see elevation F). The only continuous vertical joints are those shown by thick lines at K.

A stone *pad* or *template,* as shown in each elevation, is usually provided at the top of a pier to ensure a firm bed for a beam, etc., and to effectively distribute the load. Pillars which do not support loads(such as gate pillars) are often finished with copings (see Figs. 166 and 167).

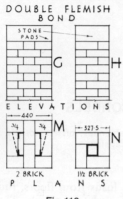

Fig.110

Square detached piers in double Flemish bond are shown in Fig. 110, although in neither case is the true face appearance of this bond presented, as the headers are not centrally over stretchers; this can only be obtained in piers exceeding 2-brick dimensions. In the 1½-brick pier (which is the smallest that can be built in this bond) at N and H continuous vertical joints are produced, as indicated by thick lines. This pier is therefore relatively weak. The short straight joints shown by thick lines at M can be avoided if bevelled closers (see broken lines) are used as an alternative.

Piers may be formed with rounded arrises by using bullnose bricks. Thus, double bullnoses (Fig. 27) may be used in the construction of pier J, Fig. 109, and single bullnose bricks (Q, Fig. 114) for the remaining piers.

Detached piers may be rectangular on plan.

Plans of alternate courses of a detached octagonal pier are given in Fig. 111. These may be constructed of standard bricks, cut to shape as required, but a better appearance is of course obtained if purpose-made bricks (p. 52) are used.

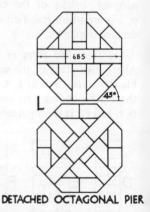

DETACHED OCTAGONAL PIER

Fig.111

A plan and part elevation of a larger detached octagonal pier (typical of many adopted in churches upon which arches are supported) are shown at R. 18, Fig. 112. The 65 mm thick bricks shown in the elevation give a pleasing appearance and a suitable finish at the floor level is provided by a plinth (see p. 177) of bricks placed on edge. Other polygonal forms, especially the hexagonal, are sometimes preferred.

An alternative design (occasionally employed in modern churches) is shown in plan and part elevation at R. 19, Fig. 112. The plan includes a steel pillar (such being used to support steel beams or steel roof trusses) which is encased in concrete and finished with brickwork. The bricks forming the two longer faces of the pillar shaft are arranged diagonally (those in alternate courses being laid in the opposite direction) to give a *serrated* (saw-edged) effect. As shown, these bricks are not purpose-made. The concrete is placed in position as the brickwork proceeds. Although

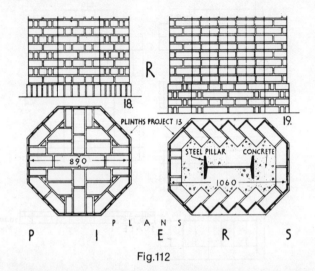

Fig.112

this brickwork does not support any load, other than its own weight, it is advisable to tie the shorter faces into the concrete by placing 25 mm by 6 mm by 150 mm long copper strips in the bed joints at every sixth course; these strips project into the concrete and are well tied in during the placing of the latter. The plinth is four courses high above the floor and has a 12 mm projection.

Two examples of *detached squint piers* (such as are required in the construction of bay windows) are shown at J and K, Fig. 113. These plans of alternate courses show that much cutting is necessary if standard bricks are used. The number of joints would be reduced, and greater strength thereby obtained, if purpose-mades were employed instead of cut standard bricks.

(b) *Attached Piers or Pilasters.*—Alternative details of a pier attached to a wall, such as that at B, Fig. 108, are given in Fig. 114. These are in English bond. The width of a pier is usually a multiple of a ½-brick and the projection may be either a ½-brick (as at O and P), 1-brick (as at Q) or upwards. The stability of walls is increased by the use of these piers at intervals and, like those of the detached type, they may be used to support concentrated loads.

Two additional examples of this type of pier are shown in Fig. 115. The projection may be increased as required. These plans of alternate courses of the piers and adjacent bonding show double Flemish bond.

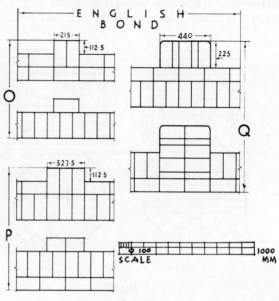

Fig.114

Plans of alternate courses of an attached octagonal pier are given in Fig. 116. Either standard bricks are cut as required or purpose-mades are used, the latter producing a much better appearance.

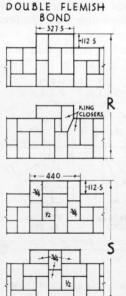

Fig.115

BUTTRESSES are external attached piers which are provided to resist thrusts from certain roof trusses or to strengthen boundary, etc., walls. Examples of buttress cappings are given in Fig. 122.

DETACHED PIER FOUNDATIONS.—An elevation of a typical foundation for a pier (such as that at F and L, Fig. 109) is shown at H, Fig. 117. This shows brick footings having ¼-brick offsets; these serve a useful purpose in gradually transmitting the concentrated load to

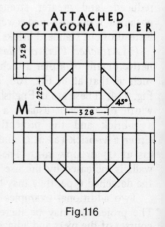

Fig.116

the concrete. The plans of the footing courses are given at J, K, L and M; these show that the maximum number of headers have been employed and there are no continuous vertical joints.

OFFSETS

These are narrow horizontal surfaces which are formed when walls are reduced in thickness. They were once used for footings (see p. 82); and were a ¼-brick wide. The width of offsets is increased when they are required to support floor joists, roof timbers, etc., the minimum width being a ½-brick. Walls of tall buildings are provided with offsets. Thus, a 15 m high wall may

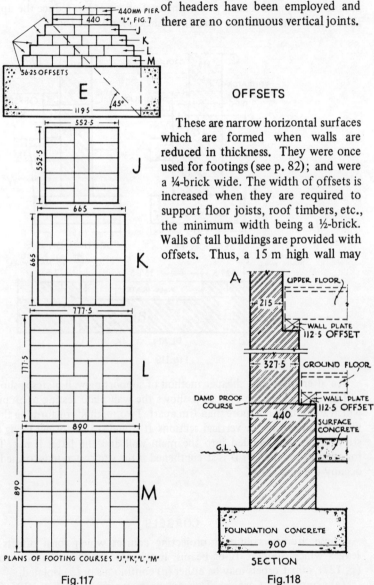

PLANS OF FOOTING COURSES "J","K","L","M"

Fig.117

SECTION

Fig.118

be 2-brick thick at the base, 1-brick thick at the top, with an intermediate thickness of 1½-brick; two ½-brick wide offsets (or ledges or shelves) are thus formed. A broken vertical section through such a wall is shown in Fig. 118. This shows two ½-brick offsets, the upper supporting a wall plate (p. 87) to which the top floor joists are fixed, and the lower providing a continuous bearing for a wall plate which supports the ground floor joists. This type of construction is used to reduce the upper thicknesses of a wall as the load diminishes towards the top.

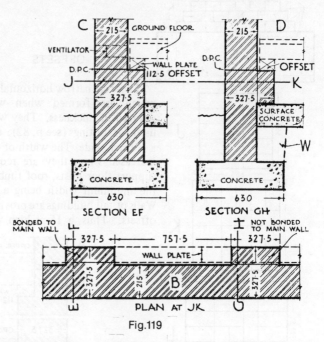

Fig.119

An alternative and cheaper method of supporting wall plates is shown in Fig. 119, where the plan at B shows the wall plate resting upon piers which are usually not more than 1 m apart. Two methods of forming these piers are shown in the vertical sections at C and D, the former being the stronger, as it is bonded into the main wall and the latter is not. The foundation for the pier D is strengthened if the site concrete is formed to occupy the space at W.

CORBELS

These are oversailing or projecting courses which form offsets or ledges which support floor beams, lintels of concrete, stone or wood (p. 127), etc. Corbels may be either (a) continuous or (b) isolated.

(a) *Continuous Corbels.*—Two examples are shown in Fig. 120. The vertical section at L shows a portion of a 1-brick wall with a corbel consisting of two courses each of which projects ¼-brick to form a ½-brick bearing for an upper floor. The vertical section at N is that through an internal wall with a corbel on each side composed of two ⅛ brick projecting courses; the reduced thickness of the upper portion of this wall assists in providing adequate (½-brick) bearing for the wall plates. The part elevation at M is the same for both sections; the two projecting courses forming the continuous corbel are shown by thick lines.

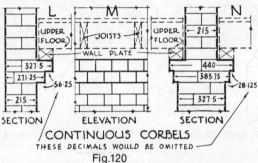

Fig.120

(b) *Isolated or Non-continuous Corbels.*—The part vertical section O and sketch P in Fig. 121 is an example. This provides a support for a beam (which may be of wood or steel) or a roof truss, etc. If the load which has to be transmitted is heavy, the projecting courses forming the corbel do not exceed ⅛ brick, as shown. The stone pad is provided to distribute the load more effectively. The stone slab (or *lintel*) forming the top of the opening (or *pocket*) supports the brickwork above.

As a load carried by a corbel tends to overturn the wall, certain precautions are taken to ensure a stable structure. These are: (1) The maximum projection of the corbel must not

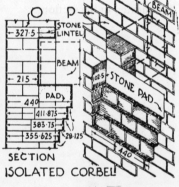

Fig.121

exceed the thickness of the wall, (2) each corbel course must not project more than ¼-brick, (3) headers must be used, as they are more adequately tailed into the wall than stretchers and (4) only sound bricks and workmanship should be employed.

OVERSAILING COURSES.—These are decorative features which are adopted, for example, at *eaves* (top of a wall covered by the lower portion of a roof), *string courses* (provided between the base and top of a wall) and *chimney stacks* (see p. 161). These courses project beyond the face of the walling.

A typical oversailing course at the eaves consists of a brick-on-edge course which has a projection beyond the face of the wall of about 20 mm. Brick-on-end and brick-on-edge courses are commonly adopted for string courses; such may be given a slight projection or they may be flush. A chimney stack with an oversailing course is shown at U, Fig. 159.

Formerly, oversailing courses of moulded bricks were used to form *cornices* (crowning members of walls), but these rarely appear in modern construction.

BUTTRESS CAPPINGS.—Two simple examples of cappings (tops) of buttresses (p. 122) are shown in Fig. 122. The sketch R and section Q

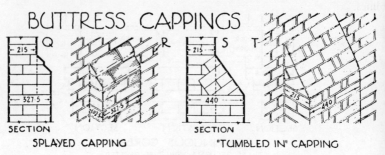

Fig.122

show two courses of splay bricks similar to those given in Fig. 31. The sketch T shows another weathered capping formed of ordinary bricks which are tilted or "tumbled" into the wall; the brick cutting involved is indicated in the sections.

CHAPTER TEN

LINTELS AND ARCHES

Brick, concrete, stone and wood lintels; axed and gauged flat, segmental, semicircular, circular and elliptical arches; rough arches; terms; centering and construction.

LINTELS

A LINTEL is a horizontal member used to support the walling above a door, window or other opening. It may be of (1) bricks, (2) concrete, (3) stone and (4) wood.

1. BRICK LINTELS.—The bricks comprising this type of lintel are either laid on edge or on end. It is relatively weak and quite unsuited to support heavy loads. Such lintels should, therefore, be used to span small openings only (unless they receive additional support as explained on p. 130) and the span should not much exceed 915 mm.

This form of lintel has been used extensively during recent years, and failures have occurred either because adequate precautions had not been taken in their construction or the spans (see p. 130) were excessive. A common failure occurs along the vertical joints, one or more bricks dropping below the normal level.

Ordinary bricks are employed; those with frogs are best, as the frogs when filled with mortar assist in preventing failure. Cement and compo mortars (p. 21) are often used, as they are stronger than lime mortar; for faced work the colour of the mortar should be the same as that used for the adjacent walling.

The lintel shown in Fig. 123 consists of ordinary bricks on end; the *soffit* (underside) is therefore a ½-brick wide (see vertical section). Of the

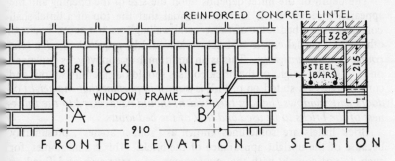

Fig.123

two methods of forming the ends that at A is the usual treatment; a somewhat stronger appearance results when, as shown at B, the first brick is slightly splayed at its bottom outer corner and supported on a similarly splayed brick in the wall course.

A portion of a brick lintel of less depth is shown in Fig. 124; its depth is equal to two courses of the adjacent brickwork. If ordinary bricks are

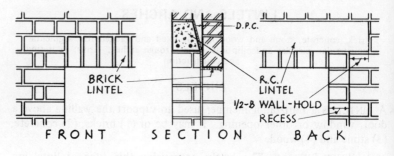

Fig.124

used for this lintel, the cut ends (formed with the bolster and dressed with the scutch) are uppermost to ensure a true face at the soffit Purpose-mades are employed in best facing work.

Brick-on-edge lintels are common and are especially effective when the soffits are required to be 1-brick wide; it will be seen that if the lintel shown in Fig. 123 has a wide soffit, purpose-made bricks must be used. Occasionally, the bricks over an opening are laid on bed; the appropriate course of general walling being continued; such a course is supported on

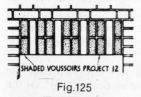

Fig.125

the window frame below or as described on p. 130.

A less simple lintel, but one of satisfactory appearance, is shown in Fig. 125. As indicated, the shaded bricks are given a slight projection beyond the face of the wall. These bricks are purpose-made.

The depth of the lintel depends upon the size of the opening and the appearance required. It is most essential that the top of a lintel shall coincide with a bed joint of the general walling (see the above Figures), otherwise a partial course of brickwork would be required. *Such a split course is most unsightly.* This is an additional reason why; as explained on p. 110, the height of the brick courses should be carefully set out and constructed. As stated on p. 113, *it is most important that the height of doors and windows (besides their width) should have regard to the thickness of the bricks to be used and that of the bed joints.*

Brick lintels are sometimes·known as "soldier arches", presumably because of the upright appearance of the bricks. This is a misnomer, for such do not comply with the requirements of a true arch as defined on p. 132. Incidentally, great care should be taken to ensure that each brick is placed vertical (by occasionally testing with the vertical level—see p. 111), as *the appearance is spoilt if one or two of them show a departure from the vertical, however slight.* An elevation of a brick lintel with a split course and several inclined units is shown in Fig. 126; that this has an objectionable appearance need not be emphasized.

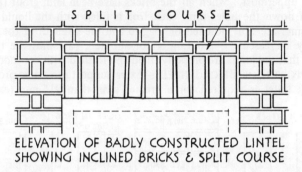

ELEVATION OF BADLY CONSTRUCTED LINTEL
SHOWING INCLINED BRICKS & SPLIT COURSE

Fig.126

A satisfactory finish is obtained if one or more courses of tiles are formed on top of the lintel and finished level with the bed joint of the walling. Two courses of tiles are shown at A, Fig. 127. Three courses of

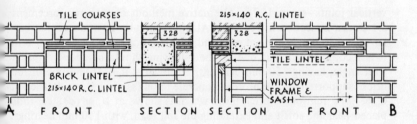

Fig.127

tiles, two of them projecting slightly, are shown at B, Fig. 127, in lieu of a brick lintel. Ordinary roofing tiles (which are made of clay or shale in a similar manner to bricks and are 265 mm by 165 mm by 10 to 12 mm thick) may be used for this purpose; as these are slightly curved in their length, purpose-made flat tiles of varying thickness are used in first-class work.

CONSTRUCTION OF BRICK LINTELS.—If the door or window frames are almost flush with the face of the wall (as in Fig. 123), it is usual to construct the lintels directly on them. In best work, however, the fixing of these frames is often deferred until the whole of the brickwork has been completed and the lintels are constructed on temporary wood supports called *turning pieces* (see p. 142).

If pressed bricks, having a frog on each bed, are used, *joggle brick lintels* can be constructed in the following manner: By means of a hammer and chisel a small channel is formed at one end to extend the frog of each brick (see broken lines at D, Fig. 128). Mortar is spread over the lower, back and front margins (leaving the frog and channel free) of the bed of each brick before being placed in position with the "frog holes" uppermost. When all the bricks have been laid, grout (p. 22) is poured down the holes until each frog is filled with the liquid mortar. The joints are thus notched or joggled and the strength of the lintel is thereby increased. If grouting is not adopted, care must be taken to ensure that the joints are properly filled and flushed with the mortar.

SUPPORTS FOR BRICK LINTELS.—Extra support should be provided if a brick lintel is required for a greater span than 915 mm (excluding

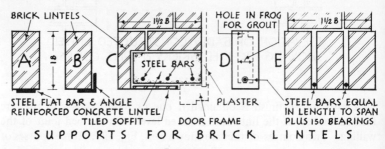

Fig.128

vertical joints—see p. 127). Alternative methods of such reinforcement are shown in section in Fig. 128. At A a 75 mm by 10 mm steel flat bar, having a 150 mm bearing at each end, is used. For spans exceeding 1·8 m it is recommended that one of the following should be adopted: (a) A steel angle, having 150 mm bearings, as shown at B, or (b) purpose-made bricks supported by a reinforced concrete lintel (see p. 131) as detailed at C, of (c) a reinforced brick lintel which is shown at D, or (d) steel rods placed near the soffit and extending the full span, with 150 mm bearings, as shown at E. Regarding detail D, a 12 to 19 mm dia. steel rod is threaded through the holes of the purpose-made bricks, and the latter are then pointed and grouted in position as described above. The exposed surfaces of the flat bar at A and the angle at B may be painted to conform to the colour of the bricks and so made inconspicuous; even if they are covered by the door and window frames, these steel members should be well painted before being fixed in order to prevent corrosion. The soffit of the concrete lintel at C may be covered, as shown, with 12 mm thick tiles cement mortar bedded to the concrete.

2. CONCRETE LINTELS.—These are now used on a large scale and are usually preferred to wood lintels. The composition of the concrete varies, a suitable mix being 1 part Portland cement, 2 parts sand and 4 parts gravel or broken brick or stone of 19 mm maximum gauge. The lintels are cast either *in situ* (in position) or are precast (formed and allowed to set before being fixed). The former is cast in a wood mould having 32 mm to 38 mm thick bottom and sides, suitably supported at the correct height, and removed when the concrete has set. The precast

method is often adopted, as the lintels can be formed at ground level in the wood moulds well in advance to allow them being sufficiently matured for fixing when required, and to permit the construction of the walling above to be proceeded with immediately after they have been fixed.

Plain concrete lintels (*i.e.*, those not reinforced) should be limited to spans not exceeding 915 mm, otherwise they may fail in tension (a stress to which the lower portion of the lintel is subjected) and shear (a stress which tends to produce diagonal cracks). Such failure is prevented if the lintels are suitably reinforced. Mild steel bars of circular cross section are usually employed as the reinforcement. Examples of reinforced concrete

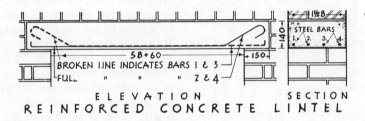

REINFORCED CONCRETE LINTEL

Fig.129

lintels are shown in Figs. 123, 124, 127 to 130. The amount of reinforcement depends upon the span and the weight to be carried; for example, the size of the four bars shown in Fig. 129 need only be 10 mm dia. Each of these bars is shaped as shown in the elevation; one end is bent up and hooked and the other is turned up or hooked. The object of the inclined bend is to resist the shear stress, and the hooked or turned up ends increase the bond or grip between the steel and concrete. The bars are placed with the bent ends alternately to the right and left (see elevation, Fig. 129). The ends of the lintels have either a ½-brick or 150 mm *bearing* or *wall-hold* (see Fig. 129). When casting such lintels, the rods are placed at about 25 mm from the bottom of the wood mould, and the concrete is deposited and well rammed round them. If precast, the top of the lintel

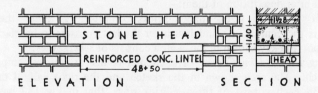

Fig.130

should be clearly marked to ensure that the fixer will bed it in position with the reinforcement *lowermost.*

3. STONE LINTELS OR HEADS.—These are rectangular blocks of stone of varying thickness and depth. These should course with the adjacent brickwork, as shown in Fig. 130, and, as mentioned on p. 113, they should be given a good bearing by being supported on stretchers (see elevation.

4. WOOD LINTELS.—These are usually of softwood, such as redwood and their use is restricted to internal walls. The size varies with the span, quality of the wood, etc., but the depth should be approximately one-twelfth of the span with a minimum of 75 mm. One form, known as a *built-up lintel*, may be used for larger spans; such consists of two or more wood pieces (of size depending upon the span, thickness of wall to be supported, etc.) bolted together. Thus, that shown in Fig. 131 consists of three 175 mm by 75 mm pieces secured with 12 mm dia. steel or wrought iron bolts near the ends and at every 380 to 450 mm of its length. A metal nut is provided to each bolt; a thin metal washer must be placed between the head of the bolt and the timber, and another between the nut and the lintel, to prevent the head and nut biting into the wood when the nut is tightened by means of a spanner. Wood lintels are prepared ready for use by the carpenter.

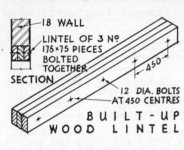

Fig. 131

ARCHES

A brick arch is composed of *wedge-shaped* bricks, joined together with mortar, and spans an opening for the purpose of supporting the weight above and providing a suitable finish. Because of their wedge-like form, the brick units support each other, the load tends to make them compact and enables them to transmit the pressure downwards to their supports.

TERMS.—Most of the technical terms applied to an arch and adjacent structure are illustrated in the isometric sketch, Fig. 132, and the following is a brief description of them:—

Voussoirs.—The wedge-shaped bricks comprising an arch; the *key brick* is the central one and is usually the last voussoir to be placed in position; the key shown in the sketch consists of several tiles.

Ring, Rim or Ring Course.—The circular course or courses comprising the arch. The arch shown in the sketch and the right half of that in Fig. 138 each consist of three ½-brick rings, that in Fig. 137 has two ½-brick rings, and that in Fig. 136 has a 1-brick ring.

Extrados or Back.—The external curve of the arch.

Intrados.—The inner curve of the arch.

Face.—The outer surface of the arch between the intrados and extrados.

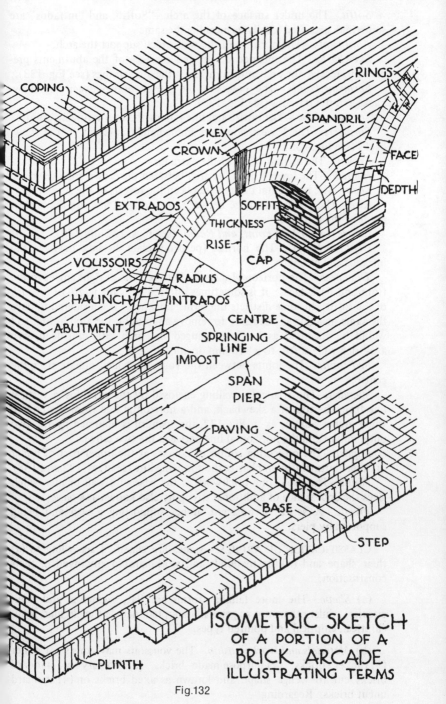

ISOMETRIC SKETCH
OF A PORTION OF A
BRICK ARCADE
ILLUSTRATING TERMS

Fig.132

Soffit.—The under surface of the arch. "Soffit" and "intrados" are sometimes accepted locally as meaning the same.

Abutments.—The portions of the wall which support the arch.

Skewbacks.—The inclined or splayed surfaces of the abutments prepared to receive the arch and from which the arch springs (see Fig. 133).

Springing Points.—The points at the intersection between the skewbacks and the intrados (see Fig. 133).

Springing Line.—The horizontal line joining the two springing points.

Springers.—The lowest voussoirs immediately adjacent to the skewbacks (see Fig. 136).

Crown.—The highest point of the extrados.

Haunch.—The lower half of the arch between the crown and skewback.

Span.—The horizontal distance between the reveals of the supports.

Rise.—The vertical distance between the springing line and the highest point of the intrados.

Centre (or Striking Point) and Radius (see Figs. 132 and 138).

Depth or Height.—The normal (perpendicular) distance between the intrados and extrados.

Thickness.—The horizontal distance between and at right angles to the front and back faces; it is sometimes referred to as the *width* or *breadth* of the soffit. In some districts the term "thickness" is considered to have the same meaning as "depth"; to remove any doubt, the arch in Fig. 133 would be specified as being a "gauged flat arch, 300 mm deep with a ½-brick wide soffit, to a 910 mm opening"

Bed Joints.—The joints between the voussoirs which radiate from the centre.

Spandril.—The triangular walling enclosed by the extrados, a vertical line from the top of a skewback, and a horizontal line from the crown; when arches adjoin, as in Fig. 132, the spandril is bounded by the two outer curves and the horizontal line between the two crowns.

Impost.—The projecting course or courses at the upper part of a pier or other abutment to emphasize the springing line (see Figs. 132 and 138).

Plinth.—The projecting brickwork at the base of a wall or pier which gives the appearance of additional strength; also known as a *base.*

Arcade.—A series of adjacent arches supporting a wall and being supported by piers.

CLASSIFICATION OF ARCHES.—Arches are classified according to (*a*) their shape and (*b*) the materials and workmanship employed in their construction.

(a) *Shape.*—The more familiar forms are flat, segmental and semicircular, whilst others not so generally adopted include the circular, semi-elliptical, elliptical and pointed types.

(b) *Materials and Workmanship.*—The voussoirs may consist of either (1) rubber bricks, (2) purpose-made bricks, (3) ordinary or standard bricks cut to wedge shape and known as axed bricks or (4) standard uncut bricks. Regarding:—

1. *Rubber Bricks, Rubbers or Cutters.*—These are soft red (chiefly), white or buff coloured bricks consisting of washed clay containing a large proportion of sand. They are usually hand-made and baked (not burnt) in a kiln. The colour is uniform throughout, and owing to their softness and fine-grained texture they are easily cut, rubbed and carved. They are used principally for *gauged arches* (see below).

2. *Purpose-made Bricks.*—These are specially machine-pressed or hand-moulded to the required shape (see p. 52) and used for good class work in the construction of *purpose-made arches* (see p. 137).

3. *Ordinary Bricks Cut to a Wedge Shape.*—These are standard bricks which have been roughly cut to the required wedge shape by the use of the bolster and dressed off with a scutch or axe (see p. 100). They are employed in the construction of *axed brick arches* (see p. 137).

4. *Ordinary Standard Uncut Bricks.*—When such bricks are used in the construction of arches, the bed joints are not of uniform thickness, but are wedge-shaped. They are used for *rough brick arches* (see p. 138).

FLAT, STRAIGHT OR CAMBER ARCH.—The extrados of a flat arch is horizontal, and the intrados is given a slight curvature or *camber* by providing a rise of 1·5 to 3 mm per 300 mm of span; thus, a flat arch with a 1·2 m span will have a rise of from 6 to 12 mm. The reason for the camber is to avoid the appearance of sagging produced if the intrados is perfectly horizontal and which defect would be accentuated if the slightest settlement occurred. A camber arch, having a flat extrados, may be given a rise of 25 to 75 mm. The angle of the skewbacks may be either (*a*) 60° (as shown in Fig. 133) or (*b*) the amount of skewback (the horizontal distance between the springing point and the top of the skewback) may equal 37 mm per 300 mm of span per 300 mm depth of arch; thus, for example, an arch having a span of 910 mm and a depth of 290 mm will have a skewback measurement of $37 \times \dfrac{910}{300} \times \dfrac{290}{300} = 108$ mm compared with 167 mm when the skewback is 60°; the adoption of the 60° rule gives a less pleasing appearance (compare the arch with 60° skewbacks in Fig. 133 and that in Fig. 134 which shows skewbacks conforming to rule (*b*)). This type of arch is weak and should be limited to spans of from 1·2 to 1·5 m unless additional strength is imparted by means of a steel bar or angle (see p. 130).

There are three varieties of this type, *i.e.*, (*a*) gauged flat arch, (*b*) purpose-made brick flat arch and (*c*) axed brick flat arch, depending upon the class of bricks and workmanship used in their construction.

(a) *Gauged Flat Arch.*—"Gauge" means "measure", and a characteristic of gauged work is its exactness. Rubbers are used; these bricks are accurately shaped as described on pp. 142-144 and the bed joints are very thin, being as fine as 1 mm, although a thickness varying from 3 to 6 mm is much favoured. Such accurate work is possible by the use of rubbers and a jointing material known as *putty lime* (lime chalk which has been

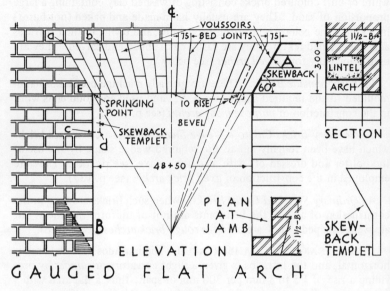

Fig.133

well slaked, worked up to a consistency resembling thick cream and passed through a fine sieve).

An elevation of a gauged flat arch is shown in Fig. 133. The wall at each side of the opening is built to the level of the extrados and the skewbacks formed (see thick lines at A) to receive the arch. The skewbacks are angled at 60°; if rule (b)—see above—were adopted, the skewback would be only 112 mm (see Fig. 134). As shown on the left, the arch may be given a "bonded face" by providing cross joints which are parallel to the *in*trados; if preferred, such joints are omitted, as shown on the right. The extrados must coincide with a bed joint of the general walling, as split courses must be avoided (see p. 128). The intrados is also shown coincident with a bed joint; this is not essential, and because of the difficulty in cutting the brick E to a fine edge (especially if the bricks are hard) it is sometimes preferable to arrange the springing point to come midway up the course, as shown at A, Fig. 136.

As the adjacent walling is shown in English bond, the span equals a multiple of stretcher units plus vertical joints (see p. 77).

When drawing this arch to scale, the student should note that all bed joints of the voussoirs radiate towards the centre and that the 75 mm measurements (or the thickness of the bricks of the general walling) are set off along the *ex*trados. Students make a common mistake in measuring off along the intrados. A satisfactory appearance results, especially if the face is bonded, if the voussoirs in the arch when divided by 4 gives a remainder of 1, for example, 13, 17 (see Fig. 133) and 21.

The construction of this arch is described on pp. 142-144.

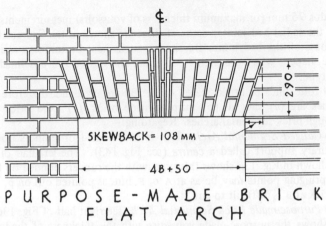

PURPOSE-MADE BRICK
FLAT ARCH

Fig.134

(*b*) *Purpose-made Brick Flat Arch* (Fig. 134).—This arch differs from
the gauged type in that the jointing material and the thickness of the

joints is the same as for the
general walling, and pur-
pose-mades are used instead
of rubbers. Rule (*b*) has
been adopted for obtaining
the size of the skewback.
This type of arch is fre-
quently employed in good
class work. See p. 145 for
a description of the con-
struction of this arch.

(*c*) *Axed Brick Flat
Arch.*—This is similar to (*b*)
except that its appearance
is not so satisfactory, as the
voussoirs are ordinary
bricks cut to a wedge shape
(see p. 135) and it is adopted for less important work.

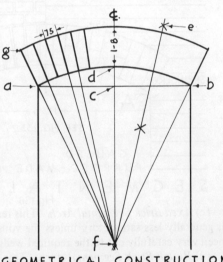

GEOMETRICAL CONSTRUCTION
OF A SEGMENTAL ARCH

Fig.135

SEGMENTAL ARCH.—
The geometrical construction of this type of arch as shown in Fig. 135 is
as follows: Draw span *ab*; bisect this at *c*; make *cd* equal to the required
rise, say 100 mm; construct the bisector of *bd* (by using compasses) and
continue this bisector until it meets the centre line at *f*. The latter is the
centre for both intrados and extrados. Continue *fa* to *g*, making the skewback *ag* equal to the depth of the arch, say 215 mm, and describe the
curves representing the intrados and extrados. Mark off along the

*ex*trados 75 mm (or maximum thickness of voussoirs) measurements and draw the radial bed joints; some of these are shown in the figure. If the thickness of the bed joints are shown, such must be uniform and not wedge-shaped, when the arch is of either the gauged, purpose-made or axed type.

All four kinds of bricks stated on p. 135 are used and, therefore, the varieties are (*a*) gauged, (*b*) purpose-made brick, (*c*) axed brick and (*d*) rough brick segmental arches. Regarding:–

(a) *Gauged Segmental Arch.*–This is constructed of rubbers upon a temporary support called a *centre* (see Fig. 143). The left half of the arch shown in Fig. 136 shows this type, with the rubbers bonded on face. The springing points may be as at A or B, but, as pointed out on p. 136, the brick at B is difficult to cut.

(b) *Purpose-made Brick Segmental Arch* (see right half of Fig. 136).– This shows the purpose-made voussoirs with the thickness of the joints the same as that of the adjacent walling. Cross joints may be used.

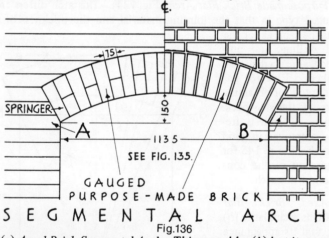

SEGMENTAL ARCH
Fig.136

(c) *Axed Brick Segmental Arch.*–This resembles (*b*) but its appearance is generally less satisfactory unless the voussoirs of standard bricks have been very carefully cut to the required wedge shape.

(d) *Rough Brick Segmental Arch.*–This type consists of one or more half-brick rings constructed of ordinary *uncut* bricks. An elevation of a two half-brick ringed rough arch is shown in Fig. 137. As the bricks are not cut, wedge-shaped *joints* result. Such arches are usually adopted when the appearance is not of primary importance (as for openings in walls which are to be plastered) because of their relative cheapness. They should be built in cement mortar.

Rough arches are always constructed in half-brick rings to avoid wide joints at the extrados. Some idea may be obtained of the very wide joints which would result at the extrados if 1-brick rings were used by reference to the three voussoirs at A. As indicated, each springer should be a stretcher (on face), as such is more effective than a header in transmitting the thrust from the arch to the abutments.

The geometrical construction of the arch is shown. The 75 mm measurements for the voussoirs in the *lower* ring are set off along the *in*trados, and those for the *upper* ring are set off along the *middle* curve. The centre of the arch is found (see p. 137) at which a 75 mm dia. circle is described (it being equal to the thickness of the bricks). Each voussoir is drawn by placing a set square against the division on the intrados (for the lower ring) and alternately tangential to the right and left of the small circle to form the wedge-shaped joints.

Rough arches are constructed over *wood* lintels which span openings exceeding 1·2 m in width. These arches relieve the lintels of the weight

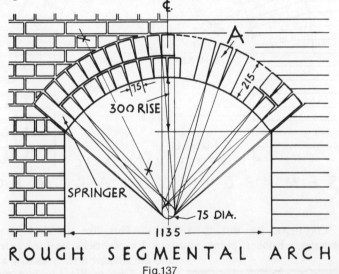

ROUGH SEGMENTAL ARCH
Fig.137

of the brickwork above and are called *rough relieving, discharging* or *jack arches*. The springing points of such an arch are at the top corners of the wood lintel. The space between the top of the lintel and the soffit of the arch is filled in with brickwork and is called the *core*. Rough relieving arches are not required if the lintels are of reinforced concrete; the latter are now generally preferred to wood lintels (see p. 130).

SEMICIRCULAR ARCH.—There are also four types of this shaped arch.

A gauged semicircular arch having a bonded face is shown on the left in Fig. 138; the cross joints may be omitted.

An example of a purpose-made brick semicircular arch is illustrated on the right in the same figure. Three half-brick rings are shown, although the number varies according to the span and appearance required; if preferred, a single ring of varying depth may be adopted. An impost, such as that shown, is sometimes formed.

The axed brick semicircular arch is similar to that shown on the right in Fig. 138, but the bricks are axed standards.

The rough brick class, like that of segmental shape, has V-shaped joints.

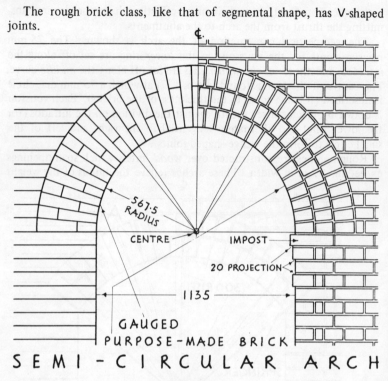

SEMI-CIRCULAR ARCH

Fig.138

CIRCULAR OR BULL'S-EYE ARCH.—This, like the above, has four varieties. Rubber, purpose-made and axed bricks are used externally,

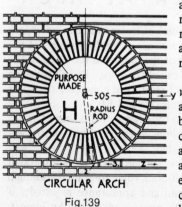

CIRCULAR ARCH

Fig.139

and an internal arch is usually a rough ring. That in Fig. 139 is a purpose-made bull's-eye. Circular openings are adopted chiefly as decorative features to receive windows.

Construction.—The lower half or *invert* of this arch is built first. The adjacent brickwork, which will form the base for this lower half, is built from course z and racked back up to course Y at the centre. A wood batten is laid across the opening and weighted at the ends on course Y. A piece of wood, called a *trammel rod* or *radius rod,* is lightly screwed at one end to the batten at the centre of the arch; this rod is indicated by broken lines and, as shown, its length equals the radius of the extrados plus the thickness of the bed joint. Course Z is completed; stretchers 1, 2 and 3 are laid temporarily in position and marked to the required curve as the radius rod is traversed; these bricks are cut with a bolster and trimmed accurately to shape with a scutch; they are then laid permanently. Each course up to the middle line is completed in this manner, after which the purpose-made voussoirs forming the lower half of the arch are bedded in position, the radius rod (upon which the depth of the arch is indicated) being used to check the curve of the intrados. The upper half of the arch is constructed on a *wood centre* (see p. 146) supported on struts.

SEMI-ELLIPTICAL ARCH.—Fig. 140 shows a half elevation of an axed or purpose-made brick arch of this type; it also shows a half arch in three

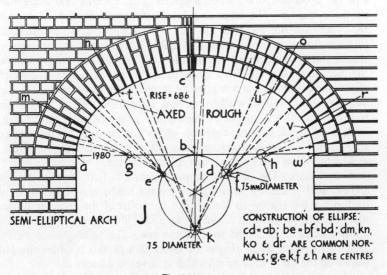

Fig.140

rough half-brick rings. A true elliptical curve cannot be constructed with compasses, but the "five centres" method shown gives a good approximation. The geometrical construction is as follows: Draw the springing line or major axis *aw* and the minor axis, making the rise *bc* at least one-third the span; make *cd* equal half span *ab*; construct circle with *d* as centre and *db* as radius, and mark *be* and *bf = db*; draw lines *dem, dfr, ken* and *kfo*; *g, e, k, f* and *h* are the five required centres for both the intrados and extrados. Describe tangential curves *as, st, tu, uv* and *vw* with *g, e, k, f* and *h* as centres respectively; construct the extrados in a similar manner. Mark off the thickness of the voussoirs on the extrados (if the bricks are axed, purpose-made or rubbed); it is important to note that these joints are radial, as shown by the broken lines; thus, the voussoirs within the portion of the arch *mnts* radiate from centre *e*, and those within portion *nout* radiate from centre *k*. It will be seen that the bricklayer will only require three differently shaped *templets* (thin pieces of wood cut to the shape of the voussoirs to which axed or rubber voussoirs are shaped—see below), *i.e.*, one for the central voussoirs, one for those within the intermediate portions *mnts* and *orvu*, and one templet for the voussoirs within the two end portions. Also for purposemades, three similarly shaped but slightly larger (to allow for shrinkage) moulds will serve the brick-moulder to shape the bricks. For a rough arch, the thickness of the voussoirs is marked off along the *intrados* of *each* ring and the V-shaped joints are drawn as explained on p. 139 by using the set square and placing it tangentially against the 75 mm dia. circles at *h, f, k,* etc., and at the divisions on the curves.

CENTERING AND CONSTRUCTION OF ARCHES.—Arches are constructed upon temporary wood supports called *centres*. These are made by the carpenter. The shape and details of a centre are dependent upon the type, span and width of the arch to be supported. In practice, any suitable timber which is readily available is converted to the required shape, and thus there is a big variation in the sizes and arrangement of the members. A centre must be sufficiently rigid to support the weight of the brickwork to be constructed on it, and, in addition, provision must be made to permit of a slight vertical adjustment (see p. 144) of the centre. A centre is supported on vertical *props* or *posts,* and *folding wedges* are placed between the heads of the posts and the centre to effect adjustment. The term *centering* includes the centre, wedges and props.

The following description is of typical centering.

Flat Arches.—The simplest form of centre is that required for flat arches; such is called a *turning piece* and is a solid piece of timber having its top surface shaped to conform to the soffit of the arch. A turning piece suitable for the arch shown in Fig. 133 is illustrated in Fig. 141. The upper surface is cambered to a 10 mm rise. The turning piece rests at each end upon a wood *sleeper* or *sill* (although this is often omitted) placed on the brick window sill which it serves to protect.

The wall at each side of the opening will have been built and the skewbacks prepared to receive the arch. When several arches of the same shape and size have to be constructed, it is convenient to use a wood *templet* or *pattern* to ensure that all of the skewbacks are made to the correct angle. A templet is shown in Fig. 133 and its application at *a, b, c* and *d.* The bricks forming a skewback can be accurately cut if a line parallel to it is marked on the wall, as shown by the broken line at B, Fig. 133, when the measurements taken along the arrises of the shaded bricks which are intercepted by the mark are transferred to the bricks to be shaped; the latter are cut with the bolster and dressed with the scutch.

Briefly, the rubbers to be used for the arch are shaped in the following manner: A full size drawing of the arch (showing the voussoirs and the thickness of the joints) is made from which the bevels (inclinations) of the voussoirs are obtained at the soffit and transferred to a thin (10 mm) wood templet called a *face mould.* The latter is shaped to that of the key voussoir and is slightly longer. As all of the bricks comprising one half of a flat arch (from the springer to the key) vary in shape, it follows that a different bevel for each voussoir is required. The bevels are obtained by means of the bevel (Fig. 90) applied as indicated by broken lines in Fig. 133, the blade being adjusted and the screw tightened. As each bevel is obtained it is marked on the face mould and numbered according to that of the voussoir on the drawing.

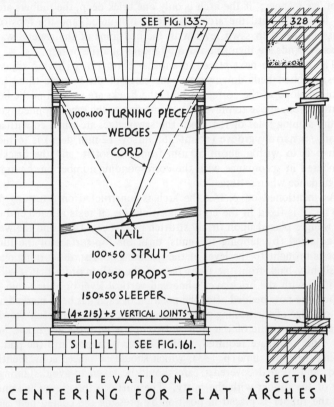

SEE FIG. 133.

328

100×100 TURNING PIECE
WEDGES
CORD

NAIL
100×50 STRUT
100×50 PROPS
150×50 SLEEPER
(4×215)+5 VERTICAL JOINTS

SILL   SEE FIG. 161.

ELEVATION   SECTION
CENTERING FOR FLAT ARCHES

Fig. 141

The bed (*i.e.*, that on which the manufacturer's trade mark or initials are impressed) of each brick is rubbed by a circular motion on the rubbing stone (p. 101) to a smooth, level surface. One face is next rubbed until it is straight and square with the bed, as tested by the try square (Fig. 79).

The bricks are now ready for shaping. They are usually shaped together in pairs (one for each half of the arch) in a wood *cutting box* which has a base, two sides and one end. The soffits of the bricks are first cut to the required bevel; the two bricks are placed closed together on edge in the box, squared faces downwards, the rubbed bed of one of them next a side of the box, and the ends projecting slightly at the open end; the bevel (Fig. 90) having been set to the bevel on the face mould is applied against the side of the box at its open edge; a piece of wood, about the size of a brick bed, is placed vertically next the outer bed of the second brick with its vertical edge in line with the blade of the bevel, and tightly wedged in the box. A vertical cut is formed at the bevel mark by the saw (Fig. 91), being guided by the edges of the box and wood strip. The two bricks are removed, reversed and wedged in the box, and cut to length by sawing the opposite ends to the same bevel in a similar manner; if the arch is only one brick deep, the rubbers are not cut to length until the arch has been constructed, and the tops of the voussoirs are then sawn level with the bed joint of the general walling. The sawn ends are then smoothed by means of a file or rasp.

The bricks are next placed in another cutting box (having adjustable sides), rubbed beds downwards; the sides of the box are tilted to the required slope at the correct height, the bricks are wedged in the box or strutted from above to prevent them moving as the saw is applied, guided by the sloping sides of the box; the sawn edges are trimmed with a file. Finally, a narrow groove (about 25 mm by 12 mm deep) is formed in each bed to within about 50 mm from the soffit, and the bricks are numbered in accordance with the corresponding number on the drawing for guidance when setting.

As mentioned on p. 142 the arch is constructed on a turning piece. The latter is fixed in the correct position, *i.e.*, it rests at each end upon the wedges placed upon firmly strutted props (Fig. 141), and the wedges are adjusted (by tapping the ends) until the top surface of the turning piece is brought to the level of the springing points; the turning piece is set slightly back from the front face of the wall in order that it will not interfere with the bricklayer's line and vertical level or plumb-rule. The rubbers are now bedded after the position of each has been marked along the top edge of the turning piece. It is usual to work from each skewback towards the middle of the arch and complete with the key brick. When very fine joints are required, each voussoir is dipped into the pan containing the putty lime (p. 135), which should be placed conveniently to hand, and its bed covered; care should be taken to avoid staining the face of the rubber with the putty. The putty in the groove is removed and the rubber is placed in position by pressing the coated bed against the adjacent voussoir. Whilst setting the bricks, frequent use should be made of the short straight-edge and vertical level. When all of the voussoirs have been bedded in position, cement grout (p. 22) is poured down the joggles formed by the bed grooves.

If thicker joints are desired, the mortar (usually cement mortar) is applied by a trowel in the usual way, care being taken that the joints are of uniform thickness and radiate to a common centre. This is ensured by using a cord or line as shown in Fig. 141; one end of the cord is fastened to a nail driven into the strut at the centre; the position of each voussoir and its bed joint is marked along the top outer edge of the turning piece, and as each brick is placed in position the bed is made to coincide with the line which is stretched taut.

The removal of the turning piece does not take place until the mortar has set, and often it is left in position until the window or door frame is required to be fixed; this removal is called *"striking the centre"*, and is effected by first loosening the wedges.

For the construction of a purpose-made brick arch, the bricks used are moulded by hand (p. 13). A full size drawing is made of the arch to "shrinkage scale", *i.e.*, each metre of the scale used in setting out the arch is increased by an amount equal to that which the clay shrinks in the drying and burning processes, which may be from 6·2 mm per 100 mm, depending upon the clay; the wood moulds are made to this increased size, and after the bricks have been moulded, they are stamped according to the corresponding numbers on the drawing. When these purpose-mades arrive on the site, they are usually set out on the scaffold, etc., in the form of the arch and arranged in order according to the numbers. The arch is constructed in lime or cement mortar as described on p. 144.

The bricks employed in the construction of an axed brick flat arch (which are facings or "selected commons") are marked according to the bevels obtained from the face mould (as described for rubbers) after the beds have been rubbed to give straight arrises; they are cut with the bolster and surfaced with the scutch.

A turning piece suitable for an arch with a 65 mm camber is shown at D, Fig. 142; this includes the wedges and props.

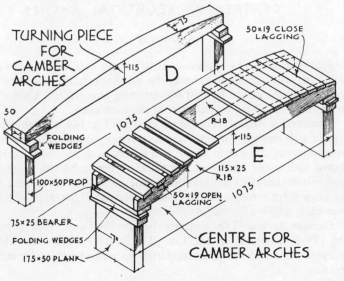

Fig. 142

Segmental Arches.—Arches which have wider soffits than a ½-brick are "turned" upon centres which are constructed of *ribs* and *laggings.* Such a centre with a similar camber to that at D is shown at E, Fig. 142. The laggings or narrow battens are nailed across two shaped ribs. The centre is completed by nailing a 75 mm by 25 mm cross member, called a *bearer,* to the underside of the ribs at each end. Both open and close lagging are shown; the former is suitable for purpose-made, axed and rough arches (with one lagging per voussoir or spaced at about 25 mm apart) and close lagging is adopted for gauged arches.

A suitable centre for a segmental arch, such as that in Fig. 136, is shown in Fig. 143. Both types of laggings are shown. The construction of the arch is similar to that described for a flat arch; the cord should be used to ensure that the bed joints of uniform thickness are radial, the

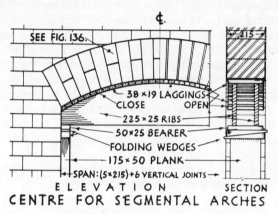

ELEVATION   SECTION
CENTRE FOR SEGMENTAL ARCHES

Fig.143

straight-edge should be applied to make certain that the voussoirs are in alignment with the bricks forming the skewbacks, and the vertical level (or plumb-rule) should be used for obtaining plumb faces. Unlike those in the flat arch, all the voussoirs are of the same shape.

Semicircular Arches.—The centre shown in Fig. 144 is suitable for the type of arch illustrated in Fig. 138. As it is not economical to use timber which exceeds 250 mm in width, it is necessary to construct the ribs as shown with upper and lower *ties* nailed to them. Narrow laggings are used in order that they will conform to the curve. As the voussoirs are of the same shape throughout, only one templet cut to the shape of the key voussoir is required for shaping the bricks.

Circular Arches.—The centering for the bull's-eye arch shown in Fig. 139 is illustrated in Fig. 145. The built-up centre for each arch (purpose-made and rough) is supported on wedges carried by inclined struts.

The construction of the lower half of this arch is described on pp. 140 and 141. The upper half of the external arch is built, bed joint accuracy being obtained by use of the cord (p. 144). The internal rough arch (assuming it to be covered with plaster) may consist of two half-brick rings as indicated in the section, or the upper half only may consist of two half-brick rings with the lower half of one half-brick ring (as indicated in the sketch).

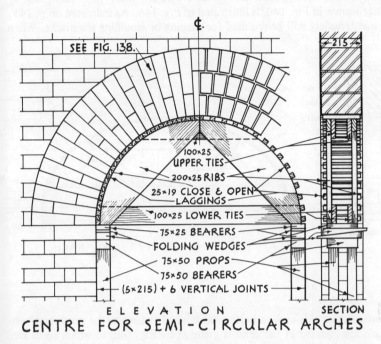

SEE FIG. 138.

215

100×25
UPPER TIES
200×25 RIBS
25×19 CLOSE & OPEN
LAGGINGS
100×25 LOWER TIES
75×25 BEARERS
FOLDING WEDGES
75×50 PROPS
75×50 BEARERS
(5×215) + 6 VERTICAL JOINTS

E L E V A T I O N   SECTION

CENTRE FOR SEMI-CIRCULAR ARCHES

Fig.144

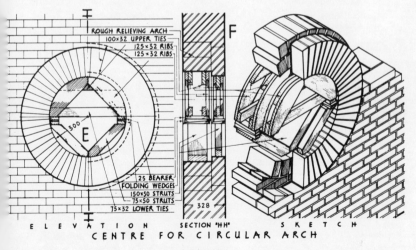

ROUGH RELIEVING ARCH
100×32 UPPER TIES
125×32 RIBS
125×32 RIBS

F

300
E

25 BEARER
FOLDING WEDGES
150×50 STRUTS
75×50 STRUTS
75×32 LOWER TIES

328

E L E V A T I O N   SECTION "HH"   S K E T C H

CENTRE FOR CIRCULAR ARCH

Fig.145

Semi-elliptical Arches.—A typical centre for this type of arch, such as that shown in Fig. 140, is illustrated in Fig. 146. As indicated on p. 141, three templets will be required for shaping or moulding the bricks. When

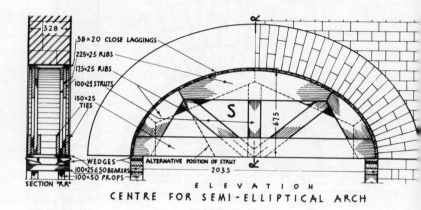

ELEVATION

CENTRE FOR SEMI-ELLIPTICAL ARCH

Fig.146

constructing this arch, a horizontal board is nailed to the props and two nails are inserted at the centres *e* and *f* (see Fig. 140) to which cords are fastened for checking the radial joints, and another board is provided to receive the nail for centre *k*. A radius rod (see Fig. 139) at each of these centres is desirable for checking the intrados, extrados and cross joints.

CHAPTER ELEVEN

CAVITY WALLS

Description of 280 and 380 mm cavity walls; advantages of this construction;
precautions to be taken.

THIS form of construction is now the most common and, for the reasons
given on p. 153, is generally preferred to solid wall construction for many
types of buildings, especially houses.

A cavity or hollow wall is usually an external wall. It is a double wall,
consisting of two brick *leaves* or *skins* with a cavity between; the leaves
are connected together by metal ties. It is generally 275 or 280 mm thick,
with ½-brick inner and outer leaves and a 65 or 70 mm cavity (see
Fig. 149); such a wall is adequate for a two-storied building of the
domestic type. The *inner* leaf is increased to 1-brick when heavier floor,
etc., loads have to be supported; the wall is then 380 mm thick (having a
62·5 mm cavity—see Fig. 152). The maximum width of cavity is 75 mm.

The *cavity ties* now employed are generally of metal. Those most
commonly in use are of wrought iron or steel; these must be thoroughly
galvanized (given a coating of zinc) or dipped in hot tar and sanded to
protect them from rust. Either copper or bronze or similar durable and
non-corrodible metal ties are
selected for important buildings. They must be so shaped
that water from the outer leaf
will not pass along them to
the inner leaf. Three types of
ties are shown at F, G and H,
Fig. 147. The galvanized
wrought iron wire tie at F is

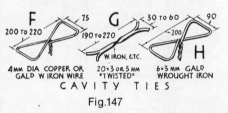

CAVITY TIES

Fig.147

very popular; the ends, which are twisted together and turned downwards, cause any water travelling along the tie from the outer leaf to drip
into the cavity clear of the
inner leaf; as the wire is comparatively thin, large accumu-
lations of mortar droppings
which are a frequent cause of
dampness (see p. 152) do not
readily lodge on them; the
wire should preferably be
3·25 mm thick, but lighter
ties 2·6 mm thick are used for
cheap work. That at H is a similar pattern but of narrow flat bar section,

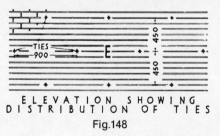

ELEVATION SHOWING
DISTRIBUTION OF TIES

Fig.148

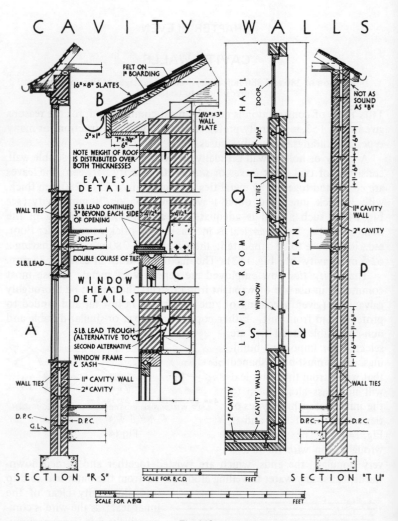

Fig.149

and is a good type. The flat bar tie G is twisted in the middle and affords a stiff and durable connection.

These ties are distributed as shown at E, Fig. 148, during the construction of the wall. As indicated, they are placed at a maximum horizontal distance apart of 900 mm and 450 mm vertically; they are staggered. At door and window jambs and at angles they should be placed at 300 mm vertical intervals to increase stability.

The plan of a portion of a building showing external walls is given at Q, Fig. 149, and two vertical sections are shown at A and P. The outer leaf is usually built of facing bricks and the inner leaf of commons. Stretching bond (see p. 55) is generally adopted, but as this has an unattractive appearance, the monotony is sometimes relieved by constructing the external leaf with a row of *snap headers* (half bricks) to three or five rows of stretchers; the face appearance of English garden wall bond is thus obtained (see p. 115). Flemish garden wall bond (p. 116) is occasionally preferred.

Alternative methods of constructing the base are shown at A and P, Fig. 149. That at A, showing the cavity extending down to the concrete foundation, is common; sometimes the cavity is filled with 1:2:4 concrete to a height of *not less* than 150 mm below the damp proof course as shown at P. Narrow outlets, called *weep-holes*, are provided in the course immediately below the damp proof course in the outer leaf at every third or fourth vertical joint between the stretchers. The joints are not filled with mortar but are just left open to allow the escape of any rain-water which may have penetrated the outer leaf and passed down its inner face.

The position of the damp proof course is at least 150 mm above the ground level (p. 87). This *must not* extend across the cavity (see pp. 152 and 153) and each leaf must therefore be provided with a separate damp proof course.

It is essential that the inner leaf shall be entirely disconnected (except for the cavity ties) from the outer skin if the wall is to be effective. Where this is not possible, as at door and window openings, special

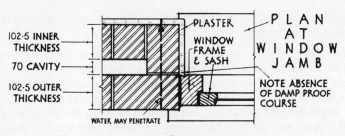

Fig.150

precautions have to be taken. Two alternative methods of construction adopted at the jambs of such openings are shown in Figs. 150 and 151. That in Fig. 150 shows a solid jamb; this is *unsound* construction, as water may penetrate in the direction of the thick broken arrow and cause dampness. This is avoided if, as shown in Fig. 151, an impermeable material such as a double layer of slates or a 150 to 215 mm wide strip of

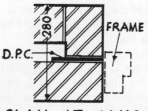

PLAN AT JAMB

Fig.151

fibrous asphalt felt (p. 88) is bedded in the position indicated as the work proceeds; this damp proof course should be at least slightly wider than the ½-brick portion of brick-work (see Figure) to ensure complete discontinuity.

Dampness is very liable to be caused at the heads of door and window openings if proper precautions are not taken. Thus, water passing through defective joints, etc., in the outer leaf will stream down its inner face until it comes into contact with a lintel, when it will spread along the top to the inside face of the inner leaf and also drip at the soffit. The protection should take the form of a fibrous asphalt felt or lead covering, stepped down from the inner leaf and continued over the door or window frame as shown at C, Fig. 149; this covering should extend for at least 75 mm (preferably 150 mm) beyond each end of the lintel in order that the water may drip clear into the cavity; a few open vertical joints may be left in the brick lintel to allow any water to escape. The alternative method shown at D, Fig. 149, where a lead or asphalt felt trough is provided, is *not* sound, as this does not prevent water from gaining access through defective joints in the brick lintel (or porous bricks) and causing dampness; the damp proof material should be continued over the head of the window frame as indicated by broken lines.

Alternative details at the eaves are shown at A and P, Fig. 149. That at A is sound, as the solid 1-brick portion of wall at the top distributes the weight of the roof over both leaves, and the overhanging eaves prevents the transmission of moisture through this wall. This is a better detail than at P, which shows the roof supported chiefly by the inner leaf. The additional alternative shown at B, Fig. 149, indicates sound construction.

SUMMARY OF SPECIAL PRECAUTIONS.—1. Wherever possible, contact between the two leaves should be avoided.

2. The cavity should be kept clear of droppings, and any on ties should be removed. Unless care is taken, a good deal of mortar will drop from the trowel, etc., into the cavity during the construction of the wall. Besides resulting in a waste of material, these droppings may cause dampness if they fall on the ties and are not removed owing to the cavity being bridged; water may thereby be transmitted to the inner face. A clean cavity will result if a wood batten is employed during construction; its thickness is slightly less than the width of the cavity and a piece of cord is attached at each end; this is supported on the ties, raised as the work proceeds, and any intercepted mortar, brick chippings, etc., removed.

Temporary openings should be left at the bottom of the cavity to afford access for the removal of droppings.

3. The main horizontal damp proof course must be in two separate widths and the bottom of the cavity must be at least 150 mm (290 mm are often allowed for "excessive mortar droppings") below this. Otherwise mortar droppings may accumulate above the D.P.C. through or over which water may be conducted to the inner face of the wall.

4. Heads of openings must be properly protected by a damp proof material. Jambs must not be solid unless damp proof courses are provided.

5. Weep-holes should be formed immediately below the main horizontal damp proof course and above the damp proof course over openings. No other ventilation to the cavity should be provided. Formerly, air bricks (Fig. 66) were provided at both the bottom and top of cavity walls to ventilate the cavity. This is not now advocated, as the insulating value (see below) is thereby greatly reduced. The usual ventilation to ground floors of timber construction must, of course, be provided (see p. 87 and Fig. 152).

6. Cavity ties must be rust-proof, capable of preventing rain-transmission and easily cleaned of mortar droppings.

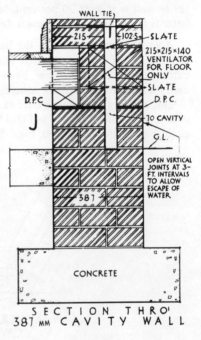

SECTION THRO'
387 MM CAVITY WALL

Fig. 152

ADVANTAGES OF CAVITY WALL CONSTRUCTION.—The following are the chief merits of cavity walls:—

1. *Prevention of Dampness.*—They are more reliable than solid walls of corresponding brick-thickness. Thus, a 280 mm cavity wall in an exposed position will prevent water from penetrating to the inner leaf, provided adequate precautions are taken in its construction, and sound materials and workmanship are employed. But an external 1-brick solid wall (which is equivalent in thickness of brickwork to a 280 mm hollow wall) in an exposed position will *not* prevent rain from penetrating to the internal face unless the wall is rought-casted or similarly treated; hence solid external walls should be at least 1½-bricks thick.

2. *Insulation*.—A building of hollow external wall construction is warmer in winter and cooler in summer than one built of solid outer wall. The air cavity is responsible for this, as air is a good non-conductor of heat and therefore that in the cavity reduces the transmission of heat through the wall (*i.e.*, it impedes in summer the flow of hot air from the outside to the inside, and in winter there is less heat lost from the inside to the outside). Consequently, an economy in fuel consumption results.

3. *Economy*.—It is estimated that the approximate cost of a 280 mm cavity wall is at least 20 per cent. less than a 1½-brick solid wall (which latter is the minimum thickness if dampness is to be avoided).

A vertical section through the base of a 380 mm cavity wall is shown in Fig. 152. It will be seen that this involves a certain amount of brick-cutting; this would, of course, be avoided if, as shown at A, Fig. 149, the cavity were continued to the concrete bed.

The bonding of alternate courses at an obtuse squint quoin (see p. 72) of a cavity wall is shown in Fig. 153, and alternative plans of 280 mm circular work are shown at D, Fig. 154.

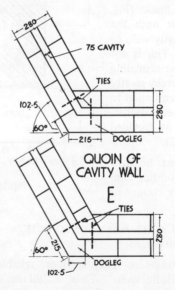

Fig.153

CHAPTER TWELVE

CIRCULAR WORK

Details of solid and cavity walls curved on plan; setting out and construction.

CIRCULAR work is occasionally required as, for example, in the construction of segmental and semicircular bay windows, walls of staircases and tall factory chimney stacks. Some details of circular work are given in Fig. 154. The plan of a portion of a room with a semicircular bay window is shown at A, that on the left being above the sill level and that on the right below it. The given details show alternative construction at the intersection between the curved and straight walls.

It will be seen at E and F that uncut standard bricks are not suitable for circular work if normal bonding is to be maintained, as the stretcher faces of the bricks only conform approximately to the curve, and very wide joints on the convex surface are produced. The width of the joints can only be reduced by cutting each brick to a wedge shape to form radial joints. Not only is this an expensive procedure but the appearance is not satisfactory (especially if the curve is to a small radius), as the "curve" is made up of a succession of straight stretcher faces. In order to conform more closely to the curve, and when ordinary standard bricks only are available, heading bond (p. 55) may be adopted; such a wall is, however, both unattractive in appearance and deficient in strength.

It is now the general practice, even in cheap speculative work, to use only purpose-made bricks for the external faces of circular walling. Such bricks are moulded to the required shape either by hand (p. 13) or by the machine-pressure process (p. 13). Many of the larger manufacturers keep stocks of circular stretchers and headers, machine-pressed in dies shaped to curves of radii varying from 610 mm to 2·4 mm, as shown at L and M, Fig. 33. The contractor states the radius of the curve when ordering the bricks. If these do not conform to a stock radius, the plan of the wall is chalked out on the setting-out board, and the position of the bricks marked after due allowance has been made for shrinkage in drying and burning. Two zinc templets (p. 142) are cut to the shape of a header and stretcher. Wood moulds (p. 13) are prepared from these and handed to the moulder who proceeds to shape the bricks by hand.

Alternate plans of a portion of a 1½-brick wall in English bond are shown at C and of a 280 mm cavity wall at D. Unless both faces of a curved wall are to be exposed, and as purpose-made circular bricks are relatively expensive (especially if hand-made), it is customary to back the curved facings with common bricks which are axed to give radial joints, as shown at C. If the internal face of a cavity wall is to be plastered, the

CIRCULAR WORK

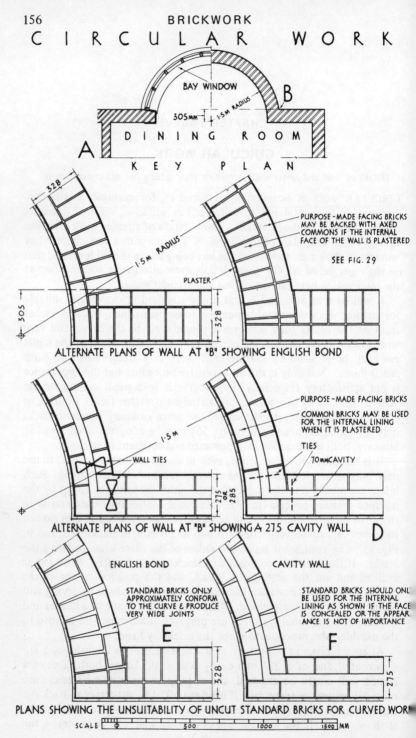

KEY PLAN

BAY WINDOW

1·5 M RADIUS

DINING ROOM

305MM | 1·5 M RADIUS

A   B

328

1·5 M RADIUS

305

328

PURPOSE-MADE FACING BRICKS
MAY BE BACKED WITH AXED
COMMONS IF THE INTERNAL
FACE OF THE WALL IS PLASTERED

SEE FIG. 29

PLASTER

ALTERNATE PLANS OF WALL AT "B" SHOWING ENGLISH BOND   C

1·5 M

WALL TIES

275
OR
285

PURPOSE-MADE FACING BRICKS

COMMON BRICKS MAY BE USED
FOR THE INTERNAL LINING
WHEN IT IS PLASTERED

TIES

70 MM CAVITY

ALTERNATE PLANS OF WALL AT "B" SHOWING A 275 CAVITY WALL   D

ENGLISH BOND

STANDARD BRICKS ONLY
APPROXIMATELY CONFORM
TO THE CURVE & PRODUCE
VERY WIDE JOINTS

328

E

CAVITY WALL

STANDARD BRICKS SHOULD ONLY
BE USED FOR THE INTERNAL
LINING AS SHOWN IF THE FACE
IS CONCEALED OR THE APPEAR-
ANCE IS NOT OF IMPORTANCE

275

F

PLANS SHOWING THE UNSUITABILITY OF UNCUT STANDARD BRICKS FOR CURVED WORK

SCALE   0   500   1000   1500 MM

Fig.154

inner leaf is usually built of common bricks (see D), and unless the curvature is too sharp these commons are not cut to give radial joints.

SETTING OUT.–Circular work may be set out by using either a (a) *trammel* or a (b) *templet.*

(a) *Trammel Method.*–The application of a trammel for the bay window illustrated at A, Fig. 154, is shown in Fig. 155. A trammel is a

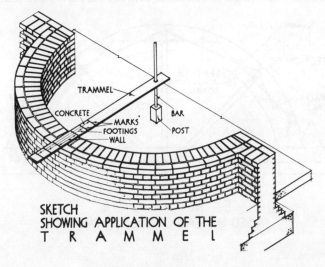

Fig.155

12 mm thick board, about 75 mm wide, and holed at one end. A 20 mm dia. metal bar is set up vertically (aided by the plumb-rule) in a slab of concrete at the centre of the circle. The trammel is threaded over and passed down the bar, and the width of the concrete (and footings–if provided) and the thickness of the wall are accurately marked on its upper face. The setting out and construction of the semicircular (or segmental) wall are aided by the trammel as it is caused to rotate, and by plumbing. As the brickwork proceeds above the ground level, the trammel, which must be horizontal, is supported at its holed end by a piece of cord which is fastened under it to the bar, the cord being raised as each course is completed. The plumb-rule or vertical level is applied near to the intersections and at approximately every fourth brick.

(b) *Templet Method.*–This is often preferred to the trammel on account of its convenience and the accurate check which it affords. A templet consists of two wide thin pieces of board, overlapped and nailed to each other, as shown in Fig. 156. The outer edge is sawn and carefully planed to the required curve. A wood tie connects and projects beyond the two ends, and the outer edge of this tie must coincide with the external face of the main wall. Three wood struts or stays are fixed as shown; these make the templet rigid and convenient for handling. The templet is placed on top of each course during and after its construction, any bricks not conforming to the curve being tapped in or out until their outer faces correspond to the curve. Plumbing provides a further check on the work. Each time the templet is used it is most important that (*a*) the outer edge of the tie is in true alignment with the main wall face, and (*b*) the two points of intersection between the outer curve of the templet and tie correspond to the intersections between the curved and straight walls.

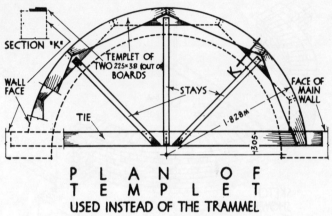

P L A N   O F   T E M P L E T
USED INSTEAD OF THE TRAMMEL

Fig.156

CHAPTER THIRTEEN

REINFORCED BRICKWORK

Application of reinforcement to walls, piers and lintels.

As implied, this form of construction is brickwork which is strengthened by the introduction of steel or wrought iron. This reinforcement consists of either flat bars or rods, woven wire or expanded metal, and is placed in the mortar joints or in perforations in the bricks. This brickwork is capable of resisting tensile and shear stresses, in addition to compression stress (p. 131). The following is essential: (1) The bricks must be sound and well burnt, those of the engineering type (p. 17) being most suitable when heavy loads have to be supported; (2) the work shall be well bonded in cement mortar (1:3) to which one-tenth part of slaked lime may be added (lime mortar should not be used, as this may have an adverse effect upon the metal); and (3) the reinforcement must be protected against corrosion (rusting may cause serious damage to the brickwork).

It is generally accepted that a reinforced brick wall is as strong as a brick wall a ½-brick thicker; hence, a 1-brick thick reinforced wall is considered to be equivalent to the ordinary un-reinforced 1½-brick wall.

Fig. 157 shows two sketches of reinforced walling. That at B illustrates the application of steel meshed strips called "Exmet" (produced by The Expanded Metal Co. Ltd.). This is made from thin rolled steel plates which are cut and stretched by a machine to a diamond meshwork form; it is known as "expanded metal". It is supplied in coils (or long flat strips) in three widths, *i.e.* 60 mm (suitable for ½-brick walls), 165 mm (for 1-brick walls) and 275 mm (for 1½-brick walls). It is given a coating of paint. A piece of the 60 mm wide Exmet is shown at A.

The amount of reinforcement used depends upon the magnitude of the stresses to be resisted, but it is usual to provide reinforcement at every third or fourth course. The example at B shows the application of 60 mm, 165 mm and 275 mm wide Exmet at every third bed joint. As indicated, the strips should be lapped 75 mm at the intersections and also at longitudinal joints. Cavity walls may be reinforced by a 60 mm strip at every third course of each leaf. The 60 mm wide strips are suitable for curved walls, as this width can be readily bent; one strip is provided per ½-brick thickness of wall at every third or fourth course. Such reinforcement can also be employed effectively to strengthen arches over wide openings by reinforcing the bed joints of the brickwork which they support.

Reinforcement of brickwork also improves the longitudinal bond of thick walls. Whilst thick walls are strong transversely, they are weak longitudinally as, with exception of the outer stretchers, they consist wholly of headers which give a lap of a ¼ brick only.

Another form of meshed reinforcement, called "Bricktor" (manufactured by Johnson's Reinforced Concrete Engineering Co. Ltd.), is shown at C, Fig. 157. It is made of steel wire, black japanned as a protection against rust, produced in 50 and 60 mm widths and sold in coils. One strip is provided at every ½-brick thickness of the wall and at every third or fourth course (see D).

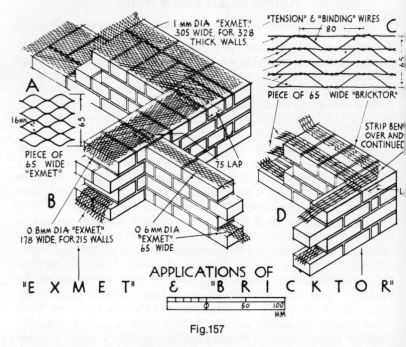

Fig.157

Vertical bars of circular section are used to reinforce walls. These are usually 12 mm dia. mild steel bars, spaced at about 450 mm centres as near as possible to one or both faces of the wall. They are placed either in the vertical joints, or perforated (or purpose-made slotted) bricks are employed and threaded over the bars. This form of reinforcement has been used extensively in air-raid shelter, etc., construction.

Brick pillars are reinforced with these vertical bars, one being provided at each corner at from 25 to 50 mm from the faces; perforated or slotted bricks are used. In addition, pillars may be strengthened by bedding 6 mm thick mild steel plates at every fourth course; these plates are holed and passed over the rods during the construction.

Brick lintels are also reinforced as shown in Fig. 128 and described on p. 130.

CHAPTER FOURTEEN

FIREPLACE, ETC., CONSTRUCTION

Chimney breasts, fireplaces, flues, stacks and hearths; fireplace interiors.

THE open fire is still the most popular means of heating a living room in this country. It also provides effective natural ventilation, and a cheap and convenient supply of hot water is obtained when a boiler is provided in the fireplace. In order to prevent pollution by smoke the Building Regulations require that heating appliances must be capable of burning a clean fuel like coke, anthracite, gas or oil.

A fireplace opening is formed in a thickened wall, and this brick structure, which usually projects, is called a *chimney breast*. The breast is continued above the roof by a *chimney stack*. A fireplace is provided with a duct, called a *flue*, for the removal of smoke, and the flue terminates at the top of the stack.

Chimney construction must comply with the Building Regulations and the main requirements of these have been incorporated in Fig. 158. This shows the plan B, vertical section C and elevation A of a two-storied chimney breast, together with several inset plans. Two fireplaces are provided for, and the flue from each is indicated in the elevation by broken lines. The Regulations give differing requirements according to the type of heating appliance and differentiate between a high rating appliance and Class I and Class II appliances. A high-rating appliance is a solid fuel or oil burning appliance with output ratings exceeding 45 kW or a gas appliance with an input rating exceeding 45 kW or large incinerators—these are beyond the scope of this book.

Most domestic appliances are Class I or II:— Class I are solid fuel or oil-burning types with an outout rating not exceeding 45 kW/hr and medium sized incinerators; and Class II appliances are gas burning types having an input rating not exceeding 45 kW/hr and small incinerators.

Briefly the Building Regulations state that:—

1. The foundations of a chimney must be similar to those of the adjacent wall. The wall shown in Fig. 158 is 1½-bricks thick and the foundations are indicated by broken lines at A.

2. The brickwork at the sides of an opening are called *jambs* and these must be at least 200 mm wide. The width of the chimney breast varies according to the size of fireplace and the size and importance of the room. The size of the fireplace opening and the projection of the chimney breast depend upon the type and size of range to be accommodated. Thus, a medium-sized kitchen range with oven will require a 1 m wide by 1·2 m high opening, whilst a small bedroom fireplace opening need only be 450 mm wide and 0·6 m high. The *head* of an opening is finished with a stone or concrete lintel (as shown at A) or a rough segmental brick arch (Fig. 137).

3. The *back* of a fireplace in an *external* wall, as at B, must be at least 100 mm thick. If this were an internal wall the minimum thickness

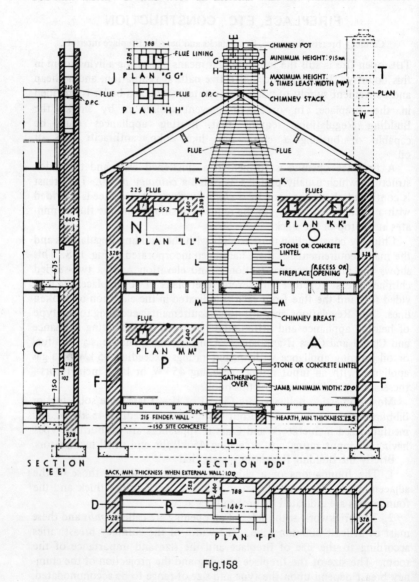

Fig.158

would be 200 mm, unless it were backed by another fireplace in the adjacent room of the same house when 100 mm is permissible.

4. The size of a flue for a Class I appliance is usually 215 mm by 215 mm (see N, Fig. 158). The brickwork above the fireplace opening is

corbelled or *gathered over* (see broken lines at A) to the size of the flue; in gathering over, the bricks are cut to the required splay, and the aim should be to avoid a large space which would produce smoke eddies and reduce the upward current. Whilst a flue should be as straight as possible for most of its height, it should have at least one *gradual* bend (not less than 45° to the horizontal) to reduce down-draught and the admission of rain; if the short flue from the upper fireplace opening at A were straight throughout, a "smoky chimney" would result.

Flues for Class I Appliances must be lined with any one of the following: rebated or socketed flue linings of clay (a) complying with B.S.1181 or of (b) kiln-burnt aggregate and high alumina cement; or (c) glazed vitrified clay pipes complying with B.S. 65 (*i.e.* drain pipes); or (d) glass (vitreous) enamelled salt glazes fireclay pipes and fittings complying with B.S. 540 (*i.e.* drain pipes). The most commonly used liners are (a) above, one of which is drawn at V, Fig. 158. An alternative to the use of flue liners is to construct the chimney with concrete flue blocks made of kiln-burnt aggregate and high alumina cement. Both linings and blocks must be pointed with 1:4 cement mortar and the linings must be built with the socket uppermost, care being taken to keep the bore of the flue free from mortar. Linings are built into the flue as the chimney is constructed and backed with mortar; they should not be cut as it is important to preserve the socket or rebate intact. The bottom length of liner should rest on small corbels projecting from the brick flue.

Before the insistence of flue linings by the Building Regulations applicable to England and Wales the inside of brick flues was rendered (known as *parged*) to a thickness of at least 12 mm with a mixture of 1 cement: 3 lime: 10 sand; the Regulations for Scotland still permit this method for open fires. Parged flues have proved very satisfactory for many years but with enclosed heating appliances there is a danger, particularly when the cross joints in brick flues have not been properly filled with mortar, that tarry compounds from the products of combustion could leach through the flue and discolour internal walls.

An alternative to the use of a brick flue is to use a *flue pipe*; this can be conveniently used when fixed outside the wall of a building to serve, for example, a central heating boiler which is being added to an existing house that is without a conveniently situated chimney. Short lengths of flue pipe are also used to connect a range or room heater to a brick flue. A flue pipe for the above purposes must be of 5 mm thick cast iron (usually 100 or 150 mm dia.—in any case of not less diameter than the flue outlet from the appliance) for the first 1·8 m of length of flue pipe from the appliance. The length beyond this distance can be of 9·5 mm thick heavy quality asbestos-cement pipe.

Flues for Class II Appliances. As these are for gas burning appliances which produce a greater amount of water vapour in the products of combustion than is the case with an open fire the linings have to be of a high standard. The linings described at (a) above may be used but they must be glazed; those at (c) and (d) above may also be used; these three must be jointed and pointed with high-alumina cement mortar. An alternative type of flue is built with dense concrete blocks having a flue area of 300 mm by 64 mm made with high alumina cement and jointed and pointed as above.

Flue Pipes for Class II Appliances may be as (c) and (d) above; or of cast iron conforming to B.S. 41; or of sheet steel to B.S. 715; or stainless steel; in certain circumstances asbestos-cement pipes may also be used.

Wherever flue pipes are used in preference to solid brick chimneys care must be taken to see that they are not in contact with or near to combustible materials.

5. If the chimney breast penetrates the ridge of the roof (see A, Fig. 158), it is gradually reduced in width above the ceiling until the width of

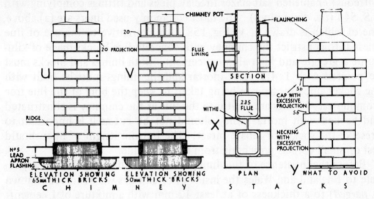

Fig.159

the stack is obtained. The minimum height above the ridge is 915 mm. If, as indicated by broken lines at T, the stack is at the eaves or partially up the slope of the roof, this minimum height is measured from the back gutter; the maximum height is six times its least width, as shown. Alternate plans showing the bonding at the stack are shown at J; see also X, Fig. 159; the divisions between flues, called *withes* or *mid-feathers*, must be at least 100 mm thick and well bonded into the external walls. The latter are at least 100 mm thick; if this thickness is increased to 1-brick when the stack contains a single flue, the appearance is improved. Chimney stacks should be built in waterproofed cement mortar (see p. 28), from 300 mm below the roof intersection, to prevent rain from entering and soaking down the walls and be provided with a d.p.c.

Usually a fireclay chimney pot, of varying shape and size, is fixed at the top of each flue (see Figs. 158 and 159). It should be supported on the flue lining, securely built in cement mortar, and the top should be *flaunched, i.e.,* brickwork covered with cement mortar sloped or weathered to throw off the water.

Two chimney stacks of simple design are shown at U and V, Fig. 159. The appearance of a stack is much improved if, as shown at V, thin bricks are employed. The upper portion of a cap is called a *capping*. Ugly chimney pots, thick flaunching, and oversailing courses with excessive projection (as at Y, Fig. 159) should be avoided.

6. The bottom of a fireplace opening between the jambs is called the *back hearth*. A *front hearth* (that in front of the opening) must also be provided. Hearths must be of non-combustible materials, such as concrete or stone. A hearth for a Class I appliance must be of concrete at least 125 mm thick projecting at least 500 mm in front of the jambs and 150 mm beyond each side of the opening. No combustible material must be built under a hearth within 250 mm from its upper surface unless such material is separated from the underside of the hearth by an airspace of at least 50 mm. (An exception to this requirement permits the use of timber fillets supporting the edges of a hearth where it adjoins a floor—such fillets are often used, when fixed to a trimming joist, to support the front edge of a hearth which is placed at first floor level, see below.)

A hearth for a Class II appliance must be of non-combustible material at least 12·5 mm thick extending 150 mm beyond the back and sides of the appliance and 225 mm forward from it (these provisions need not apply in the case of an appliance having its flame 225 mm or more above floor level).

There are several methods of forming a ground floor hearth. Usually a ½ or 1-brick wall, called a *fender wall*, is built round the fireplace to retain the concrete hearth (and material supporting it) and carry the ends of the floor joists. A 1-brick fender wall is shown at A, B and C, Fig. 158, and in the section in Fig. 160. A stone slab (Fig. 160) is supported on the main wall and the fender wall; a wall plate, bedded on the fender wall, supports the floor joists. The stone slab supports the concrete which is brought level with the top of the floor boards (as at C, Fig. 158), or the concrete is finished with tiles as indicated in Fig. 160. Alternatively, instead of the stone slab, the space between the fender wall and the main wall is filled with broken brick or stone and covered with 150 mm of concrete. A damp proof course, as shown, must be provided at the top of the fender wall. Sometimes the fender wall is dispensed with and the opening for the front hearth is *trimmed* for the floor joists as for upper floors (see below).

A hole in the floor is trimmed by the joiner for an upper front hearth, *i.e.*, a thick trimmer joist (parallel to and 500 mm from the chimney breast) is provided to receive the ends of the floor joists (see C, Fig. 158). As shown, the 150 mm stone or concrete slab forming the front hearth is supported on the wall and on brick corbels at the sides of the opening while at the front it is supported on a fillet (63 mm by 38 mm) which is well nailed to the side of the trimmer joist.

7. Chimney walls which are only ½-brick thick must be rendered outside with a 12 mm thickness of cement or lime mortar.

8. No combustible material (*e.g.* a floor joist) is to be placed nearer than 200 mm from a flue or fireplace opening (150 mm in the case of a wood plug).

Where the thickness of solid non-combustible material surrounding a chimney flue is less than 200 mm no combustible material, other than a floor board, skirting, dado rail, picture rail, mantle shelf or architrave shall be placed as to be nearer than 38 mm to the outer surface of the chimney. Metal fastenings such as nails, screws, etc. shall not be placed within 50 mm of a flue or fireplace recess.

Particular care should be taken in observing these regulations as fires have been caused by plugs, etc. having been driven through joints to actually penetrate the flue. It is therefore important that joiners should be aware of the position of flues when fixing wood members round chimney breasts.

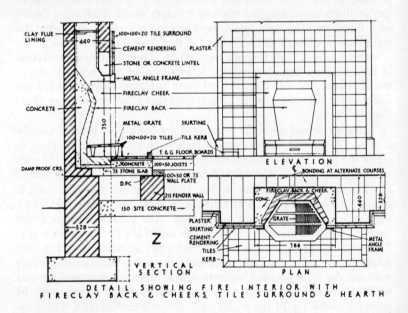

DETAIL SHOWING FIRE INTERIOR WITH
FIRECLAY BACK & CHEEKS, TILE SURROUND & HEARTH

Fig.160

FIRE INTERIOR.—A simple fire interior suitable for the ground floor opening in Fig. 158 is shown in Fig. 160. This consists of a fireclay block with base, inclined back and splayed sides or *cheeks* (inclined and splayed to throw the heat into the room), a cast-iron grate, stainless steel angle frame, surround (vertical facing) of 100 mm square glazed tiles, and a tiled front hearth with a raised tile kerb. The fireclay block is bedded on mortar and backed solidly with brick in cement mortar or concrete. The top surface of this backing is sloped to prevent the accumulation of soot; if left square, the soot collecting on the ledge would be blown into the room in the event of down-draughts. The portion of the breast to be tiled is given a rendering coat of cement mixture, 1:3; the latter is well scratched immediately it has been formed to give a key for the tile bedding. The rendering should be allowed to set hard and then well watered before the tiles are bedded. Commencing at the bottom, the tiles are bedded in cement mortar, the latter being applied to the back of each tile which is then placed and tapped in position on the wall. A "guide" tile is bedded temporarily near the top of the rendering so that its face is plumb (as tested by a vertical level) with that of the first or bottom guide tile. The rest of the tiles are bedded, a straight-edge being used to ensure that they are in alignment with the guide tiles. In good tiled work the joints should be about 1 mm wide and free from mortar. Therefore, as each tile is laid, care should be taken to wipe any mortar off the edges. The tiled hearth is formed after the fireclay base has been fixed; the tiles being level bedded on the concrete.

The bonding of the brickwork at the chimney breast is shown in the plan in Fig. 160.

CHAPTER FIFTEEN

V BRICKS

V bricks; special bricks; square quoins, jambs, stopped ends; foundations.

V BRICKS (Fig. 161), so named because of the vertical perforations, have been developed[1] by the Building Research Station to provide a brick which has adequate strength for normal purpose building and better thermal insulation than the usual standard brick.

They are used to provide an alternative to the ordinary 280 mm cavity wall (see Chap. XI) which is different in five respects. A V brick wall (1) is only 230 mm wide; (2) provides a "cavity" which is bridged by four thin diaphragms per brick (see A) which have been found not to impair the weather resistance of the wall; (3) gives better thermal insulation because of the perforations which amount to about 50 per cent. of the total volume of the V brick; (4) is less heavy permitting smaller foundations and (5) produces a 219 mm cavity wall about 30 per cent. faster than the traditional 280 mm cavity wall with about the same saving in mortar used.

One V brick corresponds in volume to *two* standard bricks and weighs about 4 kg in comparison with the weight of *one* standard brick, in the same clay, of 3·23 kg. The V brick can be lifted by the bricklayer very easily for the two outer larger perforations provide convenient handholes for lifting.

The V brick (see A) is 219 mm by 219 mm by 67 mm and is most economically laid in stretcher bond but other traditional bonds can be used by cutting the brick.ʼ In laying V bricks mortar is spread along the two outer parts of the bed (*i.e.* over the area of the small perforations). The bricks are thus laid on two separate strips of mortar, care being taken to prevent mortar from entering the centre handholes. This divided mortar joint is best made by using a special tray, alternatively a batten 75 mm wide and 16 mm thick can be placed along the centre of the wall to keep this part free of mortar; the mortar being spread on either side of the batten. When the bricks are bedded on the strips some of the mortar is pressed into the small perforations giving a strong key and producing the normal 10 mm thick bed joint.

Special Brick. Provided with the V brick is a special brick for use at .quoins, stopped ends and jambs; this is the special perforated return brick shown at B.

Square Quoin.—This is detailed at D and makes use of the special return brick; as an alternative to using the latter a king closer cut from a standard brick (of the same clay as the V brick) can be laid.

[1] The manufacturer of the V bricks shown in Fig. 162 is The Sussex and Dorking Brick Co. Ltd.

Square Jamb.—This is detailed at C and shows one course ending in a pair of the special return bricks with the other course ending in two half bats. Again, king closers may be substituted for the return bricks.

Stopped End.—This is the same as the jamb detail.

Foundation Detail.—Shown at E, this gives the construction at ground level where the wall starts as a normal 1-brick wall in standard brickwork from the footing which need only be 460 mm wide for many subsoils(see p. 82-87) instead of perhaps 610 mm wide for an 280 mm cavity wall. Near the floor level two courses of split V bricks are laid allowing the d.p.c. to be positioned. A split brick is made by cutting a V brick parallel to the face and removing the cross divisions.

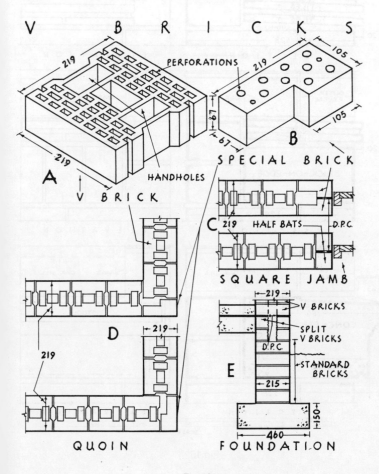

Fig.161

WINDOW SILLS

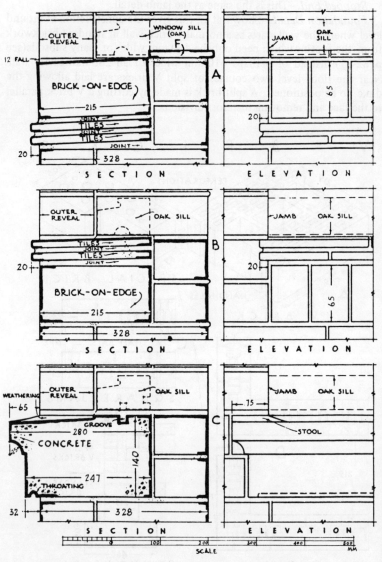

Fig.162

CHAPTER SIXTEEN

MISCELLANEOUS CONSTRUCTION

Window sills; thresholds; copings; plinths; jointing and pointing;
concrete floor construction.

WINDOW SILLS.—A sill provides a suitable finish to a window opening
and affords a protection to the wall below. Sills are of brick, brick with
one or more courses of tiles, tiles, stone, concrete, terra-cotta and wood.
The top of a sill should have a slight fall outwards to prevent the lodg-
ment of water; this is called the *weathering* of a sill.

Three sills are shown in Fig. 162. That at A shows a section and part
elevation of a brick sill upon two courses of tiles. Ordinary standard
bricks are placed on edge and are slightly tiled. The tiles vary from 12 to
45 mm thick. Ordinary roofing tiles (size, 265 mm by 165 mm by
12 mm) are sometimes used. The tiles are given a slight projection
beyond the face (see section) and jamb (see elevation) and are laid to
break joint. They must be solidly bedded in mortar, otherwise they may
be easily damaged.

An alternative arrangement is shown at B, where a double course of
tiles is bedded on a brick-on-edge course.

A simple but effective finish is provided by a double course of tiles (as
above) bedded on the top course of the general walling. If desired, the
tiles may be given a greater tilt than that shown.

The sill at C consists of two courses of purpose-made bricks or terra-
cotta blocks (made from shale and are often glazed). The top course is
weathered and slightly moulded. It has a groove to receive a metal
"water bar"; the latter is bedded in the groove (and also in the groove in
the oak sill) and prevents the
admission of water through
the joint. The bottom course
is grooved or *throated* on the
underside to throw off the
water and prevent it from
passing along the underside of
the sill and staining the brickwork below it. The ends of
the sill are called *stools* or
seatings and provide level beds
to receive the jambs.

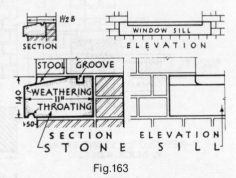

Fig.163

The relative position of the
wood window sill is shown in each of the above by broken lines. As
already stated, windows are often fixed much nearer to the outer faces of
of walls, and for such the above details would require slight amendment.

An internal sill of one course of tiles (sometimes called *quarry tiles*) is shown at F (see A).

A typical stone window sill is shown in Fig. 163. As indicated, this is weathered, grooved and throated. A concrete sill is usually of this section.

Sills should course with the adjacent walling if unsightly split courses (p. 113) are to be avoided. They should be protected (by pieces of wood fitted tightly between the reveals) during the construction of the building, otherwise falling bricks, etc., may cause damage.

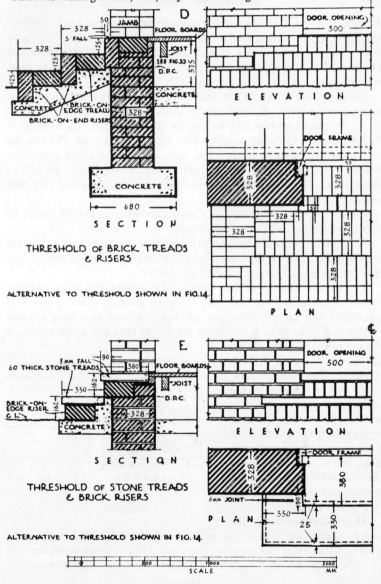

Fig.164

THRESHOLDS

The bottom of an external door opening is provided with one or more steps which form a threshold. Such may consist of bricks, stone or concrete.

A vertical section, part plan and part elevation of a threshold consisting of three brick steps is shown at D, Fig. 164. The bricks must be very hard, otherwise the arrises will be readily damaged. A good foundation in the form of a concrete bed must be provided for the steps. The height (or *rise*) of a step varies from 115 to 175 mm and the top surface (called the *tread*) should be not less than 230 mm wide in order that it may afford ample foot space. In this example the risers consist of bricks laid on end and the treads are completed with bricks on edge. The top step is given a slight fall to discharge water from the door. The whole of the brickwork should be in cement mortar.

A brick-on-edge step is shown in Fig. 132.

The threshold at E, Fig. 164, has two steps having brick-on-edge risers and 57 mm thick stone treads. The stone must be extremely hard, otherwise it will wear badly and the arrises will become chipped; sandstone (or granite), specially selected, should be used. The edges may be slightly rounded or chamfered. The treads must be well and uniformly bedded in cement mortar if fracture of the thin slabs is to be avoided.

An example of a stone threshold consisting of three steps is given in Fig. 165. The bottom step is formed of three stones. The top step is

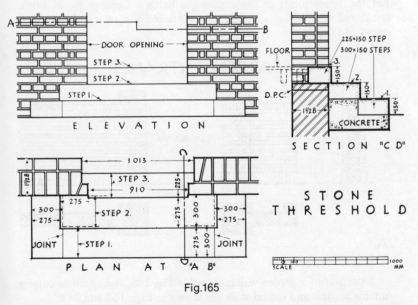

Fig.165

notched at the jambs and is bedded on the wall. Each step is given a fall of 3 mm.

Concrete steps are similar in shape to those of stone. They are usually pre-cast and formed like lintels (p. 130) in wood moulds. A concrete threshold may be made *in situ* (in position on the job); edging boards of riser height are fixed in position, and the treads are floated and trowelled (see p. 184); the bulk of the concrete may be composed of a 1:2:4 mix (p. 23), and a suitable granolithic finish is given to the treads and risers by facing them with a mixture described on p. 183.

The construction of thresholds is usually deferred until most other building operations have been completed in order to minimise risk of damage; otherwise, they must be adequately protected by wood strips or casings.

COPINGS

Copings are provided on top of certain walls, such as boundary walls (of yards, gardens, etc.) and parapet walls (those projecting above the lower portions of roofs). Their object is to exclude water from the walling below and to provide a suitable finish.

Serious damage may be caused to a wall if water gains access, especially if in winter the water freezes; the expansion which takes place when the water becomes frozen may rapidly disintegrate the upper courses of the brickwork. Furthermore, dampness may be caused if the water penetrates sufficiently.

The most effective coping is that which throws the water clear of the wall below. The jointing and bedding material should be *cement* mortar, and the fewer joints in the coping the better. Copings are of bricks, bricks and tiles or slates, stone, terra-cotta and concrete, and all must be sound and durable.

GARDEN ENTRANCE

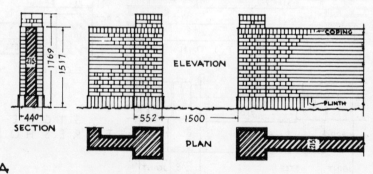

Fig.166

A portion of a garden wall is shown in Fig. 166, and alternate copings suitable for this and similar walls are shown in Figs. 167 and 168.

BRICK COPINGS.—Those at B and D, Fig. 167, are *brick-on-edge copings*. Both are often employed. That at B is formed of standard bricks and those at D are bull-nosed; the part elevation at C is common to both. Both have a satisfactory appearance, and the former especially is relatively inexpensive. Sometimes the bricks are placed on end. The coping shown in Fig. 132 is a combination of both, the lower course being of bricks on end and the upper consisting of bricks on edge. Each course is set back slightly (from 12 to 19 mm).

A *semicircular coping* is shown at E and F, Fig. 167. The purpose-made semicircular bricks are bedded upon an oversailing course of standard

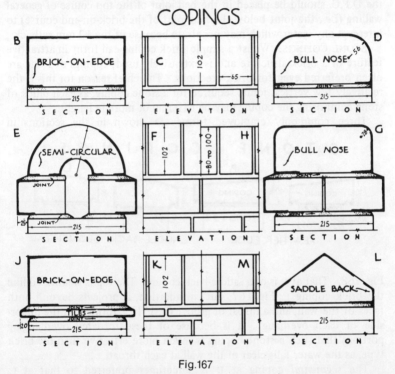

Fig.167

bricks. The space between the stretchers which form this projecting course should be filled solid with pieces of brick and mortar if the dwarf wall is likely to be subjected to side stresses from traffic, etc. The curved surface of the crowning course, and the weathered or *flaunched* bed joint, cause water to run off quickly and the oversailing course assists it to drip clear of the wall. Two semicircular copings are shown at N and O, Fig. 33. A somewhat similar coping is shown at G and H, Fig. 167, the top course being bull-nosed and the oversailing course consisting of bats.

A brick-on-edge coping bedded on a course of tiles (known as a *tile creasing*) is shown at J and K, Fig. 167. Two or more tile courses may comprise the creasing; sometimes these courses are flush with both wall faces. A slate creasing, consisting of two or more courses of slates, is occasionally used as an alternative to tiles.

A *saddle-back coping*, shown at L and M, Fig. 166, provides an effective finish. A tile or slate creasing (preferably the former because of its better appearance) may be added. A *double cant* or splayed coping is shown at P, Fig. 34.

One of the demerits of all these brick copings is the large number of vertical joints, as each is a potential weakness. Hence it is advisable to *provide a horizontal damp proof course* (p. 87) *on the top course of the brickwork* before such a coping is formed; in the type shown in Fig. 132 the D.P.C. should be placed in the bed joint of the top course of general walling (*i.e.*, the joint below the bed joint of the brick-on-end course) to intercept any water which may penetrate because of the 12 mm setback.

STONE COPINGS.–Whilst a simple brick coping can form an attractive feature of a brick structure and is extensively used, copings of stone are often preferred even for brick erections. The chief reason for this is the relatively few vertical joints required for a stone coping, as each block of stone comprising the coping may be 610 mm or more in length.

Three commonly employed forms are shown in the sections in

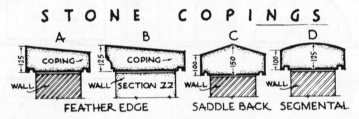

Fig.168

Fig. 168. That at C is of a saddle-back coping. The top is weathered like the brick coping L, Fig. 167, but, in addition, it projects beyond both faces of the wall, and a throat or groove (p. 171) is formed on the under-side of each overhang. It is because of these throated overhanging portions that such a stone coping is much more effective than the brick type, as the water falls clear of the wall at each throat.

The *segmental* coping at D is sometimes preferred to that at C, especially if the wall which it surmounts is low and the curved surface can be seen to advantage.

A *feather-edge* coping is shown at A and is often used. This is also throated. Sometimes this coping, having a throated overhang only at the back, is set back slightly from the front face of the wall; whilst such a coping presents a satisfactory appearance, the lack of protection afforded the front face is a demerit and has been responsible for defects arising in the work below. A moulded feather-edge coping is shown at B.

Terra-cotta blocks are made in the above three shapes. These blocks are generally hollow, the thickness being not more than 32 mm (to minimize shrinkage and distortion in the kiln–p. 12), and the voids are filled with concrete as each block is laid.

Concrete copings are of similar section to the above stone copings.

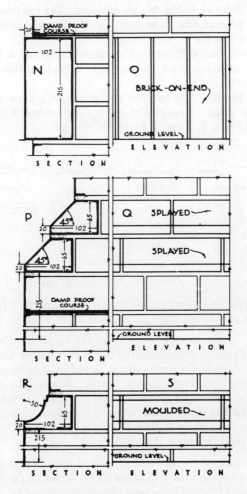

Fig. 169

PLINTHS

A plinth is a projecting (usually) feature at the base of a wall and is adopted to give it the appearance of additional stability. Three examples are given in Fig. 169.

177

BRICK-ON-END PLINTH (see N and O, Fig. 169).—This simply consists of a course of bricks laid on end which is given a slight projection beyond the face of the wall. The horizontal damp proof course is usually bedded immediately above it.

SPLAYED BRICK PLINTH.—One or more courses of purpose-made splayed bricks are bedded on the projecting base of the wall. In the example shown at P and Q, Fig. 169, two stretching courses of bricks similar to those at R, Fig. 31, are provided. The top splayed course may consist of headers, like those at S, Fig. 31. This and similar work should be in cement mortar.

MOULDED BRICK PLINTH.—That shown at R and S, Fig. 169, is one of several moulded brick courses; the curved portion is known as a *cavetto* mould.

STONE PLINTHS.—Sometimes the plinth of a brick building is constructed in stone. Examples of the upper portions of stone plinths are shown at Q, R, S, T, U and V, Fig. 170.

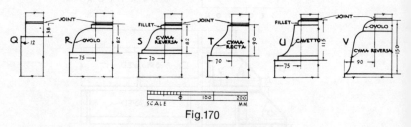

Fig.170

JOINTING AND POINTING

The appearance of brickwork is greatly influenced by (*a*) the colour of the mortar and (*b*) the shape and texture of the joints.

(*a*) The colour of lime mortar (p. 20) varies from white to black. Ordinary Portland cement mortar is grey in colour and has a "cold" appearance; white Portland cement mixed with suitable sand produces white mortar; different shades can be obtained by using coloured cements, *i.e.*, ordinary Portland cement to which various pigments (such as black, red and white oxides of iron) have been added. The colour of sand varies from white to dark brown or red, and the colour of mortar depends a good deal upon that of the sand.

(*b*) The face of the bed and vertical or cross mortar joints is usually compressed by the trowel or other tools. When this is done during the construction of the walls the operation is called *jointing*. When it is done at a later stage it is known as *pointing*. The various shapes imparted to joints are shown in Fig. 171. In faced work it is important that the texture (surface finish) of the joints shall conform with that of the bricks, and therefore a smooth finish to the joints by trowelling is most unsuitable for richly textured sand-faced bricks. Most of the following joints are shown in Fig. 171.

STRUCK OR WEATHER JOINT.—This is frequently used for external work consisting of smooth-faced machine-pressed bricks. It is a good weather joint, as the pores in the mortar (along which water may pass) are sealed by the application of the trowel, and the bevel (about 60°—see Figure) allows the water to run off the top edges of the courses. Because of its smooth mechanical appearance, it must never be used in conjunction with rough textured bricks. As the top arrises of the courses are straight (p. 111), this joint has a tendency to exaggerate any inaccuracy of the *lower* edges of the bricks when the latter are of uneven thickness.

JOINTS

STRUCK

This joint is formed as the walling proceeds when the mortar is sufficiently stiff, usually after four stretchers or their equivalent have been laid. The joints should be well filled with mortar, any hollows being brought flush with the face by additional mortar before final trowelling. After removing any projecting mortar with the edge of the trowel, the bed joint is formed by drawing the slightly inclined blade along to give the necessary bevel. The vertical joints are made by pressing the point of the trowel down each centre to produce a V-section. The cross joints are first struck, followed by the bed joints. In better class work the bed joints are formed and trimmed or cut off with the frenchman (p. 101) aided by the pointing rule (see p. 101); such is called *struck and cut jointing*.

FLUSH

RECESSED

The reverse bevel is sometimes formed, as indicated by the broken line at x. Such are known as *overhand struck joints*, as they are indicative of overhand work (*i.e.*, that constructed from an internal scaffold from which the bricklayer must lean when jointing) which is apt to be scamped. This is inferior work, as water collecting on the ledges may pass through the mortar, and frost action may destroy the upper edges of the bricks, especially if they are not of good quality.

KEYED

PLASTER

PROJECTING

FLUSH OR FLAT JOINT.—As shown, the joint is flush with the brickwork. This is an excellent joint and is formed in different ways.

In one method the mortar is pressed into the joints during the progress of walling, any depressions are filled by additional mortar flush with the bricks, and when the mortar is "semi-stiff" each joint is carefully rubbed in one direction by a piece of rubber held flat against the wall. This gives a satisfactory texture to the joint which conforms agreeably with a sand-faced class of brick.

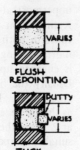

FLUSH
REPOINTING

PUTTY
VARIES

TUCK
POINTING

Fig.171

Provided the mortar is of good quality, this joint gives a good finish to rustic brickwork if it is just left as the mortar is cut off with the trowel, no attempt being made to smooth the joints. The fairly rough texture which results is preferred to that of the smooth struck joint for richly textured bricks. Care should be taken not to stain the face of the bricks with mortar.

It is preferable to adopt a flush joint, which has been trowelled, for internal walls which are to be limewashed, distempered, or painted.

RECESSED OR SUNK JOINT.—The section shows the mortar set back from the face of the bricks. The depth of the recess varies, the bricks should be carefully selected of uniform thickness, and the bed joints should be at least 10 mm thick.

The tool used for making this joint is either a jointer (Fig. 92) or that shown at V, Fig. 172, the thickness of the rubber strip inserted in the latter being equal to that of the joint. Jointing is proceeded with at once, the rubber accommodating itself to any irregularities of the brick edges, as it is pressed into the joint and worked to and fro until the mortar is removed and the sinking formed. The tool at V is suitable for the bed joints, a similar but shorter one being used for the cross joints.

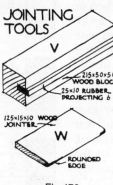

Fig.172

Recessed joints give an attractive appearance to richly textured brickwork, the shadows formed clearly defining each brick unit in the mass. The bricks must be hard and durable, otherwise any water collecting on the surfaces may freeze and cause pieces of brick to spall off.

KEYED JOINT.—It will be seen that this is a form of recessed joint. It is formed by using a convex-rounded edged jointer or the hardwood jointer shown at W, Fig. 172, of varying thickness. The cross joints are formed first, followed by the bed joints. The jointer is used in conjunction with the pointing rule (Fig. 93) when forming the bed joints; the long rule is held by two men against the wall with the bevelled edge uppermost at the same level as the lower edge of the joint; the jointer, resting upon it, is pressed into the soft mortar and passed along several times in both directions until the required depth is obtained, the surplus mortar falling between the distance pieces of the rule. If only one man is engaged upon the work, the rule will not be more than 1·5 m long. Usually the bed joints are given a slightly greater impression than the cross joints. Its appearance is quite attractive, although it is not so bold as that of recessed jointed brickwork. The V-*joint* shown by broken lines at Z is another form of keyed joint. It is formed by a jointer, having a suitably shaped edge, in a similar manner to that described above. The appearance of narrow joints is produced, especially if the mortar and bricks are similar in colour, and is not altogether satisfactory.

PROJECTING JOINTS.—The inside faces of walls to be plastered are sometimes left with the mortar projecting slightly as shown. A good key for the first coat of plaster is thus obtained.

Another projecting joint, called a *beaded joint*, is shown by broken lines at Y. It is made by the application of a concave-edged jointer and the pointing rule (for bed joints). It is not recommended, unless good quality cement mortar is used, as it is liable to become damaged by frost action.

A combination of some of these joints can be adopted with good effect. Thus, if the bricks are uniform in colour and the mortar is of a similar colour, horizontality is emphasized by flush jointing the vertical joints and recessing the bed joints. A similar effect is produced by colour only; thus, the vertical flush joints are made inconspicuous as described, and a lighter coloured mortar is used for the flush-jointed bed joints.

Undoubtedly the soundest work is obtained when the jointing is done during the construction of the brickwork, and the latter is cleaned down on completion of the work. Cleaning down is commenced at the top and continued downwards as the scaffolding is removed. If cement mortar has been employed, water can be used copiously as the brickwork is scrubbed; this is known as *wet cleaning*. *Dry cleaning* must be resorted to if lime mortar has been used, as the application of excessive water will dissolve the lime and discolour the bricks; marks (such as dust from the scaffolding and mortar droppings) are first removed by carefully rubbing the bricks with a piece of similar brick, the wall is then wetted in relatively small portions and the bricks only lightly and carefully scrubbed.

Another method of dealing with the joints, which many consider to be bad practice, is to defer finishing them until the walls have been completed. *Pointing* the joints is then resorted to, commencing at the top. As a preliminary, however, the joints of the brickwork must be raked out squarely, like the recessed joint in Fig. 171, to a depth of at least 10 mm (preferably 12 mm) as the *walling proceeds*, and therefore before the mortar has set; this is immediately followed by brushing the joints with a bass broom to remove any loose mortar. The joints are again brushed to remove dust, and well wetted before pointing is commenced.

Any of the forms of joints shown in Fig. 171 and described above can be adopted for pointing with suitably coloured mortar. The colour of the mortar used for constructing the walls is immaterial, as this is covered with the pointing material. Pointing and cleaning down is proceeded with until the ground level is reached, the scaffolding being removed in stages during the process. Unless sound workmanship and materials are used for pointing, the work will become defective, due to the pointing material falling off on account of it being inadequately keyed to the "wall mortar".

Sample Walls. —Before deciding upon the colour, shape and texture of the mortar joints, it is often desirable to build a sample wall of the bricks to be used. Several short courses are built, the more the better, and various coloured mortars are employed, the colour being influenced by mixing different coloured sands in varying proportions with the lime until the desired results are obtained. Various textured finishes and shapes of joints are also tried out before deciding upon those best suited to the bricks.

Any defect in the face bonding will be conspicuous after the mortar has dried, and it is most important that the perpends (p. 111) shall be truly vertical (Fig. 20 and G, Fig. 37) if a restless appearance is to be avoided.

Pointing walls of existing buildings is necessary when the joints have become defective, as evidenced by their sunk appearance due to the mortar perishing. Such is sometimes called *re-pointing*. If this is not attended to, dampness will result and the brickwork will be reduced to a dilapidated condition. The joints *must* be raked out to a depth of *at least* 10 mm, after which they are well brushed down with a bass broom to remove particles of mortar and dust. Any lichen, moss, etc., must be scraped off the bricks. The pointing material is usually cement mortar or cement: lime mortar (see p. 21). The mortar may be waterproofed by the addition of from 2 to 5 per cent. of waterproofer (see p. 28). The work is done in easy stages, as only a small quantity of the cement mortar should be mixed at a time and used immediately before it has been "killed" or partially set. The wall should be well drenched with water before the pointing is commenced, as this prevents the old mortar from absorbing moisture from the new; incidentally, it also ensures a clean surface. A flush joint, as shown in Fig. 171, or a struck joint is adopted for re-pointing. If preferred, the colour may be made to conform to that of the bricks by using suitably coloured cement and sand. It is emphasized that deep raking out is essential; the recess should be square, as shown (see the recessed joint in Fig. 171), with the edges of the bricks free from mortar; if this is scamped and scratched to a V-shape, as indicated by broken lines at Z, the mortar will flake off owing to the key being inadequate.

TUCK POINTING to existing work is occasionally adopted if the joints are defective and the brick arrises have become ragged. This is illustrated at the bottom of Fig. 171, and is used instead of flush re-pointing, as the latter would produce very wide joints.

Tuck pointing is performed as follows: The joints are well raked out, brushed and watered as described above. Coloured cement mortar may be used to match the colour of the bricks, and this is trowelled flush and rubbed; a small trowel is used, together with a hawk (Fig. 94) to hold the mortar. A neat 5 or 6 mm wide by 3 mm deep groove is at once made along the centre of each joint. Aided by the pointing rule (Fig. 93) and a flat edged jointer (Fig. 92), the groove is filled or "tucked in" (hence the name given to the pointing) with putty lime (p. 135) to which a small amount of silver sand has been added. The putty is given a maximum projection of 3 mm and both top and bottom edges are neatly cut off by means of the frenchman (p. 101), the bent pointed end of which removes the surplus material as the knife is drawn along the edge of the rule. The bed joints are formed first, in about 2·4 mm lengths (when two men are working together), followed by the cross joints. Tuck pointing gives a neat and satisfactory appearance to a building—the shadows cast by the projecting white putty assist in producing the illusion of narrow joints—but the bands of putty are not durable and in course of time become defective.

BASTARD TUCK POINTING is a more durable but less attractive looking imitation of tuck pointing. The shape of the joint is the same, but in bastard tuck pointing the projecting bands consist of the same material (usually coloured cement mortar) as that used for flushing up the raked-out joints.

CONCRETE FLOOR CONSTRUCTION

A concrete floor may consist of a single layer, known as (a) *one-course work*, or two layers called (b) *two-course work*.

(a) *One-course work* is often adopted for floors of garages, cellars, coal-houses, etc., and those which are to be covered with other materials such as boarding and asphalt. Site concrete (p. 90) is an example of one-course work.

(b) *Two-course work* is generally employed in good practice, and consists of a base layer covered by a finishing surface of wearing coat which should not be less than 30 mm thick. A common mix for the base is 1:2:4 of cement, clean coarse sand and 25 mm down of coarse aggregate (see p. 23); just sufficient water should be added to give a 50 mm slump (see p. 26). A hard-wearing surface, called a *granolithic* finish, is obtained from a mixture of 1 part cement, 1 part sand and 1½ to 3 parts clean granite or whinstone chippings (crushed granite) capable of passing through a 6 mm mesh sieve and excluding dust; the surface concrete should give a 25 mm slump. The concrete is either machine or hand mixed, as described on pp. 23-26. An excess of water, cement and trowelling (see p. 184) should be avoided, as this brings the cement to the surface and produces what is called a "dusty floor". The surface should be applied to the base before the latter has hardened. The ground should be firm, any soft patches being replaced with concrete or hard stone. Sometimes a 150 to 300 mm layer of broken bricks or stone (the latter being hand-set and hammer broken on top) is first laid to receive the base layer; this sub-base is called a *hard core* or *penning*.

Large floors are formed in a series of bays or sections, a convenient size being 3 m square, concreted alternately. One of several methods of forming a two-coursed floor is as follows: As shown in Fig. 173, 38 mm thick *edge-boards* or battens are nailed to wood stakes driven in along the boundaries of the bays at about 1·2 m centres, the top edge of the battens being brought to the required level by use of a long straight-edge and a spirit level. The base concrete is deposited in a bay, spread, and shovelled up to a height slightly more than the finished level. A wood *strike-board*, *tamper* or *striking-off board* is then used to consolidate and bring the concrete to a uniformly level surface; as shown at B, this

strike-board is notched at each end, the depth of the notch being equal to
the thickness of the surface coat of the floor. It is manipulated by a man
who, holding it in the middle, works it in a zigzag fashion towards himself
as it traverses the battens, and as he proceeds backwards any hollows are
filled in before the surface is given a final light tamping.

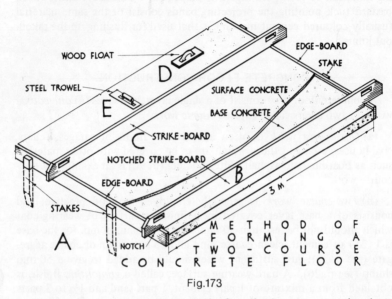

Fig.173

The wearing coat should be laid after the base concrete has been
allowed to harden for about twelve hours. The ends of the strike-board
used for forming the finishing coat are not notched (see C). The granolithic mixture (see p. 183) is deposited, and then levelled as the strike-
board is caused to traverse the edge-boards with a to-and-fro and zigzag
motion. When sufficiently hard, the surface is tamped and floated with
the wood *float* D, any irregularities being made good. The surface is
finally trowelled smooth by means of the *steel trowel* E, which is worked
in a circular motion. Excessive trowelling brings to the surface a liquid
scum, called *laitance*. Such should be avoided, as this destroys the initial
set and produces a friable, non-wearing surface having a glossy finish
which has a tendency to dust and craze (crack).

Not all surfaces are finished in this manner. Thus, for common work,
the concrete is often *spade-finished*, *i.e.*, the surface is beaten down and
smoothed over with the back of the spade. Another finish, often adopted
for paths and roads, is produced by jumping the strike-board up and
down as it traverses the edge-boards, to form a series of small corru-
gations. An alternative finish can be provided by using a machine having
rotating wheels which is applied to the wet concrete; the machine con-
solidates and smoothes the concrete. A hard-wearing surface of attractive
appearance may be produced by mechanically operated grinding discs

which are applied to the floor after it has become sufficiently hard; this exposes and polishes the coarse aggregate.

Terrazzo is another finish used in first-class work. One method is to cover the concrete base with a 25 mm thick wearing coat composed of 1 part cement and 2 parts sand; crushed marble of 6 mm gauge (free from dust) is sprinkled and rolled into this coat whilst it is still soft. When sufficiently hard (three or four days after laying) it is ground down to a smooth surface by stone discs mechanically operated. Another terrazzo finish consists of a 25 mm thick coat of 1 part cement and 2½ parts crushed marble of 12 mm gauge or less, which is machine ground after it has been allowed to partially harden.

An alternative method of forming a two-course floor is as follows: The floor is divided into bays (about 3 m square) by temporarily bedding wood battens, called *screed rules*, on narrow strips of concrete. These rules are firmly tapped in position until their top edges are brought to the required level by means of a straight-edge and spirit level. Each alternate bay is dealt with in turn. The base concrete is deposited and levelled off to the top of the screeds by a straight-edge which is drawn over them in a zigzag manner. The concrete is compacted or *punned* with a *wood rammer* or *iron rammer* or *punner* (Fig. 9). The top layer of concrete is then spread over the base, brought to a level surface with the screeds by means of the straight-edge, floated (D, Fig. 173) and trowelled (E) as already described.

The floor should be covered with damp sacks, and kept moist by occasionally spraying water on it from a hose, to prevent the concrete from drying too rapidly; if allowed to dry out too quickly the strength of the concrete is considerably reduced. It should be kept damp for at least ten days. This is known as *curing* the concrete (see p.28).

INDEX

INDEX